THE WONDERING JEW

THE WONDERING JEW

ISRAEL AND THE SEARCH FOR JEWISH IDENTITY

MICAH GOODMAN

TRANSLATED BY EYLON LEVY

Yale UNIVERSITY PRESS

NEW HAVEN & LONDON

Published with assistance from the Louis Stern Memorial Fund.

Yale University Press books may be purchased in quantity for educational,
business, or promotional use. For information, please e-mail sales.press@
yale.edu (U.S. office) or sales@yaleup.co.uk (U.K. office).

Set in Meridien and Futura types by Tseng Information Systems, Inc.,
Durham, North Carolina.
Printed in the United States of America.

Library of Congress Control Number: 2020935677
ISBN 978-0-300-25224-8 (hardcover : alk. paper)

A catalogue record for this book is available from the British Library.

This paper meets the requirements of ANSI/NISO Z39.48-1992 (Perma-
nence of Paper).

10 9 8 7 6 5 4 3 2 1

CONTENTS

INTRODUCTION

A Twenty-First-Century Dilemma

Many religious Jews offer arguments for why their faith represents the truth. They try to prove that God exists, that a revelation took place at Mount Sinai, and that the Torah is the word of God. At the same time, many secular Jews offer arguments for why their lack of faith represents the truth. They try to prove that God does not exist, that the revelation at Mount Sinai is a myth, and that the Torah is a fable. These opposing views represent a profound clash of ideas—but they are not the core of the argument tearing the Jewish people, and particularly Israeli-Jewish society, apart.

The argument stirring up the Jewish world is not over which side is right about God and revelation, but which belief offers a better, more empowering way forward. Does a religious life enrich our world or limit it? Does a secular life liberate us or limit us? This polemic will become clear in the two arguments with which I begin this book.

Let us try to be persuaded by them both.

THE FAILURE OF RELIGION

In their most fanatical forms, religions cultivate intolerance, bigotry, and even violence. Human history is replete with catastrophes provoked by religious energies that became destructive. When taken to extremes, religion brings out the ugliest side of humankind. This is why critics of religion choose to assail it in its most radical guises. But we need not focus on religious extremism to find flaws in religion. Even less extreme versions of religion can harm their devotees. They might not sow destruction worldwide, but they can sow the seeds of self-destruction in the hearts of individual believers.

As a religion, Judaism nurtures in its adherents a sense of guilt. The halakha (Jewish religious law) consists of myriad detailed rules to which observant Jews are expected to adhere. It is a foregone conclusion that any Jew who aspires to obey faithfully every single halakhic law will fail, and this inevitable shortcoming causes many religious Jews distress. But Judaism not only instills feelings of guilt within its adherents; it also fosters judgmentalism toward others. Religious Jews tend to measure the worth of others by the level of their religious commitment. Guilt and judgmentalism, after all, are two sides of the same coin: guilt turns inward; judgmentalism, outward. Critics argue convincingly that this combination of guilt and judgmentalism limits religious Jews' horizons and is emotionally damaging.

These are not the only disadvantages of the Jewish religious tradition. Judaism demands that its members make an even more painful sacrifice: their intellectual integrity. Religious Jews who are conscious of modern science and its findings, and are alert to the logical flaws at the heart of their religious faith, often feel that they must put their critical thinking aside whenever they enter a synagogue or *beit midrash* (religious study hall).

No wonder religion is subjected to such sharp criticism. If we agree that its extreme forms cultivate intolerance, bigotry, and violence, and its moderate forms foster guilt, judgmentalism, and uncritical thinking, then we will likely concur with the philosopher Yeshayahu Leibowitz that religion should be measured not by what it contributes to individuals but by what it deprives them of.[1] Leibowitz was speaking specifically of the effort required to keep halakha, but more than exhausting adherents' time and energies, religion seems to rob them of something of *themselves*. Religious Jews sacrifice aspects of their own personality for their faith.

Judaism demands an additional sacrifice. Orthodox Jews are often called on to surrender their humanistic values. Having grown up in modern societies and absorbed and internalized those societies' values, they often experience a clash between the conscience that guides them and the tradition that binds them. And their values, which they feel compelled to live by, are silenced in favor of their religion, which they feel compelled to obey.

Consider three modern examples. The first and most prominent concerns the status and role of women in religious Jewish society. In the modern world, women can be prime ministers, chief justices, or CEOs of major corporations. Our world is one in which, in principle, all opportunities are open to women. But this world stops at the door of the synagogue. In Orthodox synagogues, for example, women are prohibited from leading the congregation in prayer—in fact, they cannot even take part in the minyan (prayer quorum), which is open only to men. Effectively, they are denied full membership in their own congregation. This gulf between their modern and religious worlds sets up a cognitive dissonance for many observant Jews. What are they supposed to do? Must they stifle their moral instincts in the name of their religious obligations?

One further ideological clash that religious Jews have difficulty escaping concerns another form of exclusion. Many religious Jews believe that nobody should be excluded, insulted, or rejected because of his or her sexual orientation. The Torah, however, calls homosexual intercourse an abomination. How should Orthodox Jews resolve the conflict between their own moral sentiments and what appears to be an explicitly clear verse in the Torah?

Third, religious Jews who have internalized humanistic values take it almost for granted that all human beings share a basic equality. They find it jarring to think of one people or one nation standing above others. But this is exactly how Jewish tradition is conventionally understood. The *Kuzari*, by the medieval Spanish Jewish philosopher Judah Halevi, for example, states that just as human beings stand above animals, so Jews stand above other humans. How can Jews who believe in equality belong to a tradition that sanctifies hierarchies?

These three ideological conflicts illustrate the painful tension between modern values and ancient traditions. Religious Jews feel compelled to sacrifice their conscience for their faith. And this demand comes not from religious radicalism but from the traditional, mainstream form of the Jewish religion. Such beliefs neither threaten democracy nor endorse violence; they are not a source of physical harm or destruction. But they create violent conflicts within the psyches of believers, asking them to sacrifice aspects of their personalities, their intellectual integrity, and often also their humanistic values for their religious beliefs.

How can religious Jews shake free of the harms caused by their religion? The answer offered by secular Jews is to shake free of religion altogether. Modern secular Judaism cultivates a different kind of character. It nurtures people who do not ignore their values but live them out on a daily basis; who do not suppress their personalities but express them; who obey moral injunctions guided by their conscience and are free of religion-induced feelings of guilt. Jews who make this transition from obedience to self-actualization find it both dramatic and liberating. No wonder some Enlightenment thinkers believed that secularism itself was redemptive. It did not offer redemption in the name of religion, but redemption *from* religion.

THE FAILURE OF SECULARISM

The twentieth century, however, was the century in which Enlightenment secularism failed. The most secular pockets of Europe, the Soviet Union, and China witnessed the worst atrocities in human history. Not only religion, it turned out, sows destruction. Human beings who had no faith in a higher being and felt no connection to an older tradition had nothing to restrain the evil they harbored inside themselves. In the twentieth century it transpired that faith in humanity had not replaced faith in God—it had turned humanity into its own god. It was within this cultural climate that leaders appeared who believed that large-scale social experiments—fascism, communism, and so on—held the keys to redemption. The result was catastrophic. The philosopher Karl Popper summarized this history aptly when he concluded that those who promise paradise on earth never produce anything but hell.[2]

Critics of secularism also tend to take aim at its most radical guises. But again, we need not look only at extreme forms of secularism to spot its weaknesses. Even more moderate forms of secular humanism, which do not deify humanity and are skeptical about the possibilities of redeeming it, have had their weaknesses exposed over time.

In his book *Lost Connections,* the British journalist Johann Hari demonstrates that human beings have emotional needs that Western societies tend to neglect. Just as we have physical needs that must be satisfied to enable us to live physically healthy lives, we also have emotional needs that must be satisfied to enable us to live emotionally healthy lives.[3] Human beings need to feel that they are part of, and have a part in, a story that is bigger than themselves. Another no less important emotional need is for strong, intimate, and empowering communal ties. Social scientists have found, however, that secularism undermines both these needs. It erodes a person's sense of belonging by casting doubt on the truth and sanctity of any larger story and fraying the warm community ties forged around houses of prayer.

Countless studies have explored the emotional effects of religious and secular lives on those who lead them. Many researchers have reached the same conclusion: those who lead secular lives are on the whole less happy than followers of a religion. Perhaps counterintuitively, those who opt to live secular lives are choosing, for the most part and without knowing it, to be less happy. Of course, it is certainly possible to find religious people who would be happier leading secular lives. But such people would be the exceptions to the rule that there is a psychological cost to secularism.[4]

The evidence that, statistically, secular people are less happy than religious people exposes an intellectual flaw in secularism.

Were the opposite the case—that a *religious* life most impinges on personal happiness—the findings would represent neither a problem nor a challenge for religious people, who might argue that they are willing to sacrifice a portion of their individual happiness in the service of God. But for what purpose do secular people sacrifice a portion of *their* happiness? If the studies are accurate, there is an absurdity lying at the heart of secularism. Ironically it is the people who believe there is no higher being who are willing to sacrifice for *this* belief their own quality of life. Secular people who have replaced a commitment to God with a commitment to themselves may discover that they are actually hurting themselves.[5]

Community and family are under constant threat in the secular world. The results can be seen across the European continent. The population of the rationalist, secular, and modern Europe is shrinking and aging, the family is in decline, divorce rates are soaring and birthrates declining. These are the fruits of the core tenet of enlightened secularism: individualism.[6]

Individualism places individual will at the center. This belief has consequences. It creates a cultural climate that is not conducive to family and community life. If people consider their own individual will to be paramount, they leave no room for others. The French philosopher Alexis de Tocqueville foresaw this process as early as the nineteenth century. He analyzed modern, revolutionary culture and predicted that individualism would turn into egoism.[7] Tocqueville saw that cultures in which everyone was considered exceptional would eventually create self-centered people who were apathetic toward their peers.

Nowadays, individualism has been joined by two powerful forces that undermine community and a sense of belonging: consumerism and digital technology. Consumerism feeds people the myth that self-actualization does not mean realizing their dreams through individual efforts but through material consumption. Consumerism invades our sense of identity; we come to associate the value of the life we live with that of the items we own. Cars, houses, and designer fashion are not just possessions—they become part of who we are.

Consumerism, which is becoming hardwired into our identities, has now been joined by digital technology, which hacks into our consciousness. Technology enables people to record—and share with the world—every second of their lives. It is turning the modern belief in self-determination into a reality of self-worship.

The phenomena of consumerist culture, technological addiction, and the myth of individualism do not operate in isolation but are mutually reinforcing. The three have combined to create an aggressive force that assails personal relationships and undermines feelings of belonging. In one study that has become a classic, the political scientist Robert Putnam explored how Americans' connections to groups and their surroundings weakened toward the end of the twentieth century.[8] Americans' primary concern had become a concern for themselves. Using figures and graphs, Putnam demonstrated objectively what many of us feel instinctively, that Tocqueville's prediction has come true and individualism has turned into egoism. The hidden temptation in the secular Enlightenment—to make everyone self-sufficient—has left everyone feeling isolated.

Is there a way out of the crisis of the secular Enlightenment?

According to one recent study, people who attend a place of worship at least once a week give on average twice as much to charity as those who do not, and volunteer on average three times as often.[9] Religious traditions liberate people from a preoccupation with themselves. They instill a sense that the individual will is not the most important thing in life, and this feeling pushes people to make room in their lives for others. In Judaism, religious tradition creates both "islands in time" for people to disconnect themselves from technology and sanctuaries for family intimacy.[10] More broadly, all religions offer their believers a sense of belonging to something greater than themselves, and thus restrain and moderate the powerful forces of modernity that push people toward self-absorption. It might not be possible to prove that religions connect people to God, but religions certainly bind people to one another. According to this theory, modernity does not render religion irrelevant—it makes it more relevant than ever.

RECONCILING THE IRRECONCILABLE

Many people, however, accept both these viewpoints as accurate. They are convinced that secularism is the solution to the crises of religious tradition but also that religious tradition is the solution to the crises of the secular Enlightenment. How do they reconcile such beliefs?

Not everyone faces this dilemma. Secular people who are not tempted to believe that religion has the answer to the crises of loneliness and emptiness provoked by modernity have nothing to reconcile. Conservative religious people who reject the claim that religion warps their personalities share the certainty of their secular counterparts. But those who accept both propositions will feel the effects of the dissonance between them and find themselves in a state of great confusion.

The dilemma used to be different. In his *Guide for the Perplexed*, the medieval Jewish philosopher Maimonides describes a Jew who hopes to remain loyal to the beliefs and traditions of his ancestors and decides to study the rationalist philosophy of the age. The Jew is concerned that if he remains true to his ancestors' traditions, he must turn his back on reason—and if he follows reason, he must abandon the faith of his forebears. *The Guide for the Perplexed* was written precisely for this perplexed soul.[11] For hundreds of years, the great philosophical challenges facing the Jewish people resembled Maimonides' own challenge. The question was almost always how to bridge the gap between two distinct sources of authority: reason and revelation. How can Jews accept the fruits of human reason, when they seem to contradict what is expressly written in Holy Scripture? And of course, this question became only more pressing as science reached conclusions that undermined the credibility of Judaism's traditional story. Archaeology began to dispute the historical accuracy of the Torah; the theory of evolution, the story of creation; and biblical criticism, the belief in the Five Books of Moses as the word of God.

But postmodern thought and the postmodern spirit of the present day have somewhat dispelled this ancient dilemma, not by solving Maimonides' question, but by minimizing it. Postmodernism has undermined human beings' belief in reason.[12] In this new intellectual climate everything is relative, nothing is objective, and profound doubt in the power of reason to transcend our innate subjectivity and reach objective conclusions is the norm. Reason has therefore lost its greatest advantage, the one that made it a threat to religion in the first place. Postmodernism challenges Maimonides' dilemma not by raising faith to the objective standards of reason but by lowering reason to the subjective standards of faith.

But the decline of one dilemma brought another to the fore. The dilemma of the twenty-first century does not follow from a clash between two distinct sources of authority, nor from a rift between different sources of knowledge, but from a collision between two different human needs—the need to belong and the need to be free. One of human beings' most profound needs is to adhere to ideas that are greater than themselves, which fill their lives with meaning. But the desire for liberty, to be separate and individual, is equally powerful. And these two fundamental needs clash. How can one adhere to an idea that is bigger than oneself but also remain free? How can one live a life of self-actualization but also of self-transcendence?

This puzzle should trouble anyone who accepts both the arguments I raised. It is not a uniquely Jewish puzzle; it is a universal one. More generally we can say that most religions, traditions, and faiths attempt to address the same problems, but they do not offer the same solutions. In this book I shall show how Judaism, and in particular Israeli Judaism, confronts these profound universal challenges.

In the course of the twentieth century, Israel's Jewish society produced thinkers and philosophers whose grand visions would offer answers to the challenges of the twenty-first. We should not find this surprising: in Israel the longing for freedom and the devotion to identity frequently and forcefully collide. And the more painful the tension, the more fascinating and urgent the attempts to resolve it.

PART I THE CLASH OF IDENTITIES THAT RUPTURED ISRAELI JUDAISM

INTRODUCTION

The State of Israel is not only the nation of all citizens who live there, it is also the home of all Jews who do not. Israel is an open house, one that Jews around the world are invited to enter. Any Jew who wishes to do so can immigrate to Israel, obtain citizenship, and settle there. All are welcome. But this open invitation has a catch. All Jews are welcome, but their preferred form of Judaism might not be. Israel has an official state Rabbinate, which decides what constitutes "authentic" Judaism. Most Jews identify with strands of Judaism that are liberal, even progressive—but these strands are not considered authentic forms of Judaism by Israel's Chief Rabbinate. Hence the painful irony that Israel accepts every type of Jew but not every type of Judaism.

This situation is not new. From the moment of its inception, the Jewish state granted the rabbinical establishment a monopoly on matters relating to Judaism. One might infer, therefore, that Israel's founders were extremely religious. In fact, the opposite was true. The founding fathers of the State of Israel were extremely secular. Their dream was to build a free country, secular in character and liberated from the chains of the past. They conceived of Zionism as nothing less than a Jewish revolt against Judaism. Speak to ideologically secular Israelis today, and you will still hear echoes of the founding generation's strident antireligious secularism. But political necessity compelled Israel's secular founders to compromise with Orthodox Jews and grant them a monopoly over Judaism in the Jewish state. Thus emerged the paradox that Israel's founders, Jews who revolted against religion, ended up establishing one of the few countries in the world that enshrines a form of religious coercion in its laws.

This is a disturbing situation for many Diaspora Jews, especially in the English-speaking world. Israel's cultural elite rejects religion altogether, but its political system enforces religious coercion. Why does one side shut itself off from Judaism, while the other shuts itself off from modernity? To uncover the source of this paradox, let us delve more deeply into its roots.

Modernity burst onto the stage of history some three hundred years ago, when free thinkers of all stripes—philosophers, revolutionaries, political leaders—struck blow after blow at the traditions of the past. They strove for a future in which humanity would slough off the heavy burdens of history, including the ones imposed by the faith of generations. The Enlightenment included a specifically Jewish strain, the Haskala, and among the targets of Jewish intellectuals was the Jewish tradition. At the forefront of this revolt against Jewish history were the Zionists.

Zionism was a modern ideology. As Israel's founding prime minister, David Ben-Gurion, once noted, the Zionist revolution was different from the American, French, and Russian revolutions because whereas revolutions are generally mass, popular movements against oppressive regimes, Zionism was a revolution of Jews against themselves.[1] Long before Zionists waged a military struggle against the rule of a foreign power, they waged a cultural struggle against the rule of the past. And indeed, some of the main Zionist thinkers saw Zionism as a Jewish revolt against Judaism.

But not all did so, and those who did, did not do so fully. There was another side to Zionism, which became clear during the argument over the Uganda Scheme—the Zionist visionary Theodor Herzl's proposal to build a Jewish national home somewhere other than the Land of Israel. At the root of the fierce resistance provoked by the plan was the demand that Jews not surrender their ancient land to establish a new state. The resistors' insistence expressed an additional undercurrent in the Zionist ideology: the desire of a people to return to its past. And that undercurrent also found expression in the daring project to revive the Hebrew language, a development that reflected the Zionists' desire to resurrect their ancient national past, a project that was virtually unparalleled in human history.[2]

Zionism, therefore, is both a revolt against the past and a return to it. This tension underlies all that is enigmatic in the Zionist mindset. The Zionists sought to complete their disconnection from tradition in the Land of Israel, of all places. And the banner they wanted to raise in their revolt against religion was to be in their ancient, sacred language.[3]

Human experience is replete with relationships that are based on conflicting emotions. Some couples have tempestuous relationships in which feelings of attraction and rejection coincide. This is precisely the nature of Zionism's relationship with Jewish history. It embodies a revolt against the past alongside a resurrection of the past. Revolution, alongside renaissance. The unreconciled tension that comes from the polar ends of Zionist identity and consciousness creates the movement's cultural electricity.[4]

The Zionists' fervor produced a revolution. Their dream came true, their state was founded; later it began to prosper. But over time, Zionism's dual identity fractured into its constituent parts. Religious Israelis became the exclusive masters of one side—the connection with the past. Secular Israelis became the exclusive masters of the other—the revolt against the past. The proportion of Israelis who believed in both declined. What used to be a conceptual tension between two contradictory impulses developed into a societal tension between different Israeli factions. An identity full of contradictions was replaced by a society full of divisions.

Today two main disagreements are tearing Israelis apart: the conflict between the political right and the political left, and the conflict between religious and secular Jews. I have devoted two books to these disputes. In the first, *Catch-67*, my aim was to explore the ideas behind the political debate. The book you are reading now dives into the ideas behind an even more fundamental and profound argument—the argument over Judaism.

The transition from an identity crisis within Zionism to this social tension within Israel is the result of a twofold process: the emergence of an authoritarian form of Judaism whose adherents claim a monopoly on Jewish tradition, and the emergence of an angry, rebellious form of secularism whose adherents feel threatened by any contact with tradition. The rift between the two sides opened up when the aspiration of modernists to create a new kind of Judaism, one that would be liberated from the authority of religious tradition, collided with a reactionary response from authoritarians who sought to retain a stranglehold on both Judaism and its tradition.

1 THE GREAT REVOLT

Nathan Birnbaum, the late nineteenth-century Austrian Jewish writer who coined the term "Zionism," described the Jews as
an inferior people: "[The Jews] lack personal courage, external
dignity, tact and an aesthetic sense."[1] His harsh remarks expressed
a rarely mentioned truth about the early Zionist movement: the
Zionists disliked "the Jews." His contemporary Zionist theorist
Nachman Syrkin declared that modern Judaism was the garbage
of human history.[2] The early twentieth-century author Yosef Haim
Brenner said Jews had brought a curse on the world: "The Jew and
Jews. It seems the world would have been happier without this
curse—the Jew."[3] Among the Zionist pioneers in Israel, the term
"Jew" was often used as a pejorative; some even used the word ye-
hudon, "Jew boy."[4] These expressions are jarring. At times it can be
difficult to distinguish between Zionist and anti-Semitic rhetoric.[5]

Textbooks taught in Israeli schools nowadays identify Zionism as a reaction to anti-Jewish hatred. Every Israeli high school
student is taught that Theodor Herzl devised the idea of a Jewish

state when he discovered the danger of anti-Semitism. But the connection between Zionism and anti-Semitism turns out to be more complicated. Zionism arose not just as a means of confronting anti-Semitism but also as a camouflaged version of the same thing.[6]

Yet despite the many similarities, there is a profound difference between the two. The Zionists and anti-Semites both agreed that Jews were diseased creatures. But whereas the anti-Semites reasoned that this disease was innate and genetic, the Zionists thought that it was environmental. They believed that the disease was a result not of the Jews' genes but of their life circumstances. Exile had warped the Jewish character. If the Diaspora were ended and Jews reunited in their homeland, they believed, the Jewish character would heal.[7] If the Jews relocated to the Land of Israel, if they started exercising their muscles by working the land, if they bore arms and cast aside their religious observance, they would be cured of the psychological maladies they had accumulated in exile.

Zionism was a grand project to heal the Jewish character. The early Zionist thinkers, including the authors Yosef Haim Brenner and Micha Josef Berdyczewski and the poet Shaul Tchernichovsky, believed that more than being a political project, Zionism was chiefly a therapeutic project. More than establishing a new state, its objective was to forge a new Jew.[8]

What was it in Diaspora Jews that provoked such great revulsion among the Zionists? For the most part, their aversion came from their perception of Jews as submissive and cowardly. Jews were submissive because they were ruled by two oppressive authorities: the temporal power of the gentiles and the spiritual power of the rabbis. Under these authorities, the Jews also suffered from a twofold fear: of gentiles and of God. Zionism purported to liberate the Jews from both. To create a new generation of Jews freed from authority and fear. Or as the early Zionist leader Ze'ev (Vladimir) Jabotinsky put it, "a psychologically new race of Jew."⁹

THE CRITIQUE OF THE JEWISH RELIGION

The Zionists were not the first Jewish thinkers to criticize the Jewish religion. They were, rather, internalizing the reasoned and persuasive critiques of Enlightenment Jewish thinkers.

These critiques took two forms: a theological critique and an anthropological critique. Theological criticism typically focuses on a religion's precepts. It may, for example, challenge the belief that the Torah was handed down at Mount Sinai or dispute the divine origin of the religious legal tradition. Anthropological criticism concerns a religion's results. It questions not the divine origin of halakha but the character of its adherents.

The thrust of the Zionists' criticism of the Jews was anthropological. They did not reject the claims of the Jewish religion so much as they felt repulsed by religious Jews. To their minds, the nub of the problem was not that Judaism was wrong but that it was repellant. Religious Jews, they believed, had developed defective characters. And what was the defect in the character of those who obeyed Jewish religious law? The answer was first articulated by the Dutch Jewish philosopher Baruch Spinoza in the seventeenth century.

Halakha, Spinoza wrote, creates submissive and obedient characters. Every aspect of the lives of religious Jews is governed by ancient laws. Religious Jews are not even free to choose which shoe to put on first or which laces to tie first. Halakha decides everything for them. The psychological result, Spinoza felt, was debilitating: religious Jews became habituated to suppressing their own individual desires, and obedience became a natural part of their character.[10] Spinoza's critique of Judaism gained followers and became a point of consensus. In the eighteenth century it became common to say that in contrast to all other world religions, Judaism was not a religion of faith but a religion of laws. The Jews were not spiritual, many believed, but merely submissive.

The main point of tension between tradition and modernity did not concern their respective worldviews but the perceptions of the type of person they cultivated. Modernity had changed not only people's beliefs but also their aspirations: during the Enlightenment, philosophers asked, What constitutes an ideal person? To what should individuals aspire? Whereas for religious Jews the goal was self-abnegation, for secular Jews it was independence. Religious Jews admired those who eschewed personal development; secular Jews admired those who achieved self-actualization. Parallel to the clash developing between religion and science was a clash between different conceptions of heroism. And of the two types of hero described here, the modernist hero became the Zionist hero. The Zionists dreamed of a liberated Jew, independent and fulfilled. In Tchernichovsky's Zionist fantasy, a new generation of Jews would arise in the Land of Israel and "shake off its chains."[11] This dream of a new personality was accompanied by reservations about and disgust at the old personality. Everything that traditional Jews once considered inspirational, Zionist thinkers found antithetical.

Halakha, they believed, trained Jews to be obedient, the opposite of Zionism's intent. The novelty of Zionism was its historic attempt to liberate the Jews from the religious tradition that, Zionists claimed, was keeping them chained. Micha Josef Berdyczewski explained that in exile the Jews were not an authentic nation: they did not exercise self-determination but worshipped their own heritage. "We are slaves of our memories, slaves of our inheritance; we have been mummified by our devoted, limited thought." The new Jew, however, would be neither enslaved to his past nor a slave of his memories. He would recognize one authority alone—his own. "We are Hebrews," he wrote, "and we will serve our own hearts."[12]

THE CRITIQUE OF JEWISH POWERLESSNESS

Zionists did not act solely to liberate the Jews from the rule of rabbinic and halakhic Judaism. Zionism was first and foremost a movement to liberate the Jews from the rule of non-Jews, and its criticism of the Jewish religion was only one element in its critique of the Diaspora condition. The main criticism centered on Jewish powerlessness.

In 1903, the Jewish community leadership in Odessa sent a young poet to Kishinev to investigate the massacre of the town's Jews and write a detailed report. But when Hayim Nahman Bialik returned from Kishinev, he published something that was much more than a report. Bialik had written a prophetic poem, one that caused an upheaval in the Jewish world. His report took the form of a poignant poem that reflected the historic shift in Jewish aesthetic tastes that Zionism had prompted.[13]

In his poem, Bialik decried the atrocity perpetrated against the Jewish community of Kishinev. That in itself was nothing new. After almost every pogrom in Jewish history, someone had penned a piece lamenting the suffering and horror. These writings had a common name: *kinnot*, or "lamentations." After the 1096 Rhineland massacres, in which tens of thousands of Jews were butchered by the Crusaders, a lamentation was written in memory of the victims which is still in use: the prayer *Av HaRachamim* (Merciful Father), recited in Ashkenazi synagogues every Sabbath before the Musaf prayer. It describes the victims thus: "Holy communities who gave their lives for the sanctification of the Divine Name. They were beloved and pleasant in their lifetime, and in their death are not parted [from Him]. They were swifter than eagles and stronger than lions to do the will of their Possessor and the desire of their Rock. Our God will recall them favorably together with the other righteous of all time."[14]

Traditionally, Jews massacred in pogroms were considered holy and pure. But Bialik's poem broke with tradition. Instead of exalting the victims, he blamed them. For the first time in Jewish history, the Jewish victims of violence were described not as "beloved and pleasant" but as weak, even degraded. Consider, for example, how Bialik described the reaction of the Jewish men to the rape of their wives during the pogrom:

Where seven heathens flung a woman down,
The daughter in the presence of her mother,
The mother in the presence of her daughter,
Before slaughter, during slaughter, and after slaughter!

· · · · · · · · · · · · · · · · · · ·

Note also do not fail to note,
In that dark corner, and behind that cask
Crouched husbands, bridegrooms, brothers, peering from the
cracks,

· · · · · · · · · · · · · · · · · · ·

Crushed in their shame, they saw it all;
They did not stir nor move;
They did not pluck their eyes out; they
Beat not their brains against the wall!
Perhaps, perhaps, each watcher had it in his heart to pray:
A miracle, O Lord,—and spare my skin this day![15]

These verses cannot but spark fury in their readers' hearts, but that fury is not necessarily directed at the violent "heathens." It might also be directed at the frightened, wretched men who hide and peek through the cracks as their wives, sisters, and mothers are abused. More than victims of the gentiles, these Jews are victims of themselves, of their own miserable characters. Perhaps for the first time in Jewish history, the victims were not holy—they were repugnant.

Bialik was expressing a new sentiment in his poem, one that would persist and develop in the Zionist movement: the belief that weakness, in Jews, is a deformity.[16] This was the second, complementary, aspect of Zionism's critique of diaspora Jewry. Zionism attacked both the Jews' inaction against God and their inaction against the gentiles.

ZIONISM AS A TWOFOLD LIBERATION PROJECT

There was a clear connection between these two forms of criticism, a profound link between the Zionists' revulsion at powerless Jews and their aversion to religious Jews. Powerlessness and obedience to religious law went hand in hand. In fact, many Zionist theorists believed that religious law was a central reason for the Jews' submissiveness.[17] Bialik's poem, which criticizes that submissiveness, is also a vicious parody of Jewish religious law. Consider his description of the men who, after the massacre ends, go to the synagogue to thank God for their salvation:

> They crawled forth from their holes, they fled to the house of
> the Lord,
> They offered thanks to Him, the sweet benedictory word.
> The *Cohanim* sallied forth, to the Rabbi's house they flitted:
> *Tell me, O Rabbi, tell, is my own wife permitted?*
> The matter ends; and nothing more.

All the men can do after the massacre, after abandoning their wives to sexual violence at the hands of the gentiles, is make an inquiry about halakha: *"Tell me, O Rabbi, tell, is my own wife permitted?"* — that is, May I have sex with her now that she has been raped?

Bialik presented here a scathing caricature of religious law as a deformed legal code that had created a deformed breed of people. His poem was a clear expression of the prevailing mood among the founders of the Zionist movement. They believed that religious Jews had exchanged their vitality and spontaneity for the mechanistic formalism of the Jewish legal code.[18]

This double enslavement, to God and to gentiles, had led in Berdyczewski's damning words to a double rot: the degradation of the character of the religious Jew. For the Jews to be cured, they needed to be liberated from these two authorities. Zionism was thus a movement to liberate the Jews twice: politically and psychologically. Politically, Zionism would liberate the Jews from the rule of the gentile. Psychologically, Zionism would liberate the Jews from the rule of the past. This was why the Zionism of Israel's founding fathers could only ever have been secular. If the Jews were controlled by two authorities, they had to be liberated from both—from God and from gentile alike.[19]

But this is only one side of the story of Zionism's relationship with Jewish tradition. The story has another side. Zionism was not just a revolt against the authority of tradition. Strangely enough, it was also a movement that bolstered the authority of that tradition.

2 THE NEW ORTHODOXY

For some two thousand years, religious law has stood at the heart of Jewish life. How has it survived the trials and tribulations of Jewish history? One surprising answer comes from a sage of the Jerusalem Talmud, Rabbi Yannai: "If the Torah had been given sliced (i.e., with one clear answer to every question) there would be no room for the leg to stand [i.e., no room to maneuver] . . . so that the Torah will be interpreted 49 faces impure and 49 faces pure."[1] The obscure nature of the Torah's text invites multiple, contradictory interpretations, which allowed the rabbis to adapt it to ever-evolving circumstances. Had the Torah been "clear-cut" — that is, clear and unambiguous—it would not have produced the interpretative flexibility that made it adaptable to different eras. The Hebrew word *halakha* comes from the root meaning "to proceed," and halakha retained its important status because it kept moving forward.[2]

Jewish religious law continued evolving until the cultural upheaval of the modern era, which threw Jewish life into turmoil. Modern science, politics, and values all posed new challenges to the old Jewish way of life. Many members of Jewish communities in western Europe could not resist the temptations offered by modernity. They left their Judaism behind, abandoned their communities, and embraced modern life. The Reform movement was founded as a response to this great exodus, in order to staunch its flow and neutralize the temptation of Jews to assimilate completely. Its founders believed that the way to stop Jews abandoning Judaism was to change it. They offered the new assimilating Jews an attractive deal: instead of abandoning Judaism for modernity, they could modernize Judaism.

This was a turning point. Jewish religious law had always evolved, but change had hitherto been slow and organic. The Reform movement's precipitous change, however, broke with the familiar pace of change in Jewish law and threatened to empty it of content. The Orthodox rabbis and leaders of various Jewish communities grasped this momentous threat and reacted accordingly. Attempting to defend themselves from the winds of modernity, and traditional Judaism from a cultural onslaught, they developed a stubborn resistance to any changes in halakha. In response to movements that sought to make new and dramatic changes in the religious tradition, these rabbis declared that "what is new is forbidden by the Torah." Ironically, since Jewish religious law had always undergone change, the declaration that Judaism must not change was itself a change within Judaism. The prohibition on innovation, observed the historian Jacob Katz, was itself a massive innovation.[3]

So it came to pass that the Reform movement was a reaction to modernity, and ultra-Orthodoxy was a counterreaction to the reaction to modernity. In reality, two modern movements emerged:

one championed an ideology of changing Judaism, the other an ideology of not changing Judaism.

During the nineteenth century, this new Jewish orthodoxy identified two threats to Jewish continuity: openness and change. In response it took two defensive measures: seclusion and stasis. Ultra-Orthodox Jews closed themselves off from the threatening modern world and placed their halakha in a deep freeze. As a result, the more authoritarian aspects of Judaism were bolstered. The progress of halakha was halted, and its evolution ended.

Of course, there are many shades to Orthodox Judaism, which has more moderate as well as stricter forms. For my own part, I am a member of an Orthodox congregation and raise my children within it, but I am also well aware that the stricter Orthodox Judaism becomes, the more acute the paradoxes at its heart: Orthodoxy is a modern movement that is perceived as traditional. It opposes change and in so doing creates change; it makes the Torah "clear-cut" and thus undermines the force that made it a source of continuity during changing times.[4]

RELIGIOUS CONSERVATISM AND ISRAELI POLITICS

When the State of Israel was established, Judaism gained the coercive powers of a modern state—and out of all the possible groups, movements, and interpretations in Judaism, it was the most deeply conservative form that came to be the official Judaism of the State of Israel. As the world began to change, halakha remained static.

Why did Israel's secular founders allow their new country's laws to be based on religious law? The answer lies in the deliberations preceding the decision by the United Nations to partition the Land of Israel into two states, one Jewish and one Arab, on 29 November 1947. The U.N. resolution was based on the recommendations of a special committee, sent by the United Nations to Palestine to investigate whether the Jews and the Arabs could establish their own independent nation-states. This committee, known as the United Nations Special Committee on Palestine (UNSCOP), interviewed various representatives of the Jewish community to determine whether they were capable of creating a sovereign state. In the course of their inquiry, the committee spoke with representatives of the ultra-Orthodox Old Yishuv—Jews who lived in Palestine before the modern waves of Jewish migration. But this move alarmed David Ben-Gurion, who feared that these deeply conservative and mainly anti-Zionist Jews would voice their opposition to the establishment of a Jewish state, thereby leading the committee of inquiry to conclude that the Jews were incapable of establishing a stable state rooted in a cross-societal consensus.

To avert this threat, Ben-Gurion initiated a dialogue with representatives of the Old Yishuv, and the two sides reached an agreement. The ultra-Orthodox community would not oppose the diplomatic efforts to create a Jewish state, and in exchange it would have a say in the form of Judaism adopted by the state. This is the "status-quo" agreement, whose effects are felt to this day in the relationship between religion and state in Israel. To establish the State of Israel, Ben-Gurion was forced to surrender its secular character.[5]

The status-quo arrangement, reinforced by legislation over the years, has meant, among other prohibitions, that public transport cannot operate in many cities on the Sabbath and that the Chief Rabbinate controls matters of marriage, divorce, conversion, and burial. The ultra-Orthodox have gradually taken control of the Chief Rabbinate, and through it control the most basic, sensitive elements in the life of Israeli citizens. So it happened, in an ironic twist of fate, that the Israelis who wanted to rebel against the Jews of yesteryear found themselves oppressed by them instead.

The nineteenth century saw the creation of conservative forms of Judaism (Orthodoxy and ultra-Orthodoxy), and the twentieth century saw the creation of a political framework for the Jews (the State of Israel), and the two developments converged. The clear-cut legal code of Judaism merged seamlessly into the formal laws of the state. The result was a conservative brand of Judaism, created as a reaction to modernity, that acquired the political power of the modern Jewish state.

THE COLLISION

All this happened at the same time as the emergence of the most extreme form of Jewish secularism. As we saw, for many of the pioneers, one of Zionism's central aims was to create a secular culture unbound by the chains of the past and liberated from the heavy onus of tradition. The Zionist aim of some of the state's founders was to liberate the Jews from the rule not only of non-Jews but also of Judaism. The same Zionism that granted political authority to the Jewish religion was therefore the Zionism that nurtured an identity that rebelled against religious authority. The movement that exacerbated the more oppressive tendencies of Judaism as a religion was the same one that encouraged Jews to liberate themselves from those tendencies.

We have here two stories: the history of how secular Jews turned their backs on Judaism and the history of how religious

Jews fossilized it. And these two stories led to a collision. There is a common idea in philosophy that major tensions are a source of great growth. But here, it appears, the tension was not conducive to growth. It is not only unproductive; it is paralyzing. The psychological fantasy that inspired Zionists was to create a way for Jews to free themselves from authority, chiefly religious authority—but political necessity led the Zionists to create one of the only democracies in the world governed by religious laws. The result is not a synthesis of the two poles but an aggravation of the polarity.

Alexis de Tocqueville observed one of the great wonders of American democracy in the nineteenth century. He noted that on the one hand Americans hewed to a religious ethos, but on the other U.S. legislation forswore any religious affiliations. In America, religion and state were separate, but American society was the most religious in the Western world.[6]

How was it possible, Tocqueville asked, for a country that had erected a barrier between religion and state to be so religious? His answer was that religion remained attractive in the United States precisely because it did not enjoy state power. "They [priests] mainly attributed the peaceful dominion of religion in their country to the separation of Church and State," he wrote. In his analysis, citizens of democracies have a healthy aversion to state authority. If religion is integrated into the machinery of the state, therefore, their aversion to state power will become an aversion to religion as well.[7]

Today we can say that the experiment conducted in Israel all but proves Tocqueville's theory. Many secular Israelis have responded badly to religious coercion. The power that the state gave the Jewish religion did not promote that religion but provoked antipathy toward it.[8]

The America of Tocqueville is Israel's mirror image. American culture is deeply religious, but American legislation strives to be secular. Zionism cultivated a deeply secular culture but permitted religious legislation. Not only religion but secularism has been politicized. Some secular Israelis feel that any intimate encounter with the Torah or spiritual experience of prayer is by definition tantamount to surrender to the religious establishment. Secularism in Israel is more than a theological or emotional disposition—it is also a political protest.[9]

Micha Josef Berdyczewski aptly expressed the anger of the first secular generation: "Our souls are full of resentment against the past.... Our people are rotting from traditions, and rules, and laws their whole lives.... We have very many things in the inheritance of our forefathers that kill our souls and give them no redemption."[10]

This was the anger of a man who had grown up in a religious home, been educated in a yeshiva, felt suffocated by religious law, and yearned to breathe the air of a free culture. But this anger should have dissipated over time. The second generation of secular Israeli Jews, who did not receive Berdyczewski's stifling religious education, should not have felt such anger at the religious tradition. The more distant they grew from that tradition, the more their anger should have subsided. But secular Israelis' anger at the religious tradition refuses to go away. That anger still burns because something still fuels it: the religious establishment and its powers of coercion. Israel's religious politics are feeding the secular fury against Jewish tradition and preventing it from abating. Through a strange partnership, an authoritarian religiosity is keeping secular rebellion alive.[11]

THE ANTIRELIGIOUS SHIFT

The Jewish religion has a history, and so does the Jewish antireligious movement. In Israel, the antipathy toward religion took on a new form after the Six-Day War. When the Gush Emunim settler movement brought Jewish settlers to the hills of Judea and Samaria to live among the Palestinian population, religious voices burst into Israel's public conversation. The justifications for the settlements were rooted in the depths of Jewish tradition. Biblical verses and rabbinical texts became sources of authority and inspiration for the growing settlements in Judea, Samaria, and the Gaza Strip. Over time an associative linkage developed between the settlement enterprise and Jewish tradition, and within the secular left, distaste for the settlements in Judea, Samaria, and Gaza became distaste for the tradition that justified them. The new antireligious movement rested, consciously or unconsciously, on the following syllogism: Israel's military rule over the Palestinian civilian population was immoral, so the settlements that perpetrated that situation were immoral, and therefore the Jewish religion, which fueled that enterprise, was dangerous and immoral as well.[12]

For some members of the secular Israeli public, aversion to "the occupation" merged with aversion to "religious coercion." The politics in Israel caused many secular Israelis to feel that they were both being oppressed by their religious compatriots in matters of Judaism and oppressing the Palestinians in the name of Judaism.

Sociologically speaking, the aversion to "religious coercion" was directed mainly at the ultra-Orthodox, and the aversion to "the occupation" at religious Zionists. But the difference was not only sociological. It was also psychological: the original antireligious sentiment had been against Jews who were too passive (the exilic ultra-Orthodox); the new antireligious sentiment was against Jews who were too active (religious settlers). This was a dramatic shift. The old critique of religion, voiced by the founding fathers of Israeli secularism, was that it silenced the national element of Jewish identity; the new critique was that it ramped that nationalism up too high.

Here we come full circle to the situation described in the previous chapter. In his powerful and trenchant poem, Bialik blamed the Jewish religion and law for the Jews' weakness and feebleness toward gentiles; the new critique blamed the Jewish religion and law for the Jews' aggression and heavy-handedness against gentiles. Thus, in a process that took a hundred years, Jewish antireligiosity, which opposed religion for extinguishing national sentiments, became opposition to religion because it *sparked* nationalist sentiments.

THE NEW ISRAELI DILEMMA

In *Not Without My Daughter,* the American Christian writer Betty Mahmoody narrates her own amazing story of falling in love with and marrying an Iranian man and visiting Iran with him. There she found herself trapped in an oppressive relationship that stifled her liberty. She was forced to wear traditional dress, her freedom of speech was restricted, and her opinions about her own children's education carried virtually no weight. She agonized over whether to leave her husband.[13]

Mahmoody's struggle is still shared by many women around the world who are forced to confront a difficult dilemma: Should they surrender their freedom to preserve their relationships and marriage, or surrender their relationships to win their freedom?

This is also the dilemma of Israelis who would like to have an intimate relationship with their tradition but do not wish to be controlled by it. They think they are faced with a choice between two paths: surrendering their freedom for a relationship with the past, or surrendering their relationship with the past to win their freedom. This Israeli dilemma is the result of the collision of identities we have described, and of the collision between Zionist ideology and Zionist politics. This collision heightened the sense that the only possible authentic relationship with the Jewish tradition is enslavement. Either enslavement by the past, or liberation from it.

Is there a third way? Can Jews cultivate an intimate relationship with their past without becoming enslaved by it? This is not a cold, academic question. Behind it lies a need for meaning. There is a deep link between belonging and meaning. People who feel that they belong to something greater than themselves sense that their lives are more meaningful. But modern life in the Western world, which induces people to become increasingly preoccupied with themselves, hampers their ability to feel they belong to anything, and therefore threatens their sense that their lives have meaning. Modern Jews are trapped in an impossible dilemma concerning their identity. Are they fated to sacrifice meaning for liberty?

PART II ALTERNATIVE SECULARISM

INTRODUCTION

Judaism is a powerful spiritual force, which has survived the trials of history and shaped it. It is a force pulsating with wisdom, ideas, texts, and practices. It is dynamic and has repeatedly changed form to meet new challenges. The Judaism of the medieval rationalists was profoundly different from that of the Kabbalists. The Judaism of the spiritual, mystical Hasidim was different from that of their more scholarly rivals, the Misnagdim. But whatever their differences, each of these many forms of Judaism was authentic, and each made a contribution to the overall development of Jewish civilization.

At the core of this book is the argument that over the past century a new form of Judaism has emerged: Israeli Judaism. Just as the Middle Ages produced Kabbalah and modernity produced Hasidism, the twenty-first century has produced a distinctly Israeli Judaism.

Let me clarify here what this book is *not* about: it is not about non-Israeli forms of Judaism. This is why it contains no systematic discussion of ultra-Orthodox Judaism, which has certainly evolved inside Israel but was born and developed outside Israel and cannot be considered a uniquely Israeli innovation. Neither is this book about Reform and Conservative Judaism, or other progressive streams, simply because they are not predominantly Israeli.

This book is about Israeli Judaism and will advance the argument that such a phenomenon exists. Modern Israel is not only somewhere Jews *live*, a country like any other; it is also the soil in which a new and distinct kind of Judaism has grown. Israeli Judaism largely has two aspects, one religious, the other secular. In this section I explore the secular side of the coin: secular Zionism. Later I shall look at its twin: religious Zionism.

The form of secularism that shakes off the past, rebels against tradition, and attacks religion is only one kind of secularism.[1] The form of religion that opposes change, closes itself off from the world, and attacks Western values is only one kind of religion. There is a tendency to associate extremism with authenticity. Many people consider the most extreme forms of religion and secularism to be the most authentic. As humans we do not naturally aspire to be extreme, but we do aspire to be authentic. Often the draw of extremism is rooted in this desire for authenticity.

Many of the founders and philosophers of Israeli secularism criticized the extreme version of secularism. The academic Gershom Scholem described it as criminal, cultural violence: "To sever the living connection with the legacy of generations is an act of educational murder."[2] The first dean of the Hebrew University of Jerusalem, Samuel Hugo Bergmann, cast doubt on the possibility that secularism, if disconnected from historical roots, could survive: "I am doubtful whether the secular ideal is also capable of gaining strength for very long."[3] The philosopher Martin Buber feared that if Judaism were divorced from the Israeli state, the state would be unable to survive: "A Jewish Commonwealth is to be built in Palestine. It must not become just another of the numberless small states that are devoid of spiritual substance, a place like any other in today's Western world where spirit and people are separated.... It would become crushed in the machinery of its own intrigues."[4]

Scholem, Bergmann, and Buber saw eye to eye with such important figures as A. D. Gordon, Berl Katznelson, and Hayim Nahman Bialik.[5] They all fought against the extreme version of secularism and believed that an intimate connection with the past would not damage secularism but exalt it. But their form of secularism did not become the standard form of Israeli secularism. Although many secular Israelis maintain a connection to their past, many of them see this relationship as a compromise with their secularism, not a fulfillment of it. For the most part, they are not even aware that other, alternative forms of Israeli secularism exist.

3 CULTURAL SECULARISM

Is it possible to connect to tradition without surrendering one's freedom? Is there a way for Jews to maintain a meaningful connection to their past without weakening their secular identity? Over this mammoth task labored a thinker who was one of the founders of Israeli secularism—Ahad Ha'am, born Asher Zvi Hirsch Ginsburg. To this end, he presented a surprising idea: secular Jews can connect to their Judaism without subordinating themselves to religion—simply because Judaism is not a religion.[1]

Deep in the soul of any religious Jew is faith, a belief that above and beyond the reality we can see and comprehend exists another reality—sacred, invisible, and intangible. But according to Ahad Ha'am, this faith is not what stands at the center of the Jewish experience. Judaism is not a religion in which one *believes* but a nation to which one *belongs.* And whereas faith cultivates religiosity, nationhood nurtures solidarity. Instead of faith in a reality greater than ourselves, Judaism centers on faith in the group to which we belong. This sense of belonging replaces religious sentiments as the strongest emotional fiber in Jewish identity.

There are consequences to replacing faith with belonging. According to Ahad Ha'am, an individual's sense of belonging to his or her nation manifests itself through belonging to everything that nation creates. In the Jewish context, such a sense of attachment creates a new, secular basis for the connection to the Jewish tradition. The Torah was neither revealed nor handed down to the Jewish people, but created *by* them. And a sense of belonging to the Jewish people entails a desire to connect to their creative works.[2] If the Jewish tradition is not a religion but a culture, then the stronger secular Jews' love for their nation, the greater their love for its national culture.

In Ahad Ha'am's vision, secular Jews would devote themselves to studying their nation's Holy Scripture in the same way religious yeshiva students did. But while religious Jews scoured these texts for the divine will, secular Jews in the style of Ahad Ha'am would search for the national spirit. Nationalism would therefore become an alternative source of energy, impelling Jews to connect to their tradition. Consequently, the Jewish nationalism that would replace the Jewish religion would not abolish tradition—it would renew it.

Both religious and secular Jews can devote themselves to their tradition's founding texts, but there is still a vast difference between them. For religious Jews, the written word is a source of authority; for secular Jews in the style of Ahad Ha'am, it is a source of inspiration. Books that are sources of authority control their readers; books that are sources of inspiration enrich and empower them.[3]

Ahad Ha'am's position stands against the religious position, but it also contradicts the secular worldview—or at least the rebellious incarnation of Jewish secularism expressed by Micha Josef Berdyczewski discussed above. Ahad Ha'am likened the present to a tree and the past to its roots: "Can a tree be freed from its roots sunk deep underground?"[4] In contrast, Berdyczewski averred that "all that is past, inasmuch as it is the past, buries the present, and all that is old buries the new."[5] If in Ahad Ha'am's view the present grows out of the past, in Berdyczewski's view the past buries the present.

Just as Ahad Ha'am developed a nonreligious affinity with tradition, he also developed a non-rebellious version of secularism. Consider this eye-opening analogy, from the late author Amos Oz, which clarifies Ahad Ha'am's unique position. If the Jewish tradition is the Jews' inheritance—the accumulated, multigenerational wisdom handed down from their ancestors—Jews must ask how best to manage that inheritance. When people inherit their grandparents' property, they do not usually hoard all their possessions at home. Not every chandelier is affixed to the ceiling; not every sofa is moved into the living room. Wise heirs to family property know to fill the living room with whatever belongs there—and to move into storage whatever does not. They choose what to place in the garden as decoration, and if they have nowhere to put a particular heirloom, they might throw it in the garbage. Orthodox religious Jews are like heirs who unreflectively place everything they inherit in the middle of the house. Rebellious secular Jews are like those who would throw the whole inheritance, including priceless treasures, into the trash.[6] Neither truly grasps that the most important skill in identity-formation is to use the inheritance of the wisdom of generations in an astute manner.

For Ahad Ha'am, both religious Jews' slavish devotion to the past and rebellious secular Jews' renunciation of the past represent broken relationships with history. He believed that the greatest challenge of modern Jewish thought was to shape a Judaism that would inherit the wisdom of generations without suffocating under the weight of the burden.

THE FOUNDATIONAL DEBATE OF SECULAR JUDAISM

The debate between Aristotle and Plato was the foundational debate of Greek philosophy; without understanding their differences, we cannot understand ancient Greek thought. The debate between the rival Jewish philosophical schools of Beit Hillel and Beit Shammai was the foundational debate of the Talmudic world, and understanding it is the key to understanding the intellectual world of the Talmud.[7] The debate between Maimonides and Judah Halevi was the foundational debate of medieval Jewish philosophy; without understanding it, we cannot understand medieval Jewish thought. Similarly, the debate between Berdyczewski and Ahad Ha'am was the foundational debate of Israeli secularism. Even if most Israelis remain unaware of this debate, it is the essential window through which the nature of Israeli secularism must be observed.[8]

The question at the heart of the polemic between Berdyczewski and Ahad Ha'am was: What constitutes a free, or secular, Jew? According to Berdyczewski, a free Jew is one who is free from the past. But according to Ahad Ha'am, a free Jew is one who maintains a *free relationship* with the past.

In Talmudic times, it was decided that the halakha would follow Beit Hillel, not Beit Shammai; in the Middle Ages, most Jewish thinkers and sages followed Judah Halevi, not Maimonides. And what happened in the debate over Israeli secularism? Was the secularism that developed the type that draws inspiration from tradition or is cut off from it? The author S. Yizhar had a clear answer: "We have lost the key to the treasures of the People of the Book, so rich in history. And all that was stored from Second Temple times till yesterday is alien to us, silent and dark. Is it because the key to these treasures is primarily religious?"[9]

Yizhar compared the accumulated wisdom of Jewish tradition to a treasure chest, and the key that opens it is a religious one. Israeli secularism does not hold that key and therefore has no access to the treasures of Jewish history. The novelist Aharon Appelfeld similarly pointed to Israelis' alienation from their Jewishness: "There was an attempt here to amputate internal organs of the soul. That caused incapacity, a serious cultural incapacity.... The result is a black hole of identity. That is why there is a deep recoil from everything Jewish."[10]

Ahad Ha'am argued that Judaism was a culture, not a religion, and therefore the secular recoil from religion need not become a secular aversion to Judaism. But Ahad Ha'am's project was never fully realized. Over the years, the antipathy that secular Jews felt toward religion led many of them to become antipathetic toward Judaism. The consequences for their identity were grave. In Appelfeld's scathing words, secular Israelis suffered from a "serious cultural incapacity," and Israeli society found itself in a "black hole of identity."

The debate over the secular Jewish soul ended with a victory for Berdyczewski and defeat for Ahad Ha'am. The dominant model of secularism was one of rebellion, not inspiration, of neglecting the heritage of previous generations, not using the inheritance wisely.[11]

Berdyczewski's philosophy is certainly more complicated than I have presented. The angry Berdyczewski who declared a revolt by the present against the past and by Jews against Judaism also believed that he was rebelling against himself. "When we defeat the past, we ourselves are the defeated," he wrote.[12] Judaism was a part of Berdyczewski's being, and he was conflicted and pained by his revolt against it. "I cannot lie to myself. I regret that I will miss the sanctity of innocence, and I express this regret publicly."[13] Berdyczewski's win, one could say, was also therefore his loss.

Yosef Haim Brenner represented an even more extreme position. Brenner shared Berdyczewski's rebellious impulses, but they were not mellowed by the longing and emotional attachment to the past that drove Berdyczewski. "We . . . the free Jews have nothing to do with Judaism," Brenner declared.[14] To his mind, the ancient Jewish religion had no books or ideas with which it was worth engaging. "Have we not yet heard they've died, the gods have died, all of them? Yes, they are dead to us. Dead forever. And with them, their laws."[15]

Brenner was the torch bearer of an unambiguously resistant and defiant form of secularism. Whereas Berdyczewski could see sparks of light in the darkness of Jewish history, Brenner comprehensively dismissed the tradition. The whole of rabbinic literature was, as he put it so sharply and bluntly, "the words of a dead god."[16]

The gulf between Berdyczewski and Brenner is representative of the gulf between different generations of secular Zionists. The Jews of the Second and Third Aliyah, Berdyczewski among them, rebelled against the Jewish tradition and were emotionally wounded. They turned against the world in which they had grown up. When they dismissed the tradition, they felt they were dismissing something of themselves. In the words of the researcher Moti Zeira, their souls were torn.[17] But the generation who came after them, including Brenner, inherited their desire to revolt against the past but not their nostalgia for it. The second generation of Jewish secularists inherited the founders' secularism without the emotional baggage.[18] These secular Jews openly rejected the tradition without secretly feeling drawn to it. Their secularism was not torn. Thus, in a process that took only two generations, Ahad Ha'am lost, and the revolutionaries won.

Ahad Ha'am would not have been surprised by his defeat. He knew that history was not on his side. In his own day and age, he could already see the attraction of the rebellious version of secularism. He understood that the new secular Jews had difficulty accepting his message. When they looked at the Jewish tradition, they saw only a force that threatened them, not a cultural asset that could enrich their lives. Ahad Ha'am offered a psychological explanation for the secular Jews' emotional recoil from their Judaism. He argued that their aversion to the past was based on a problem not with the past but with the present. The new secular Jews associated the rabbinic literature with the religious Jews of their own time. And since they were put off by the religious Jews of their own time, they were also put off by the ancient tradition that their religious peers purported to represent.

In Ahad Ha'am's words: "Judging by their 'freedom,' they are still slaves to the feelings of hate that fill their hearts against the living religion of the present. And in their imagination they always see a group of fanatics persecuting them to force them to wear a tzitzit and tallit, and this is why they concede their national cultural heritage of the past, in order not to be seen as having any connection to the faith and religion of the present."[19]

Secular Jews' revulsion from religious orthodoxy in the present has become an emotional barrier blocking off intimate contact with the cultural assets of the past. Ahad Ha'am saw this as enslavement. If religious Jews are enslaved by religion, secular Jews are enslaved by their hatred of religion.

SECULAR JEWISH RENEWAL

The revolt against religion was victorious. But although Ahad Ha'am was defeated, his ideas did not die. They survived on the periphery of Israeli culture, biding their time. Now, in the twenty-first century, it may be time to resurrect them.

There are signs that Ahad Ha'am's alternative secularism is beginning to revive. Plato once noted that when a society's music changes, that is a clear sign that the whole society is changing.[20] And Israeli music is indeed experiencing a change. Ehud Banai is writing, composing, and singing a new type of songbook, as are Kobi Oz, Corinne Allal, Berry Sakharof, Etti Ankri, and many others. They are setting biblical verses, lines from prayers, and medieval poems to music, sometimes even composing their own original prayers. With so many leading artists involved, the phenomenon is reaching a critical mass in Israeli culture. "Jewish" music, which until recently was considered separate from "Israeli" music, is now an organic part of the Israeli music scene. The names of these artists might not be familiar to Diaspora Jews, but in Israel they are popular artists on par with Bob Dylan and Bruce Springsteen.

The change is coming not only in the new songs. There are also new books. In recent years, publishers have started giving prominence to books that make Judaism accessible. Books about Jewish philosophy, Kabbalah, the Talmud, and the Hebrew Bible are being written for the general public and becoming best sellers. Just as Jewish music has become Israeli, books about Judaism are no longer trapped under the category of "holy texts."

Music is composed and books are written when there is demand for them. When there seems to be a cultural hunger for them. And this hunger can be seen in the new, nonreligious *batei midrash* (Jewish study centers) that are opening up and flourishing all over Israel.[21] These new study centers teach the Gemara, the Mishnah, and the Hebrew Bible, but most of the students are not religious, nor do they intend to become religious. They are returning to their tradition—without turning to religion.

Here, then, are three signs that something new is happening: Israeli music is evolving, Israeli nonfiction is expanding, and the offerings of Jewish study halls in Israel are changing. Many secular Israelis are looking to get back in touch with the Jewish tradition without being controlled by that tradition. They are successfully overcoming the emotional barriers and drawing inspiration from the past without making negative associations, as the early secularists did, with what repels them in the present. They are not becoming religious—they are becoming another kind of secular Jew. Ahad Ha'am's secularism is back.

This phenomenon, known as the Jewish renewal, is not widespread, but it is spreading, and it shows that an alternative type of secularism can develop alongside more classical secularism. And note, this "Jewish renewal" has nothing to do with the progressive, neo-Hasidic movement that shares its name: it is the birth of a vibrant, secular culture that draws on its ancient roots. The Jewish religious world, as we know, is diverse and impassioned. Alongside the dominant streams of Judaism, each generation creates alternative interpretations of its own. And indeed, it seems that not only the religious world has disagreements; so does the secular world. Just as every few generations Jewish history throws up an alternative religious movement to the dominant religious stream, so now we are beginning to see the emergence of another form of secularism, an alternative to the central stream of Jewish secularism.

Secularism is a mindset of sovereignty. Secular people consider themselves to have complete sovereignty over their own lives. And this might lead to a surprising conclusion: as secularism becomes more *Jewish*, it also becomes more *secular*. Secular Jews who study the foundational texts of the Jewish tradition do not limit their personal sovereignty; they enhance it. They apply their own sovereignty to the Jewish tradition. This important reversal can also be seen in the sharp words of one of the founding thinkers of Israeli secularism, Berl Katznelson: "A renewing and creative generation does not throw the cultural heritage of ages into the dustbin. It examines and scrutinizes, accepts and rejects. At times it may keep and add to an accepted tradition. At times it descends into ruined grottoes to excavate and remove the dust from that which had lain in forgetfulness, in order to resuscitate old traditions which have the power to stimulate the spirit of the generation of renewal."[22]

The Jews are in control of their history, Katznelson proclaimed. From the heritage of past generations, they can choose what suits them and throw in the dustbin whatever cannot nourish them. Secular Jews who feel attached to their Judaism are therefore freer than secular Jews who cut themselves off from it. Their freedom includes the freedom to choose what they want from the past rather than simply the freedom to reject it.

Notwithstanding everything I have said about the "Jewish renewal" and the emergence of an alternative secularism, however, this idea has not been fully internalized by secular society in Israel. I say this based on my own life experience. I have often seen how surprised secular Israelis are to discover that someone they know is studying the Talmud and Hebrew Bible out of curiosity and enthusiasm. They are almost always certain that anyone who explores these texts is taking the first steps toward becoming religious. They cannot fathom the possibility that their friends might not be becoming religious but rather choosing a different kind of secular life. Their resistance to such an idea may be because they are unfamiliar with alternative models of secularism. Many secular Israelis are convinced there is only one authentic way to be secular.

The lack of secular pluralism in Israel mirrors the lack of religious pluralism. Read the founding texts of Jewish religious thought, and you will discover there is more than one way of being religious. Read the founding texts of secular thought, and you will discover there is more than one way of being secular. In modern Israel, the Orthodox religious establishment controls who can and cannot be a rabbi, and what constitutes an authentic conversion. But the secular world has its own orthodoxy: a strong, dominant voice that determines what qualifies as truly secular.

The "Jewish renewal" within Israel's secular public offers another kind of secularism. Following the path charted by Ahad Ha'am, it proposes an alternative model of secularism and another way to be free. It challenges the conventionally accepted trade-off:

that a sense of belonging that fills one's life with meaning must come at the expense of intellectual integrity and personal liberty.

WHY IS THIS RENEWAL HAPPENING NOW?

Twenty-five years ago I was a frightened soldier at an IDF infantry basic training camp. My biggest fear was of my commander, Nachshon. I was a sloppy and scatterbrained soldier, who kept on losing his military gear and was repeatedly late in performing missions. Night after night, I showed up at the gates of the base to face the punishment my commander meted out to me. I remember well those nights with Commander Nachshon when he made me run with heavy equipment on my back up and down a hill over and over again.

Twelve years later, I found myself facing Commander Nachshon again. I had just finished teaching a lesson at the Hebrew University of Jerusalem. As I was walking down the corridor at the Mount Scopus campus talking to students about some issues that had come up in the lesson, I saw him. He was a first-year philosophy student. I approached him cautiously, said hello politely, and quickly went on my way. When I noticed that my heart rate was rising, I asked myself what was happening to me. Could it be that I was still afraid of the man who had been my commander in basic training twelve years earlier? Nachshon was now a frightened freshman, and I was a university lecturer. Why was I afraid to see him? Why when I looked at him could I not see Nachshon the student but only Nachshon the commander?

It can be confusing to see someone who once had authority over one in a new light. Is it possible to meet such a person without hearing echoes of his former authority? This is also the question facing Israeli secularists. For many generations, the Jewish tradition was authoritative. Could it be stripped of its authority and a new relationship be forged with it? Ahad Ha'am believed that it could. He believed that Jews could strip the tradition of its magisterial robes and reconnect on that basis. Jews could adopt ancient ideas and ancient Jewish wisdom without getting ensnared and imprisoned by the authority of tradition. Berdyczewski thought otherwise. He thought that tradition always implied authority, such that any connection with it would eventually lead to its taking control. The only way to shake off the authority of the tradition was to shake off the tradition itself.

I bumped into Nachshon the commander again eight years later. This time, I was in no rush to run away. He invited me for a cup of coffee, and I accepted. We reminisced about times gone by. Nachshon, I discovered, was a sensitive man with a strange and infectious sense of humor. This time, he no longer appeared to me as my commander, just as Nachshon. After twenty years his authority had diminished, no longer concealing the man in front of me. When we finished our meeting, I knew that I had finally been released from the army.

During the first generations of Jewish secularism, the authoritative stranglehold that the tradition held hid that tradition from the eyes of many. But perhaps now some forces in the secular world are breaking free of their identity-related fears, and are ready to reconnect with the tradition without fearing it might swallow them whole. This seems to me one of the main reasons why the first generations of secular Jews tended to express their identity by rebelling against the past and attacking religion, while growing sections of the present generation have enough confidence in themselves and their identity as free Jews to express their secularism through renewed engagement with the tradition. The "Jewish renewal" is not an expression of the core voice within Israeli Jewish secularism, but it does express a new voice within it. It is the voice of people who have lost their fear. And this loss of fear of the tradition indicates that their secularism has gained, not lost, strength. The secularism that engages with Judaism is a secularism that has finally managed to release itself from religion.

4 MYSTICAL SECULARISM

Removing God from the Jewish tradition, as we have seen, does not destroy the tradition itself. Even without God, the ancient Jewish texts have meaning. In this chapter I shall present another form of secularism: a secularism *with* God. What follows is the radical argument of A. D. Gordon: secular Jews have a clearer pathway than religious Jews to God.

Ahad Ha'am's philosophy assumes that knowledge is power. By studying their tradition, Jews could acquire a sense of ownership over their Judaism and become the masters of their relationship with the past. Yitzhak Volcani, one of the most prominent intellectuals of the Second Aliyah, rejected this argument: "Man cannot choose the different foundations on which his soul is built, and he does not govern it. . . . We are one link in a chain of generations. . . . We can legislate new tablets of law, but they will always contain sparks from the old ones. Always, even if we make every effort to extinguish them."[1]

Whereas Katznelson argued that Jews must choose from the past the elements with which to reshape their present identity, Volcani argued that such a choice was not in their hands. The past has its own imperceptible means of insinuating itself into our consciousness. The tradition remains a presence in the minds even of Jews who are convinced that they have broken free of it.

Gershom Scholem echoed Volcani's argument eloquently in his analysis of the likely implications of the revival of the Hebrew language. Hebrew had been a holy tongue for many generations, the language of Torah study and prayer. Jews conducted their dealings with God in Hebrew and their dealings with one another in secular tongues. But with the movement to revive Hebrew, the sacred language was moved out of the synagogue and into the market and street. Suddenly, Hebrew was the language for speaking no longer only to God but to fellow Jews.

The secularization of Hebrew was part of the process of asserting secular Jews' ownership over the treasures of Jewish history. But Scholem argued that the project was doomed to fail: the day would come when the past would take back control of those who tried to seize it:

> The Land [of Israel] is a volcano. It is a storehouse for the [Hebrew] language.... Will the abyss of the sacred language, in which we have immersed our children, not open its jaws? Indeed, people here do not understand the significance of their actions. They believe they have turned Hebrew into a secular language. That they have removed its apocalyptic sting. But this is not the truth.... If we pass on to our children the language that was passed on to us, if we, the transition generation, revive in their lives the ancient mystery language so that it may be revealed to them anew—will the religious power hid-

den inside it not erupt against its speakers? … After all, with this language we are living as if on the edge of an abyss, and almost all of us walk confidently, like the blind. Is there not the fear that we or our successors will stumble into it, when we open our eyes?[2]

The Hebrew language, in Scholem's view, had been used for many generations, and each generation had left its mark on it. Over the years, the ancient words had become burdened with associations of tremendous religious power. The revival of the Hebrew language might therefore revive all its latent associations as well, which would overhaul how its speakers thought and one day bring the secular project crashing down.

"This Hebrew is pregnant with calamity," wrote Scholem. "It cannot remain in its current state. Nor will it. Our children again have no other language. And the truth must be said: they, and they alone, will pay the price of this encounter, which we have imposed on them without asking them, without asking ourselves. When the language turns its guns on its speakers—and at some moments it is already doing so now, and these are moments that are difficult to forget, leaving wounds that reveal the hubris of our task—will our youth survive the revolt of the holy language?"[3]

According to Scholem, the pioneers of the revival of Hebrew failed to understand that they were not in control of the Hebrew language and that it would one day control them. They did not understand that the words they were bringing back to life would swallow them whole. "God," said Scholem, "will not remain mute in the language in which he was made to vow thousands of times to return to our lives."[4]

Secular Israelis, in Scholem and Volcani's view, might have much less control over their world than they thought. The past has tremendous power and acts on the human consciousness in ways we cannot recognize. As we saw, cultural secularism allows Jews to control their own past. But cultural secularism ignores the unconscious power that flows from that ancient tradition to our present reality. These unconscious dimensions exist in another type of alternative secularism. This secularism diverges from Ahad Ha'am's path, seeking contact with the unconscious energy of the Jewish tradition. This radical secularism cultivates in its adherents an experiential and mystical connection to God.

BUBER AND GORDON: BETWEEN RELIGION AND RELIGIOSITY

Aaron David Gordon was one of secular Zionism's greatest thinkers, yet he was full of religious fervor. Gordon believed that the world was but an extension of God, whose fingerprints could be sensed all around us. Gordon wrote of God: "You interact with him with every thought and feeling, although you can't grasp him or understand him."[5] The external reality, including the people who live within it, is nothing but an expression of an internal, hidden divine reality.[6] According to Gordon, rather than speaking *to* God, humans could have a transcendental experience of being part *of* God: "The mental life of every living being is only a drop in the wider ocean of life, and only within that ocean and in complete unity with it is that being truly complete and whole."[7]

Human beings are prevented by mental blocks from sensing the unity of this hidden, divine reality. Humanity's greatest aspiration is to remove these blocks and become one with the divine.[8]

Gordon describes this mystical moment of unity with God in a similar manner to the analogous descriptions by Jewish Kabbalists and Hasidim, and by Sufis and Buddhists: "You will certainly have moments in which seemingly your whole being melts into the infinite. Then you will grow silent. Not only speech but also song and even thought will be sacrilege to you. You will know the secret, the holiness of silence."[9]

Gordon was one of the most important thinkers of socialist Zionism, revered by the rebellious secular Jews of the Second and Third Aliyah. If we wonder how a fervent desire for God like Gordon's fit into a movement with such a secular worldview, Gordon himself had a simple and surprising answer: he was jettisoning his religion precisely because of his strong desire to be one with God. Gordon believed that religion was not a bridge to God, but a barrier between humans and God.[10]

The tension between love for God and distaste for religion was not unique to Gordon. It runs throughout the history of religion. Martin Buber articulated it clearly when he drew a distinction between "religion" and "religiosity" as two different, almost contradictory, phenomena.[11] Religion is formalized and institutionalized; religiosity is fluid and spontaneous. Religions—such as Christianity, Islam, and to a lesser extent Judaism—have organizations, leadership, budgets, and bureaucracies. They have official doctrines, standard ceremonies, and peremptory norms. "Religiosity," in contrast, is a turbulent and emotional matter. It is neither institutionalized nor formalized, and it inhabits our inner world, sometimes bursting out at unexpected moments. Human beings can have a religious experience looking at a breathtaking vista, listening to music, or meditating and becoming absorbed in peaceful quiet. To some extent, Buber used "religiosity" to mean something like what "spirituality" means nowadays. In short, religion and religiosity are almost opposites. In Buber's words:

> Religiosity starts anew with every young person, shaken to his very core by the mystery; religion wants to force him into a system stabilized for all time. Religiosity means activity—the elemental entering-into-relation with the absolute; religion means passivity—an acceptance of the handed-down command.... Religiosity induces sons, who want to find their own God, to rebel against their fathers; religion induces fathers to reject their sons, who will not let their fathers' God be forced upon them.[12]

William James, one of the preeminent psychologists of religion, collected reports from different places and cultures about people's spiritual experiences, and found that they were quite similar.[13] Some people reported strongly sensing a mysterious presence. Others said they felt the walls between them and the cosmos disintegrating, feeling unity and oneness with the rest of existence.

Spiritual experiences are many and varied, and Buber believed that they are accessible to all who train their minds to receive them and are willing to open their hearts. And according to Buber, a strong tension exists between religion and religiosity. Religion threatens religiosity: the moment religiosity is institutionalized, it is choked off and fated to ultimately disappear.

Buber's distinction sheds light on Gordon's mystical secularism. Gordon was not seeking religion but religiosity. He wished to experience the complete unification of his soul with the divine presence that infused reality, and he felt that the Jewish religion was weighing him down and stopping him from achieving this. Why? The beliefs in the Jewish religion were too rigid, its laws immutable.[14] This stagnation was a danger to feelings of religiosity, which demanded renewal: "Like every living emotion, it [religiosity] needs a dynamic, living expression."[15] For Gordon, therefore, Jews needed to free themselves from their religion in order to renew their religiosity. It followed, then, that secularization was the force that would pave the way back to God.[16]

RELIGIOUS EXPERIENCE

What was religious experience for Gordon? He did not just describe it; he also coined a word for it, combining the Hebrew words *chayyim* (life) and *havaya* (being) to form a new word, *chavaya*, "immediate experience." *Chavaya* is the opposite of *hakara*, "intellectual knowledge."[17] Intellectual knowledge is our power of rational comprehension; immediate experience happens when we tap into our subconscious. For Gordon, the revealed and hidden parts of ourselves correspond to the revealed and hidden parts of reality. There is a visible physical reality and a hidden spiritual reality. When we successfully connect to the hidden recesses of our mind, we unite with the hidden inner soul of the whole of reality: "The unknown plane, therefore, holds for man the point of cohesion where the individual soul of man merges with the soul of all creation, and becomes one living soul. All that is original and illumined by the superior light in the soul of man, all that we call loftiness of the spirit, the spirit of holiness, if you will, issues forth from this infinite sea."[18]

Gordon's mysticism differs from other forms of mysticism. In his theory, a great cosmic experience is not the wiping out of one's consciousness. It does not stem from self-abnegation or immersion in a sea of divinity. For Gordon, connection is a substitute for self-abnegation: "A surplus of life is the quality of living one's complete self and beyond one's own boundaries, overflowing into all that is alive and exists, into infinity."[19]

In Gordon's philosophy, one can experience oneself expanding into the divine presence latent in reality and merging with it. In our regular state of conscious awareness, there is a barrier between the self and the world. We look at the world, and the world is outside us. But when we move from "awareness" to "experience" of the world, the world is no longer external to us. We expand into the world and become part of it—in effect, at one with it. "A person needs to comprehend with his entire being that he and the cosmos are one, and he is connected and united with all that exists with his entire physical and spiritual being."[20]

This is the reason why religion is a threat to religiosity. With their clear-cut beliefs and rituals, religions trap the mind within the narrow bounds of their awareness of external reality, preventing adherents from experiencing reality's hidden layers. Religion thus *distances* people from God. Gordon felt that if religion were to be the foundation of a higher, dynamic human life, it could not remain static, nor could it cleave to laws and beliefs handed down from time immemorial. "Beliefs and opinions are not religion," he wrote, "nor are laws and accepted norms—religion is a religious feeling, a feeling of the complete union of the human 'I' with all of world experience, an experiential comprehension that precedes intellectual comprehension." For Gordon, *this* was the one eternal precept of religion. It had no other laws than the obligations that followed from this feeling of transcendence.[21]

One of Gordon's greatest contributions to Israeli culture was to spread the revolutionary idea that *secular* rather than religious Jews have the closest contact with the divine. In Gordon's philosophy, spirituality is not under threat from secularism—it is *based* on it. Secularism is a condition for an intimate connection to the divine.

Gordon's philosophy expands the range of possibilities open to secular Israelis. If Ahad Ha'am teaches that secularism at its most profound maintains a relationship with the past, Gordon teaches that contact with the divine is the consequence and perhaps even the goal of secular freedom.

To highlight the difference between the theories of Ahad Ha'am and Gordon, let us briefly consider Gordon's particular approach to the study of the Hebrew Bible. Engagement with the treasures of Jewish culture is the beating heart of Ahad Ha'am's cultural secularism. How does Gordon approach the study of the greatest treasure of Jewish culture? "We think that in discovering new ideas in the Bible, we are interpreting the Bible. But the opposite is true. The external meaning of the Bible is an interpretation of the internal Bible in our souls. Without this interpretation . . . we would know nothing about our hidden treasures."[22]

According to Gordon, Jews do not interpret the Hebrew Bible so much as it interprets them. It is a text that has the power to connect Jewish readers to the depths of their souls. As Gordon put it, the Hebrew Bible animates a Jew's experience, not his or her awareness. Gordon read the Hebrew Bible selectively and only delved into the chapters that awakened his inner spiritual life.[23] If for Ahad Ha'am Torah study was an intellectual activity that expanded a Jew's horizons, for Gordon that activity was experiential.

The ultra-Orthodox Jewish world contains two branches: the Hasidim and the Lithuanians. The former crave the experience of attachment to God; the latter aspire to understand his law. For the Hasidim, Judaism makes possible the emotional experience of proximity to God. For the Lithuanians, Judaism requires a deep intellectual acquaintance with the Torah.

The secular Jewish world has its own Hasidim and Lithuanians. Ahad Ha'am, if you will, was a secular Lithuanian. His proposed connection to the past is intellectual.[24] Gordon, in contrast, was a Hasid. His proposed connection to the past is experiential and spiritual.

Once more, we discover, there is more than one way for a Jew to be religious—and more than one way to be secular, too.

5 HALAKHIC SECULARISM

In the Jewish tradition, the past is engaged in a dialogue with the future. The prophets and sages did not want people to learn *about* them but *from* them. Holy Scriptures are letters from the past to the future, in which previous generations make demands of the generations to come. Religious Jews aspire to obey these commands. Secular Jews are free of them. After all, what is secular freedom if not freedom from the commands and dictates of the past?

But here arises a new question: Does secular freedom require one to ignore and be indifferent to the desires and demands of previous generations? I am not so sure. One can be free of the past without ignoring it. Indifference to the previous generations is not the only alternative to enslavement by them. There is another way to express one's freedom from the authority of the past, and the man who tried to articulate it was another of the founding thinkers of Israeli secularism: Hayim Nahman Bialik.

Our relationship to the past is similar to our other relationships. Relationships based on obedience or apathy are unhealthy.

According to Bialik, a free life means listening to the desires and demands of previous generations without feeling the need to obey them. In Bialik's vision of secularism, the past does not control the present, but it does influence it.

Bialik was Ahad Ha'am's disciple and saw him as a guide and the prophet of his generation.[1] But he did not accept Ahad Ha'am's idea that it is enough to study the ancient tradition in order to belong to it. Bialik took one step farther than Ahad Ha'am and insisted that a life inspired by the past must be expressed through one's behavior in the present. Bialik had a daring vision: the secular revitalization of Jewish religious law.

> A generation is growing up in an atmosphere of mere phrases and catchwords, and a kind of go-as-you-please Judaism is being created out of the breath of empty words.... But where is the *duty?* ... Aspiration, good will, spiritual uplift, heartfelt love—all these are excellent and valuable when they lead to action, to action which is hard as iron and obeys the stern behests of duty.... What we need is to have duties imposed on us![2]

Bialik demanded a life of deeds, not words. The core of Judaism had always been based on religious law instead of philosophy, and therefore the revitalization of Judaism had to be reflected in the revitalization of its commands, not just its precepts. Nevertheless, it was important for Bialik to emphasize that he was not calling for a return to the *Shulchan Aruch*—Rabbi Joseph Caro's sixteenth-century code of Jewish law—nor was he hoping to duplicate traditional halakha. "Shall we, then, return to the *Shulchan Aruch?* So to interpret my words is to misunderstand them completely."[3]

Bialik's vision of Jewish secularism was far more sweeping than that of his mentor Ahad Ha'am. The challenge that Ahad Ha'am posed to the secular revival was the challenge of secular Jewish enlightenment. The challenge that Bialik posed was of secular Jewish halakha.

Of all Judaism's ancient laws, which must Zionism revitalize? According to Bialik, this bold vision of halakhic secularism should be realized first and foremost by revitalizing the Sabbath commandment ("Remember the Sabbath day, to keep it holy"): "In order to create fresh, original forms of life that have a national character and demeanor, it is necessary to take the raw material for these creations from the building blocks of ancient forms of the nation's life. And even if we need to create a new foundation, we should take the foundation stone from the foundation of tradition. And we will never find a higher form or a deeper one to create new original forms of cultural life than the creation of the Sabbath."[4]

The Sabbath is an ancient cultural institution, which must be refined and reshaped into a new, revised form. Bialik's Sabbath can serve as a shining example of the use of a valuable tradition to help rejuvenate Judaism in the present.[5]

The primary function of the Sabbath, according to Bialik, is to create another level for Zionists, above the struggle for survival. On weekdays, we struggle to remain alive. On the Sabbath, we reach for the meaning of life. Without the Sabbath, "we [would be] a debased and despicable people, not even a real people. We must exalt the value of the Sabbath among ourselves here and in every place, especially in the eyes of the young generation; and no—if we rot, we shall not have rebirth."[6] Bialik believed that the sanctity of the Sabbath must be an organic part of the secular Zionist enterprise.

This still raises the question, however: Are the words *secular* and *halakha* irreconcilable? Secularism is based on freedom; halakha sets limits to freedom. Secularism is a liberation from authority; halakha is based on obedience to authority. Surely "secular halakha" is an oxymoron. Can Jews who have freed themselves from an antiquated tradition be expected to commit to a revitalized religious code? This is an intellectual challenge for Bialik's philosophy, but his own writings do not contain the answer. Instead, it can be found in a fascinating experiment in Jewish secularism conducted in recent years in the United States.

This experiment was an initiative led by an organization called Reboot, headed by American Jewish artists who are not religious and feel no obligation to Jewish religious law. They launched an initiative called Unplug Yourself, in which they call on people to abstain from technology one day a week.[7] They do not demand a complete disconnection from technology: they travel on the Sabbath and use electricity. Their disconnection is from all contact with the virtual world. No email, no internet, no social media. The initiative has enjoyed notable success, with increasing numbers of young Americans joining it. Randi Zuckerberg, sister of the Facebook founder Mark Zuckerberg, argues that people need a weekly detox to cleanse their minds from the toxins of technology.[8] Reboot is not a rabbinical initiative. Those who answer the call to abstain from digital technology one day a week are not adherents—they are participants. So the question of how halakhic secularism can become a reality remains. How can the inherent contradiction contained in the idea of "halakhic secularism" be overcome? The answer, it seems, is already emerging: a halakha without authority is a halakha that people follow not out of obedience but out of a desire to join it.

This American test case highlights a particularly Israeli problem. It is easier for American Jews to come into contact with their past without fearing that they will be ensnared in its web of authority. This is because religion in the United States does not carry the weight of legislative authority, and religious leaders do not have the power to place coercive restrictions on freedom. Judaism in America has never been politicized and does not serve as a mechanism of control, and as such it is much less threatening to Americans than Israeli Judaism is to Israelis. In order for Israelis to feel comfortable about forging ties with their tradition, they need to overcome the trauma wrought by the politicization of religion in Israel.

Israeli secularism has not yet revitalized halakha, and Bialik's vision has not yet been realized. In modern Israel, the Sabbath has not developed as a cultural asset. Israelis who talk about the importance of the Sabbath are not seen as calling for a secular renewal—they are suspected of promoting religious coercion. Like Ahad Ha'am's cultural revival, Bialik's halakhic revival has fallen victim to Zionism's clash of identities.[9] Instead of the Sabbath empowering Zionism, Zionism has injured the Sabbath. But perhaps Bialik's idea might still be realized, and the Sabbath might yet experience a halakhic but still secular flourishing. In the Afterword, I offer some suggestions on how this challenge can be tackled.

6 IS SECULAR JUDAISM STILL JUDAISM?

I remember well the day I heard the news that Yeshayahu Leibowitz had died. I was mesmerized by Leibowitz's philosophy and was influenced by his ideas, but as soon as I had become aware of this towering figure, he passed away. I was a soldier, and I asked my course commander for permission to attend his funeral. He asked me whether I was a member of Professor Leibowitz's family, and I said no. "Reading his book doesn't make him your grandpa," my commander said, and he refused to give me leave for the funeral. I was reminded of this disappointment a few years later and asked myself: Who had more power over me? The officer who controlled my movements—or the philosopher who influenced my thoughts?

There is a profound difference between control and inspiration. Control limits opportunities and thereby restricts liberty. Influence, by contrast, enhances liberty by creating new possibilities from which to choose. Control makes us smaller; influence makes us greater. This distinction between control and influence can also be applied to tradition. Is its purpose to control us or influence us? Is it a strict commander or wise instructor?

In the European version of Orthodox Judaism, tradition is a source of authority. Jews must obey what the holy books and rabbis say; Judaism controls a Jew's life. Jewish secularism, in contrast, declared itself liberated from the authority of Judaism. But liberation from the authority of tradition need not be expressed as a disconnection from tradition. Instead of replacing control with rebellion, Jews can also replace control with influence.

This option offers a way out of the identity trap with which this book began. The dilemma—whether to sacrifice one's liberty for the sake of a link to tradition or to sacrifice a link to one's tradition for the sake of liberty—is based on the assumption that the only possible relationship between Judaism and Jews is one of control. But Ahad Ha'am devised a school of thought in which the Jewish tradition can have influence without control; Gordon created a philosophy that allows Jews to draw on spiritual and even mystical influence from the Hebrew Bible and tradition without subordinating themselves to them; and Hayim Nahman Bialik went so far as to dream of a life built around a Jewish legal code based on influence and inspiration rather than power and control. Each of these thinkers sketched out a way for Jews to return to the Jewish tradition without becoming religious. Their proposals call on Jews neither to surrender to the past nor to abandon it. They call on them to *continue* it.

But what is "continuity"? Those who *continue* the past neither subordinate themselves to the past nor subordinate the past to themselves. Instead, they make a connection between their world and the worlds that came before them. The philosopher Ronald Dworkin proposed the following analogy to illustrate this point:[1] Suppose a group of novelists decided to write a novel together, each adding a chapter in sequence: after one person wrote the first chapter, the next would write the second chapter, the next the third chapter, and so on. What will ensure that the finished book will be a success—for the story to flow and the narrative to develop from one chapter to the next? Quite simply, each author must write a chapter that follows from the earlier ones. If one novelist writes a chapter without reading the previous ones, then his or her chapter will not be a continuation. By the same token, if another novelist writes a chapter that simply copies previous chapters, it will not be a continuation either.[2]

In its rebellious version, secularism does not *continue* a story because it has no contact with previous chapters; and in its reactionary form, religion does not *continue* a story because it is stuck in previous chapters. Neither secular nor religious Jews can find a way to add a new, unique chapter to Jewish tradition for the present generation because they both refuse to *continue* the Jewish story.

Ahad Ha'am's cultural secularism, A. D. Gordon's mystical secularism, and Bialik's "new halakhic" secularism are three answers to the question of continuity. Each proposes a different kind of continuity, and together they attempt to pave a way for modern Jews to avoid being stuck in the past without being cut off from it. They offer a way to continue the Jewish tradition.

Ahad Ha'am, Gordon, and Bialik believed that the new Jewish secularism—like the Talmud, Kabbalah, medieval Jewish philosophy, and Hasidism—was a new interpretation of Judaism. They also believed that a secular interpretation was no less authentic or less Jewish than the interpretations, streams, and movements that preceded them. Perhaps the core disagreement within Israeli

Jewish secularism is best phrased thus: Micha Josef Berdyczewski argued for secularism as liberation *from* Judaism, whereas Ahad Ha'am and others conceived of it as innovation *within* Judaism.[3]

The Jewish tradition is a tradition of upheavals. Over the generations, it has taken several philosophical twists and turns, each of which has given it the gift of renewal. Each has added a new chapter to continue the Jewish story. Secularism, in Ahad Ha'am's school, is one such innovation.[4] In his mind, the shift to secularism would save Judaism and guarantee its relevance.

Ahad Ha'am's model was Maimonides. In medieval times, Judaism's esoteric philosophy needed to be laid bare for Judaism to maintain its relevance, and this is what Maimonides did. In modern times, Judaism's secular and cultural side needs to be laid bare, and this is what Ahad Ha'am did. Ahad Ha'am and his disciples argued that Judaism was not the work of God but of the Jewish people, and the desire to connect to Judaism should come not from a fear of God but from a love of nation. In such a case, modern Jews' attack on religion would not be an attack on Judaism because Judaism was not a religion. The secularization of Judaism, which many people considered an assault on Judaism, was for Ahad Ha'am a means of protecting it.[5]

Now is the time to pause and ask, Is Ahad Ha'am's sweeping argument convincing? Does the principle of continuity apply to his philosophy without conceding its intellectual integrity? We need to ask this question of Ahad Ha'am specifically, because even if Gordon's spiritual secularism and Bialik's "revitalized halakha" can be seen as continuations of Judaism, it is much harder to say the same of Ahad Ha'am's atheistic Judaism.[6] If Jewish secularism gives up on God and turns religion into a culture, it must contend with the question of whether it has gone a step too far. After God is sidelined, can whatever remains be called "Judaism"?

This is not an easy question, and Ahad Ha'am's philosophy has been strongly attacked on this front. Opponents argue that he was trying to have his cake and eat it: to liberate himself from Judaism while claiming to be adhering to Judaism. In the argument of the literary scholar Baruch Kurzweil,

> Ahad Ha'am takes the existence of the secular interpretation of Judaism and the loss of faith in a living God as a basic assumption, as a natural hallmark of the developmental stage that Judaism had reached at his time. . . . This is a pretense of continuity and contiguity, while continuity and contiguity implicitly mean the ultimate loss of faith. And all this is done quietly, modestly, without a hint of polemic. . . . This was a figment of Ahad Ha'am's imagination.[7]

Kurzweil argued that when Ahad Ha'am cut himself off from faith, he was cutting himself off from the Jewish tradition. Admittedly, he had a strong case. Faith in God had been the beating heart of the Jewish tradition for every generation. How could Jews disconnect from faith in God without disconnecting from the tradition?

We cannot know how Ahad Ha'am himself would have answered this question. It is a profound quandary, calling into question his entire enterprise. But anyone who believes, as I do, that his philosophy is relevant and vital for this generation has no choice but to try to answer it.[8]

THE PARADOX OF SANCTIFYING GOD

The ancient biblical faith was humanity's first heresy. The Hebrew Bible is a radical book, which challenged the prevailing conceptions of the ancient world. During biblical times, it was generally believed that the gods belonged to the natural world and were subject to the eternal laws of nature. The gods lived in the mountains, the forests, the seas, and the earth. The biblical tradition denied this. It presented an alternative faith, in which the forces of nature no longer represented the gods who resided within them. There was one God, and he was one. He was not part of nature but above and beyond it.[9] The Hebrew Bible removed God from the world.

But even after God was removed from nature, a connection remained between God and the world, one that was expressed through prophetic revelation. God revealed himself to the world through his prophets. He sent prophets to human societies to convey his fiery protests against their ruling powers and prevailing norms. The biblical revolution, therefore, had two parts: God was taken out of the world and he revealed himself to prophets whom he exhorted to change the world.

The Talmudic tradition continued only part of the biblical tradition. The Talmud retains a belief in a supranatural God, but prophecy is no longer part of the Talmudic world: "The Sages taught: After the last of the prophets, Haggai, Zechariah, and Malachi, died, the Divine Spirit of prophetic revelation departed from the Jewish people."[10]

According to the sages of the Talmud, God no longer reveals himself to humankind and no longer instructs people on how to act in the natural world. Moreover, even in the rare cases in which echoes of the divine will can be heard in Jewish study halls in the form of a "divine voice," these echoes possess no legal validity. "Rabbi Yirmeya says: Since the Torah was already given at Mount Sinai, we do not regard a Divine Voice."[11] In the sages' world, God had lost his authority to shape people's lives. The result was an unbridgeable gap between God and humanity. "Rabbi Elazar said: Since the day the Temple was destroyed an iron wall separates Israel from their Father in heaven."[12]

But this process did not end with the Talmud. In the Middle Ages, Maimonides took the Jewish tradition one further, decisive step toward completely removing God from the world. He declared that human language was powerless to describe God. Language would put God and the natural world in the same category, so the only way to place God beyond this world was to place him beyond language. According to Maimonides' *via negativa* proof, nothing tangible can be said about God. God is greater than language. "The idea is best expressed in the book of Psalms, 'Silence is praise to Thee.'"[13] In the face of God, Maimonides concluded, we can only fall silent.

The Talmudic sages determined that God no longer speaks *to* humanity. Maimonides judged that humanity can no longer speak *about* God. In some sense, the history of Jewish thought, from the Bible to Maimonides, is the history of God moving farther away from our everyday experience. The writers of the Bible looked at a pagan world in which the divine resided within nature and took the divine out of nature—but kept it connected to the world through the channel of prophecy. The Talmudic sages blocked the channel of prophecy. And then along came Maimonides to remove God from the bounds of language altogether. The more the Jewish faith in God developed, the farther away it distanced him from the world and humankind.

This is, of course, a generalization and it was not the only change that occurred in the Jewish tradition. The Hebrew Bible also contained voices that are incompatible with pure mono-theism. Some Talmudic sages did not accept the injunction against a "divine voice." And in the Middle Ages, Kabbalah offered a sweeping alternative to the distancing of God; in Kabbalah, God is present in the world through his *sephirot*, or emanations. So the story presented above about the distancing of God is not the only story in the Jewish tradition, but it is a *central* story in that tradi-tion. That God stands aloof from the natural world was the domi-nant belief of Hebrew Scripture; that prophecy has ended and God no longer speaks to humanity was the dominant belief in the Tal-mud; and that God cannot be described through words was the belief propounded by one of the towering Jewish thinkers of the Middle Ages.

The Hebrew word that describes God's otherness is *kadosh*, "sacred." Before the Torah was handed down at Mount Sinai, God ordered Moses: "Set bounds about the mount, and sanctify it."[14] The bounded mountain was sacred. It was not to be touched. Simi-larly, the Torah sets a prohibition on uttering the most sacred word in the Hebrew language—the name of God. Even the most sacred location in Judaism—the Holy of Holies in the Temple in Jerusa-lem—is a space that Jews are forbidden to enter. The sacred is the inaccessible, whatever is beyond the realm of human touch. We can say that in moving from the pagan world to the biblical world, from the biblical to the Talmudic world, and from the Talmudic to the Maimonidean world, Judaism sanctified God. This is the story of an audacious religious idea that produced one of the most interesting paradoxes in Jewish theology: the more *sacred* God becomes, the more secular does the world.

The power of this paradox becomes clear when we consider a theory articulated by Peter Berger, a leading twentieth-century sociologist of religion. Berger observed that monotheism leads to the secularization of nature. Once God is no longer part of the world, the world no longer contains mystery and can be examined by rational, human means. Thus monotheistic faith paved the way for modern science. According to Berger, modern secularism is a rebellion not just against ancient religious traditions but, in some way, also against their natural continuation.[15]

IS SECULARISM A FORM OF JUDAISM?

Recall: we are seeking to answer whether Jewish secularism in its atheistic form can be defined as a modern branch, or a modern interpretation, of Judaism. But what do we mean by "interpretation"?

If interpretation is an attempt to uncover the original intent behind a text, then the claim that secularism is an interpretation of Jewish tradition is absurd. The biblical prophets and the Talmudic sages were not atheists. But in the Jewish tradition, interpretation has never been limited to seeking the original intent behind specific verses. The midrashic sages who came up with ideas and religious laws by studying biblical texts were neither trying nor claiming to expose the texts' original intent.[16] Rather than seeking to go backward, to the intentions behind the original texts, they moved forward, developing them further.

The Talmudic sages analyzed biblical texts through the rabbinic method of *midrash halakha,* which they used to produce new laws. Maimonides compared the relationship between the legal code that the sages had developed and the original biblical text to the organic relationship between a tree's roots and its branches. The biblical verses are the roots of Judaism and the religious laws are its branches. According to Maimonides, midrash halakha does not *reveal* laws buried in the text, for the laws enumerated by the Talmudic sages (unless otherwise specified) are not *d'oraita* (from God)—that is, they are not commandments. Rather, midrash halakha creates laws that cannot be found in the original text but are nonetheless rooted in it. According to Maimonides, the primary purpose of the sages' interpretations was not to illuminate the biblical text but to *continue* it and make it bear fruit.[17]

The evolution of the Jews' faith in God exemplifies this well. As we saw, the Hebrew Bible distanced God from the world, the Talmud distanced him from humanity, and Maimonides removed him from human language. The changes that took place in this process did not *illuminate* the ancient tradition but continued its internal momentum. Maimonides' God beyond language does not appear in the Hebrew Bible, but he stems from it. We can also argue that modern Jewish secularism is an organic continuation of the tradition of God's ever increasing distance; it continues through the inertia that has carried every generation. The process that began with the monotheistic revolution, continued in the Talmud, and gained momentum in Maimonides' *Guide for the Perplexed* has perhaps reached its next waystation in modern Jewish secularism.

To clarify, there are two assumptions here that lead to a single conclusion. The first is that the Jewish theological tradition contains a trend in which God moves ever farther away from the natural world. The second is that interpretation in the Jewish tradition is an attempt to continue the internal logic of the object of interpretation and to make it bear fruit. The conclusion: atheistic Jewish secularism continues the traditional momentum of God's ever growing distance and stems from it, and it is therefore an organic interpretation of the Jewish tradition.

This conclusion may not seem completely convincing. It arguably conflates two different categories and fails to distinguish between "origination" and "continuation." We could say that whereas Ahad Ha'am's version of Jewish secularism does originate in Judaism, it represents not its continuation but its death throes. Just as the end of life follows life, so too secularism—which turns religion into culture—follows Judaism but represents the end of Jewish life, not its continuation. Without God, what can be left of Judaism, which for generations nurtured faith in God, worship of God, and even martyrdom in God's name? In every place and period of time in which Jews have lived, they have worshipped God. They discovered the unity of God when their journey began, and they remained faithful to him as that journey continued. Faith was what turned one hundred generations of Jews into a single continuum, so it is difficult to resist the argument that atheism unties the connections that bind Jews to their past.

But this argument is based on a faulty assumption. Widespread, perhaps, but wrong. It was not faith in God that created a continuum of one hundred Jewish generations, for Jewish thinkers have never agreed about *who* or *what* God is. In reality, God was never the basis for broad agreement across the Jewish world; he was the cause of bitter arguments within it. The Hebrew Bible describes God as having such human emotions as love, jealousy, and anger, but Maimonides argues that these are illusions; God has no feelings: "He is neither subject to death nor to life similar to the life of a living body; to Him cannot be attributed either folly or wisdom similar to the wisdom of a wise man; no sleep and no awakening, no anger and no laughter, no joy and no sadness, no silence and no speech similar to human speech; and likewise have the sages declared: 'Above there is neither sitting down nor standing up, no backward nor forward.'"[18]

According to Maimonides, it was heresy to ascribe physical or emotional attributes to God. But the twelfth-century Spanish Jewish philosopher Abraham ibn Daud (the Raavad) disagreed with Maimonides: "He who says that there is One Lord but that He is corporeal and has a form. Why does he call such one an atheist? Many greater and better than he followed this opinion."[19] The Raavad's evidence is clear-cut: there were indeed Jewish sages who believed God was corporeal! The Raavad even dared to call the sages who ascribed human attributes to God "greater" than Maimonides. Rabbi Moses Taku, for example, the author of the thirteenth-century Bohemian text *Ketav Tamim*, assailed all philosophical attempts to deny God's physicality and personality. He ruled that the Torah should be read literally.[20]

Rabbi Moses Taku was arguing that God was a personality, whereas Maimonides claimed he was an entity. Who was right? Whose position was the more Jewish? The Kabbalists complicated the situation even further. According to the Kabbalists, the Divine is divided into ten "emanations," whose dynamic connections constitute their inner secret. Let us ask again: Who has the most "Jewish" conception of the Divine? Maimonides, the Kabbalists, or those who ascribed human attributes to God? Each proclaimed the oneness of God when reading the *Shema* prayer twice daily, but each gave this oneness a different meaning. The thinkers agreed on the formulation but not on its meaning. One's conception of the divine was the other's definition of idol worship. Yeshayahu Leibowitz put it sharply and precisely: "Judaism does not have a faith—Jews have faiths."[21]

My question, therefore, is misplaced. Secularization does not undermine the Jewish faith because there is no such thing as the Jewish faith. From Maimonides' perspective, for example, Jewish atheism is no more absurd than the division of God into ten emanations. And heresy against God is no more problematic than personifying God. Judaism contains so many theological options that it is difficult not to include secularism as one of them.

JUDAISM AS AN INTERGENERATIONAL CONVERSATION

Exploring why the secular branch of the Jewish tradition can be considered constitutive of that tradition raises a new question: If *faith* was not what connected a chain of one hundred Jewish generations, what did?

One answer comes courtesy of Amos Oz and Fania Oz-Salzberger. They argue that what connects all Jews is the Jewish conversation an intergenerational dialogue based on holy texts and concerned with interpreting them, arguing about them and with them, and even rebelling against them. The conversation about Judaism is the essence of Judaism.[22] I shall rephrase their argument in my own way.

One of the most important commandments in the Torah is to study the Torah. Jews are commanded to devote time to studying the Torah. And here "Torah" means not just the Five Books of

Moses but also the debates about those books and the interpretive literature written about them. In learning about the disagreement between the schools of Beit Hillel and Beit Shammai and the debate between the Babylonian rabbis Rabbah and Abaye, Jews fulfill the commandment of Torah study as much as when they read the books of Leviticus or Deuteronomy, Isaiah or Ezekiel. The commandment of Torah study encompasses both God's words to humanity and our interpretation of God's words.

The Talmud contains a remarkable fable in which Moses finds himself sitting in Rabbi Akiva's study hall.[23] It is an extraordinary scene, in which Moses, the receiver of the Torah, learns from Rabbi Akiva, a scholar of the Torah. And what emerges from this topsy-turvy situation? Moses learns from Rabbi Akiva things about the Torah that he never knew himself. A scholar of the Torah ends up understanding the law better than the lawgiver.

In a different and no less daring Talmudic fable, readers are shown a heavenly academy in which God sits and studies Torah. More than that, God actively participates in the discussion. God cites Rabbi Eliezer ben Hurcanus's position on a particular religious law.[24] Everything is topsy-turvy in the Talmud. Not only do humans quote God—God quotes humans. The hierarchy between the divine Torah and the human debate unravels. The community that reads and interprets the Torah is part of the Torah.[25] There is no difference between past and future, divine and human—it is all the same Torah.

From a halakhic perspective, the Oral Law and the Written Law are not of equal status. The laws that originate in the Torah (the Written Law), called *d'oraita*, take precedence over laws that originate in the Mishnah (the Oral Law), which are called *dera-*

banan, from the rabbis. There is a hierarchy. The Torah is above the Talmud. But once one enters a Jewish study hall, the two are equal. Once the intergenerational conversation begins, the hierarchy collapses. God cites humans; Moses learns from Rabbi Akiva. The study of the human conversation about the divine text has religious value, of equal value to the study of the divine text itself.

Recall the question with which I began this section: If faith is not what connects one hundred generations of Jews, what does? The answer: Judaism is the Jews' ongoing conversation. The conversation about Judaism *is* Judaism. The way Jews become connected to Judaism is by joining the Jewish conversation. Even those who disagree with the content of the tradition can still be part of the tradition, because a disagreement with previous generations is still a conversation with them.[26]

From Oz and Oz-Salzberger's definition of Judaism as a civilization of words, we might conclude that secular Israelis are *better suited* to the intergenerational conversation than their religious, Orthodox peers.[27] Their analysis raises an interesting criticism of Orthodox Jews: in surrendering to and obeying the accumulated wisdom of generations, they are arguably not participating in a conversation with the past but simply subordinating themselves to it. In contrast, secular Jewish Israelis, who enjoy freedom of thought and possess a generally critical disposition, are fit for active participation in the intergenerational Jewish conversation.

This is a fascinating conclusion, but it is clouded by a major question: Do secular Israelis meet the basic conditions for participation in a Jewish conversation? After all, one precondition for joining any conversation is a basic familiarity with its context. If we want to engage in a political debate, we must be familiar with the political context; and if we want to engage in a scientific debate, we must understand something about the science. And in order to join the intergenerational conversation about Judaism, Jews need to be familiar with its contents and different strains, and such familiarity demands years of effort and study.

This intergenerational conversation is stored in many books, most of which are not new. It exists in the modern writings of S. Y. Agnon and Aharon Appelfeld and is rooted in the stories of the Aggadah and the debates of the Talmud, in the Mishnah, the Babylonian Talmud, and the Jerusalem Talmud. The argument that participating in a tradition means taking part in a conversation about the tradition eliminates confessional conditions for such participation, but it creates new ones. Scholarship replaces faith as the basic condition for participation in the Jewish tradition. Atheism does not disqualify someone from participating in the intergenerational Jewish conversation, but ignorance does. It is not atheism, therefore, that might undermine the conclusion that secularism is a stream of Judaism but ignorance.

Since it is hard to deny how profoundly ignorant many Israelis raised in Israel's mainstream education system are of Jewish matters, I must add some reservations. I argued that secularism is a stream of Judaism, and I constructed a two-layered thesis to justify the claim that even atheist secular Judaism is no less Jewish than previous intellectual revolutions. But there is a problem with this argument because it does not apply to all sections of the contemporary secular Jewish world. Only a secularism that includes familiarity with the intergenerational Jewish tradition—even one that is angry at it and rages against it—can be said to be part of it.

Let's backtrack: Is Jewish secularism a spiritual, cultural movement that cuts Jews off from Judaism, or is it a stream of Judaism? Micha Josef Berdyczewski and Yosef Haim Brenner believed that secularism allowed Jews to liberate themselves from Judaism, whereas Ahad Ha'am and his disciples believed that like the Talmud, Kabbalah, and medieval Jewish philosophy, secularism is another reinterpretation of Judaism. Both sides were right. From an intellectual perspective, Ahad Ha'am was correct: there is no bar to seeing the secular rebellion as part of the Jewish conversation. But the facts favor Brenner and Berdyczewski: secularism led many of its adherents to disengage from the intergenerational Jewish conversation.[28]

The Jewish renewal referred to earlier—including the secular and mixed secular-religious academies, the new books, and the new music—is generating a new kind of Jewish secularism. This movement asks a different question: not *whether* Israeli secularism is a stream of Judaism but *how* to transform it into a stream of Judaism. And this is no longer an academic question—it is a practical challenge. This "alternative secularism" is being created by secular Israelis who are embracing the challenge, studying the Jewish sources anew, and drawing fresh inspiration from ancient ideas. They are not letting Judaism override their secularism—they are making their secularism part of Judaism itself.

PART III ALTERNATIVE RELIGIOSITY

INTRODUCTION

When the Zionist movement was born, a fierce debate erupted between Theodor Herzl and Ahad Ha'am over its fundamental purpose. According to Herzl, the biggest threat to the future of the Jewish people was anti-Semitism. According to Ahad Ha'am, the biggest threat was the Emancipation. Ahad Ha'am explained his dissent from Herzl elegantly: Herzl's Zionism was an attempt to save *the Jews*, while his own Zionism was an attempt to save *Judaism*.

If we wished to compare Jewish life in Israel to Jewish life in the United States, we could choose between Herzl's criteria and those of Ahad Ha'am. We could ask, Where are *the Jews* safer? Or we could ask, Where is *Judaism* safer? The answer to Herzl's question is not obviously Israel. Many more Jews have been targeted and killed in Israel than in the United States. Whether Israel offers Jews a safe haven is debatable. But Ahad Ha'am's question is much easier to answer. The State of Israel is an inestimably safer environment for Judaism. In the modern State of Israel, even Jews who are indifferent to Judaism and neglect their own faith can be reasonably certain that as long as they remain in Israel, they will have Jewish grandchildren.

Lord Jonathan Sacks, the former British chief rabbi, once made the distinction that in Israel the Jews are the chosen people; in the Diaspora, they are the *choosing* people. In Israel, Judaism is chosen for, and forced on, the Jews; they live and breathe Judaism whether they want to or not. In the Diaspora, the opposite is true: unless Jews actively choose to embrace Judaism, attending synagogue and giving their children a Jewish education, they are likely to assimilate and lose their Jewish identity.

In Israel, there are four components of Jewish identity that Israeli Jews breathe in through the air: their location, their nationality, their calendar, and their language.

In Israel, even Jews who are estranged from their ancient identity live in their ancient homeland. The place where the great dramas of the Hebrew Bible unfolded is now the place where the dramatic story of modern Israel is unfolding. In addition, the majority of the citizens of modern Israel are Jewish, and the Hebrew calendar is the official Israeli calendar. When Israelis say that "the holidays" are coming up, they do not mean Christmas but Rosh Hashanah. Finally, because the ancient language of the Hebrew people was resurrected in the modern age, most Israelis are fluent speakers of Hebrew. Israelis speak, think, and dream in the language of the Bible. Secular Jews might despise religion and Jewish traditions. But if they are Israeli, they do so in places that bear biblical names, in Hebrew, and with friends who are almost all Jewish. Religious or secular, Israeli Jews are reminded daily that they are Jews.

But the fact that Jewish continuity is so assured in Israel also has its drawbacks. From a psychological perspective, when an issue seems to be settled, it tends to be taken for granted. In the American Jewish community, for example, Jewish continuity is a perennial worry. Their country is not Jewish; their calendar is the Christian calendar; the most commonly heard language is English; and the majority of Americans are not Jews. And precisely because Judaism is not indigenous, they have to create communities in which it can be practiced. Precisely because Jewish continuity is not assured, they have to fight for it. For the Chosen People, Judaism can never rest; for the Choosing People, it is a constant battle to keep it awake. The dialogue between the Jewish communities of Israel and the Diaspora is vital. The two sides complement each other. Israeli Judaism safeguards the continuity of Diaspora Jewry, and Diaspora Jewry enlivens and revitalizes Israeli Jewry.

In the modern day, Judaism—like other religions—is the subject of much criticism that is actually based on prejudice. Many people see it as a superstition that is contrary to reason, perpetuates ignorance, and is based on irrational ideas. But this characterization is totally alien to Maimonides' type of Judaism, articulated in his twelfth-century *Guide for the Perplexed*. We approach God, Maimonides writes, only when we actively engage our reason, not when we neglect it. A religious Jewish life is complete only if it is rational. Maimonides, the most important philosopher in the rabbinical Jewish tradition, also dispels another preconception about Judaism. The Jewish people are no better than other nations, he claims. *Reason* is the "image of God" that is shared with humans, and it draws no distinctions between nations and tribes.

True, Judaism also contains irrational trends and can foster thinkers who promote an ideology of Jewish supremacy. But though it would be accurate to say that Judaism *contains* irrationalities, it would be false to say Judaism itself is irrational. Judaism is richer and more varied than that. Prejudices about Judaism, like most prejudices, are based on partial truths that are mistakenly taken to be the whole truth. Many critics treat a partial reality as the entirety.

But prejudices are not just held about religion; they are also held about secularism. Just as the Jewish religion is more varied than it seems, so is Jewish secularism. Many Jews believe that an intimate connection with tradition is contrary to the free spirit of secularism. But a study of the roots of secular thought reveals the opposite. An intimate relationship with tradition can constitute the fulfillment of a liberated secularism. Jewish secularism contains antitraditional trends, but secularism itself is not antitraditional. We have seen that Ahad Ha'am sought a secularism that would contain a Jewish enlightenment, that A. D. Gordon theorized a secularism that would contain religious experiences, that Hayim Nahman Bialik went as far as to dream of a secularism that would contain a practical code of law. Prejudices about the Jewish religion and secularism treat these two worldviews as unduly superficial. Religion can accommodate rationality and universalism; secularism can accommodate spirituality and traditionalism.

Religious Zionism, as Orthodox Judaism is known in Israel, is the subject of much prejudice. It is denounced on the basis of the standard stereotypes about religion in general, but it also suffers from preconceptions that are uniquely held of Religious Zionism. Yet Religious Zionism is also more varied than it appears from the outside. It is a turbulent ideology, full of varied, even contradictory ideas. Just as an "alternative secularism" can be found to the more reactionary forms of Israeli secularism, an "alternative religiosity" can be found to the more reactionary forms of Religious Zionism.

Religious Zionism can be divided into three schools of thought: the messianic philosophy inspired by Rabbi Abraham Isaac Kook, which takes a hardline and reactionary approach to religion; a non-messianic alternative; and the Mizrahi school of thought, which currently finds expression in the writings of Sephardic rabbis. We shall look at each in turn.[1]

7 MESSIANIC RELIGIOUS ZIONISM

What is Religious Zionism? What is the glue that binds Zionism to religion and religion to Zionism? Rabbi Abraham Isaac Kook (Rav Kook), one of the most prominent thinkers active in the Land of Israel in the twentieth century, had a dramatic answer: the Redemption. Zionism had religious significance in Judaism because the return of the People of Israel to their ancient homeland would be the realization of God's messianic plan. But Zionism did not develop exactly as the messianists foresaw.

For many generations, Jews cultivated two expectations of the great upheaval they envisioned for the end of history. The Jews believed that when the Redemption came, the Jewish people would return to their land and to their God. In reality, however, when the Jewish people finally began returning to the Promised Land at the end of the nineteenth century, they did not return to God. The secular Zionist pioneers who strove to restore the Jewish people to their ancient land were among those who most rebelled against the ancient tradition. Secular Zionism therefore represented an unsolvable riddle for religious thinkers. They could not explain how the movement that was fulfilling the vision of past generations was also undermining that same vision.

Rav Kook dedicated much of his philosophy to addressing this paradox. He believed that secular Zionists were, in fact, fulfilling the prophecy. In Kook's ingenious explanation, the new secularism did not represent the abandonment of God but an unconscious return to him.[1]

In Rav Kook's conception, secular Zionism was an unconscious movement of religious renewal. He saw it as the confluence of two schools of thought. The first school is connected to one of the great philosophers of the nineteenth century, Friedrich Hegel, who saw nations as organic beings that, like all organisms, have souls that animate them. The soul of a national organism is its Volksgeist, its national spirit: an invisible force that develops over the course of a nation's history.[2]

The second school of thought emerges from the Kabbalistic tradition. As we have seen, according to Kabbalah, the divine world comprises ten emanations (*sephirot*), each of which constitutes a manifestation of the Divine. The tenth emanation, at the bottom of the tree of *sephirot*, is *malkuth*, kingdom. Another term for the tenth emanation is *Knesset Yisrael*—the Assembly of Israel—which is also the midrashic name for the Jewish collective. In light of this, some started identifying the emanation of *malkuth* with the Jewish people and treating the Jewish people as divine.[3]

Rav Kook connected these two motifs by identifying Hegel's Volksgeist with the Kabbalistic emanation of *malkuth*, and developed the radical idea that the spirit of the Jewish people is the spirit of God. In his own words: "The spirit of the nation and the spirit of God are one." This combination, Rav Kook believed, was the key to understanding the secret of secular Zionism. Secular Zionists had abandoned religion for nationalism. Instead of worshipping God, they devoted themselves to the nation. But if we identify the Jewish national spirit with the spirit of God, we are forced to conclude that Jews who devote themselves to the nation are thereby devoting themselves to God. If the divine spirit finds expression through the Jewish national spirit, then expressions of Jewish nationalism are effectively also expressions of Jewish religiosity.[4]

According to Rav Kook, secular Jews deny the religious essence of their own secularism. They are unaware of the divine will within themselves: "The spirit of the nation has awoken now, and many of those who possess it say they do not need the spirit of God ... [but] they do not know what they themselves want."[5] For Rav Kook, then, secular Zionists are Zionists who are consciously secular—and unconsciously religious.[6]

A REINTERPRETATION OF RELIGIOSITY

Rav Kook's novel interpretation of Jewish secularism arose at the same time as a dramatic realignment was taking place in Jewish religiosity. The belief in the divinity of the Jewish people, which promoted admiration for secular Jews, also led to the development of some extremely reactionary tendencies among certain religious Jews in Israel. Since the 1970s, Religious Zionism has sprouted a branch known as Haredi Leumi, an ultra-Orthodox nationalist group, which is rooted in a belief in the divinity of the Jewish people. How did they come to this conclusion? Rav Kook taught that the Torah originated in the Jewish national spirit. This was a profoundly significant inversion: the Torah was not revealed *to* the Jewish people as much as it was revealed *out of* them. This idea might sound heretical and similar to Ahad Ha'am's theory that the Torah is not God's creation but that of the nation. But Rav Kook's interpretation differs from Ahad Ha'am's in his contention that although the Torah is the creation of the Jewish nation, since the Jewish nation is *divine*, the Torah is divine too. It is precisely because the Torah was created by the Jewish people that it is a divine creation.

This interpretation leads to several important conclusions. If the Torah originated in the Jewish national spirit, then when Jews connect to the Torah, they are effectively connecting to their nation. "The more one observes the Torah and commandments, the greater one's connection to Knesset Yisrael and one's sense of the soul of the entire collective there." The more nationalistic a person is as a Jew, therefore, the more he or she should aspire to lead a religiously observant life. This represents a novel criticism of Jews who feel unbound by halakha: Jews who decline to observe the biblical commandments are not fully connected to their nation's soul. Failure to observe the commandments is not just a religious offense—it is a national affront. It was thus that a belief in the divinity of the Jewish people created a new, hardline form of religion, one in which nationalist fervor demands religious obedience.[7]

This is the key to understanding the theology of Haredi Jewish nationalism in Israel. The nationalist component of the nationalist Haredi identity is not an addendum to Haredi religiosity—it is its foundation. These are not Haredi Jews who happen to be nationalists; they are Jews who are Haredi *because* they are nationalists. They subordinate themselves to the nation's Torah and obey its laws *because* they believe in the divinity of the Jewish people.

The nationalist form of ultra-Orthodoxy is expressed through more than its strict religious observance. The whole concept of Torah scholarship is reshaped by faith in the divinity of the Jewish nation. For hundreds of years, Torah study had stood at the pinnacle of the religious values of the Jewish tradition. In the classical explanation, Torah scholarship was said to be important because the Torah was the will of God, and studying the Torah meant studying God's will. But for those who believe that the Torah originated in the national spirit, Torah study means revealing not just the will of God but also the soul of the nation. "Torah study injects into our souls the character of Israel and its unique form," wrote Rav Kook.[8] If the Torah is an expression of the national soul, then studying the Torah means tapping into the national soul.

Rav Kook's disciples developed his ideas further. One of his most prominent followers, Rabbi Zvi Tau, saw Torah scholars as men who were tapping into the latent desires of the Jewish people. For these scholars to sustain their authentic connection to the Jewish national spirit, they needed to avoid exposure to foreign sources of knowledge. Intellectual self-seclusion would thus protect the purity of a Torah scholar's connection to the national soul: "Nowadays there is an ongoing process of submission and vile subservience to Western culture," wrote Tau, "while . . . the original Israeli culture is miles and miles above human culture."[9]

This is a new, original type of self-seclusion. Whereas "classical" ultra-Orthodox Jews have also opted for cultural seclusion, closing themselves off in order to protect their tradition from modernity, Haredi Jewish nationalists have a new emphasis. Their isolation is primarily intended to protect the Jewish national soul from foreign cultures.

I must note that the vast majority of Religious Zionists oppose such isolation. The researcher Yair Sheleg has observed that although many Religious Zionist youth are taught in the messianic, self-seclusionary variety of school, they tend not to erect barriers between themselves and the rest of the world. Life has a power of its own, and in time most Religious Zionists are integrated into academic studies, pursue successful careers, and live comfortable middle-class lives, the influence of the yeshiva education of their youth slowly waning.[10]

Nevertheless, the Religious Zionist rabbinic elite is indeed nurturing a new form of ultra-Orthodoxy and encouraging isolation from foreign cultures in the name of national authenticity. In Rabbi Tau's words: "A normal, healthy national character contains a certain 'conservatism' that opposes and rejects the acceptance of foreign elements that may disrupt its spiritual harmony and cause chaos throughout its life, until it loses its character and force of life."[11]

In sum, the belief in the divinity of the soul of the Jewish people facilitated a new interpretation of secularism and a new conception of religion. On one hand, it was argued that the nationalism of secular Jews attested to their unconscious religiosity. On the other, Jewish nationalism required complete devotion to religious observance and reclusive Torah study. There is a profound paradox here, which might be the key to understanding the messianic stream of Religious Zionism: the belief in the divinity of the Jewish people has simultaneously led both to admiration for Jewish secularism and to the radicalization of the Jewish religion.

FROM A CRISIS OF SECULARISM
TO A CRISIS OF MESSIANISM

Religious Zionists believe that history is marching inexorably toward the Redemption, when the Jewish people will return to both the Land of Israel and the God of Israel. As part of the messianic process, therefore, secular Zionism is fated to become religious. But for Rav Kook and his disciples, "becoming religious" does not mean secular Zionists will change; rather they will become self-aware. If the People of Israel is a manifestation of the God of Israel, then the nationalism of secular Jews is a manifestation of religiosity, and their return to religion will simply be a process of self-discovery.

Messianic Religious Zionists believe that secular Zionism is destined to disappear, and to do so when secular Zionists' nationalism overcomes their secularism. To date, however, this forecast has not come true; in fact, the opposite has happened. The great change that is sweeping secular Zionism has been the weakening not of its secularism but of its nationalism. From the perspective of messianic Religious Zionist rabbis, the secular State of Israel has become more liberal, more cosmopolitan, and much less nationalistic. The strongest and most painful evidence they find of these trends is the willingness of many secular Israelis to uproot settlements in the West Bank and pull out of biblical areas of the Land of Israel.[12] Their disillusionment with secular Zionism began when settlements were evacuated from the Sinai Peninsula under the peace treaty with Egypt, continued with the 1993 Oslo Accords, and reached its zenith during the 2005 Disengagement from the Gaza Strip and northern Samaria. The theory that secular Zionists were the unconscious pioneers of the Redemption took a blow when it became clear that secular Zionists were the very conscious pioneers of these withdrawals. According to the messianic forecast, the secular Zionists' nationalism should have trumped their secularism. In reality, it was their secularism that overpowered their nationalism.

Rabbi Zalman Melamed, one of the most prominent rabbis in the messianic Religious Zionist movement, expressed his dismay: "Perhaps the Religious Zionist movement was wrong to think it could forge ties with secular Zionism.... Perhaps the whole dream of coexistence and of ever finding a way to bring the faithless closer to faith was a pipe dream. *Perhaps those who argued that there was no point in becoming close to secular folk because their way is the opposite of ours were right after all*" (emphasis mine).[13]

Rav Kook wrote that the secular Zionists' nationalism would restore them to the Jewish religion. But the opposite has occurred. Nationalism has not transformed secularism: secularism has transformed nationalism.[14] The disillusionment with secularism was a bitter blow to the faith of messianic Religious Zionists, because the mystical interpretation of secularism is one of the pillars of the messianic interpretation of Zionism as a whole. Zionism was supposed to restore the Jewish people to both the Land of Israel and the God of Israel as part of a single, historic, dramatic event. But if history is not steering secular Israelis toward faith, then it would be difficult to argue that Zionism is steering history toward the Redemption.

The connection between Zionism and Judaism as a religion has been weakened with the undermining of Rav Kook's messianic theories. Yet the connection might take other forms. Religious Zionism need not be a *messianic* conception of Zionism; it might be a *non-diasporic* conception of Judaism.[15]

8 NON-DIASPORIC JUDAISM

Does God have a messianic plan that he is bringing to fruition step by step, pushing history toward the Redemption? And if so, is the State of Israel part of his plan? Throughout history, key thinkers have cast doubt on our ability to know God's plan: God's infinite mind cannot be grasped by our limited understanding. So Jews who believe that God's thinking cannot be deciphered by human beings, and that his grand plans are not revealed to us, find it difficult to declare with certainty that the State of Israel is a stage of the Redemption.

The messianists' doubts about Zionism were reinforced by a series of historic events that culminated in the 2005 Gaza Disengagement. But this skepticism is not a *religious* skepticism: even if the State of Israel has no messianic significance, it can still possess religious significance. Though they may not know whether the Redemption is coming, they do know that the Exile has ended, and the end of the Exile can have profound religious significance in itself.

The path to a non-exilic form of Judaism began in the ancient

Near East, which contained the mighty kingdoms of the Assyrians, the Hittites, and the Egyptians, as well as the minor kingdoms of the Jebusites, Girgashites, and Hivites. The Near East was a diverse patchwork of ancient nations. Each had its own gods, rituals, language, and political system. But they had one thing in common— they all eventually disappeared. In time, the kingdoms collapsed and their peoples were exiled or vanquished. The national identities of the ancient Near East were wiped out. No one today speaks the Girgashite language or thinks of his or her nationality as Jebusite. Out of all of these peoples, virtually only the Hebrews survived. Like other nations, the Hebrews were exiled and scattered; unlike them, they did not disappear. The Hebrews are not only part of history, they are part of the present. Thinkers such as Hegel, Nietzsche, and Oswald Spengler have pondered the Jewish people's ability to defy the laws of history, which is widely considered an unresolved riddle: How did the Jews survive the Exile?

At least one of the reasons for the Jews' survival is Judaism. The Jews did not preserve the Torah so much as it preserved them and safeguarded their identity. And this did not happen by accident. The Jewish sages reshaped Judaism as a religion as a way to improve the Jewish people's chances of survival. Throughout the Exile, new elements were added to the Jewish religion that functioned as protective mechanisms for Jewish identity. Some pertained to religious faith, others to religious law.

But the success of exilic, diasporic Judaism has also been its greatest problem. It turns the preservation of Judaism into Judaism's central goal—and so slips into circular logic. If Judaism's reason for being is greater than Judaism itself, what is that reason? This puzzle has stood at the foundation of Jewish thought throughout the generations. Maimonides, for example, declared that the purpose of Judaism was the full actualization of our humanity. The eighteenth-century founder of Hasidic Judaism, the Baal Shem Tov, believed that the purpose of Judaism was devotion to God. The twentieth-century American theologian Abraham Joshua Heschel believed that the purpose of Judaism was *tikkun olam*, "repairing the world." These thinkers were many and varied, but they all agreed that the mere preservation of Judaism was not its raison d'être.

But the threats to Jewish identity in the Diaspora put Jews on the defensive and pushed them to focus on building protective mechanisms into their Judaism. The greater the dangers to Jewish identity, the greater the centrality of these mechanisms as a feature of the Jewish drama, and the more the preservation of Judaism seemed to become the central purpose of Judaism. And so the Diaspora disrupted Judaism.

The establishment of the State of Israel marked a major shift in the history of the Jews, and it also provoked a major change in the history of Judaism. The state was founded to protect Jews from persecution, but it also protects them from assimilation. It is not merely a refuge for Jews from places and people that reject them; it is also a refuge for Jews from places and people that *accept* them and thereby threaten to undermine their Jewish identity.

Outside Israel, many of the Jews who do not make use of Diaspora Judaism's defense mechanisms assimilate into their wider societies, but in Israel Jews who make no use of these mechanisms do not assimilate. Thanks to Zionism, Jews can begin to carefully peel away from their Judaism the mechanisms that have burdened and beleaguered it. In Israel, Jews can worry less about how to preserve Judaism and wonder more about what its purpose should be. If the Diaspora burdened Judaism, Zionism might be a way to unburden it.[1]

JUDAISM'S METAPHYSICAL STATUS

Many Orthodox Jews believe that the Jewish religion protects its adherents from harm and that Jewish religious rituals protect their participants. This belief is as common now as it was in the past. One of the first people who tried to dispel this notion was the prophet Jeremiah: "Don't put your trust in illusions and say, 'The Temple of the Lord, the Temple of the Lord, the Temple of the Lord are these [buildings].' No, if you really mend your ways and your actions; if you execute justice between one man and another; if you do not oppress the stranger, the orphan, and the widow; if you do not shed the blood of the innocent in this place; if you do not follow other gods, to your own hurt—then only will I let you dwell in this place, in the land that I gave to your fathers for all time."[2]

Jeremiah lamented that the Judean public was being bombarded by propaganda from the religious and political establishments, which proclaimed, "The Temple of the Lord, the Temple of the Lord, the Temple of the Lord are these." God's presence in the Temple, according to the propaganda, was the guarantee of the Jews' continued existence and prosperity. And the people, according to Jeremiah, believed this propaganda. They believed that the Temple would protect them and that religious practice gave them immunity. With no fear of destruction, therefore, the people had become complacent and had allowed their society to grow rotten and corrupt. According to Jeremiah, the reason the Temple was destroyed was not that the people did *not* believe in it, but that they *did*. The Temple was not destroyed because people failed to take it seriously enough—it was destroyed because they took it too seriously.

The Jewish prophets in the Bible had a strategic argument. Their society's protection against military defeat or economic collapse was conditional on the extent of its social sensitivity. They tried to convince the people to change their conception of security. They tried to persuade them that religious rituals would not grant them immunity from disaster, and acts of worship would not protect their society. What would? Caring for foreigners, orphans, and widows.

Orphans are vulnerable to threats from their surroundings and society because they have no parents to protect them. Widows, in patriarchal societies, are vulnerable to exploitation and abuse because they have no husbands to protect them. Foreigners (*gerim*) are members of minorities, who are vulnerable to oppression and mistreatment by the majority group because they have no political community to protect them. The moral fervor of the Hebrew Bible focuses on these cases.

The prophets' injunction is clear and simple: the defenseless must be defended. The prophets' equation is equally simple and clear: societies that defend the defenseless are thereby defended. Societies that fail to defend the defenseless are left undefended.

In his final speech, in the book of Deuteronomy, Moses sketches out for the Israelites the major dangers inherent in power. Power corrupts. It dazzles those who wield it, blinding them to the presence of the weak and minorities. The Torah therefore creates a psychological mechanism to prevent the bearers of power from being so blinded: an educational system that plants memories of weakness in the minds of the strong. The Israelites are commanded to tell themselves every day, every Sabbath, and every holy day that they were once *weak*. They are commanded to remember that they were once slaves in Egypt, a persecuted minority who suffered the tyranny of the majority. Many other commandments exist to embed this story into the Jewish consciousness. The tzitzit that Jewish men wear, the tefillin they don, kiddush on the Sabbath, and the synagogue liturgy are all reminders for the strong that they were once weak. The Bible encodes the psychological assumption that the greater the Jews' connection to their own weakness, the greater their attentiveness and sensitivity will be toward the weakness of others. This is the most important foundation of the Bible's system of moral education: memories of past weakness will counterbalance an awareness of present strength.

The problem with the Torah's educational function is that the logic of memory as a counterweight is only relevant to the Jewish people when they are sovereign in their own land. Only when the nation is strong can memories of weakness balance out their power. When the Jewish people are neither strong nor sovereign, memory loses its role as a counterweight. The Exile rendered the biblical injunction to constantly remember weakness absurd.

After the Jewish people were exiled and once more became weak and persecuted, they no longer needed to be reminded of their former weakness. When the Jews were a minority, they did not still need to recall other times when they were a minority. The memories of Egypt, which acted as a counterweight to the Jewish mindset in Israel, ceased to balance out the Jewish mindset outside Israel. What role remained for a religion that *moderated* the Jews' sovereign power once the Jews were no longer sovereign?

In the Diaspora, Jews found a different way of restoring balance. Jews in the Diaspora were not a strong people who needed to be reminded of their weakness—they were a weak people who needed to be reminded of their strength.

The *Zohar* quotes the painful words of a Christian clergyman to Rabbi El'azar: The ancient Hebrew kingdom was a fleeting presence, while the Roman Christian kingdom is permanent, and this teaches that the Jewish Torah is a lie, and the Christian gospel is the truth:

> I remember one time when I was walking with Rabbi El'azar. He encountered a certain *hegemona*[3] who said to him, "Are you familiar with the Torah of the Jews?"
>
> He replied, "I am."
>
> He said to him, "Don't you say that your faith is true and your Torah true, and that our faith is a lie, and our Torah a lie? Yet it is written *The lip of truth will be established forever, but the tongue of falsehood lasts only a moment* (Proverbs 12:19). We have reigned since ancient days, and dominion has never departed from us, generation after generation—*will be established forever*, surely! As for you, for a little while you had a kingdom and right away it was removed, thereby fulfilling the verse: but the tongue of falsehood lasts only for a moment."[4]

The bishop's words reflect a common theological argument in the Middle Ages, one that Christians found simple and convincing: The Jews' inferior political situation was proof of Judaism's inferior theology. But the Jews, weak and persecuted, had to continue believing that their religion was divine, although nothing in their day-to-day existence suggested that God was still with them.

How did the Jews cope with the gulf between their faith and their reality? The *Zohar* has an answer:

> Rabbi Yose opened, saying, *"Behold, shamed and humiliated shall be all who range against you ...* (Isaiah 41:11). One day the blessed Holy One will enact for Israel all those good things that He uttered through the true prophets. On account of these, Israel endured much evil in their exile; and were it not for all those good things that they await, which they see written in Torah, they could not stand or bear exile. But they go to houses of study, open books, and see all those good things that they await—written in the Torah and promised by the blessed Holy One—and they are comforted in their exile."[5]

Life in the Diaspora was humiliating, harsh, and painful. The Jewish people survived because of the biblical promise that they would one day become the rulers and the gentiles would become the ruled. This promise of future power enabled the Jews to bear their present lack of power. The Torah now offered a significant reversal: When the Hebrews entered the Land of Israel, they were ordered to remember their past as slaves. When they were exiled from the land, they tried to imagine their future as sovereign masters. This was also the secret of the balance: when Jews are strong, they must remember their weakness in the past; and when they are weak, they must envision their power in the future.

According to the *Zohar*, the study hall is where Jewish identity is realigned. It is where Jews read about who the real winners and losers are in the drama of history. The *Zohar* maintains that the Jews are a divine people whose origins are in one of the divine emanations. The gentiles, in contrast, have their origins in the *Sitra Ahra*—the realm of evil.[6] In their study halls, Jews learned that everything was contrary to what it seemed. In history, as revealed by experience, the Jews were abject, but in the metaphysical reality, as revealed by the mystic texts, the Jews were supreme and the gentiles beneath them. The study halls were a sanctuary. They were where the Jews rehabilitated their self-image.

The belief that the Jewish people were superior to their persecutors and abusers was common among Jews in the Middle Ages. In the Spanish Jewish poet Judah Halevi's *Kuzari,* for example, the hero of the story is a "friend" who presents reality as a hierarchy. At the bottom of the ladder are inanimate objects; one rung above are plants; a rung above that are animals; and above the animals are humans. But the metaphysical hierarchy does not stop with human beings. The ladder has one more rung—the Jews. The "friend" does not say that the gentiles are not human beings. He says the gentiles are *only* human beings and the Jews are a level above them. The difference between Jew and gentile, that is, is similar to that between humans and beasts. And similar to what we saw in the *Zohar,* the *Kuzari* contains the idea that the purpose of faith in the Jewish people's superiority is to compensate for their present abasement. The book's full name is *The Book of Refutation and Proof in Support of the Abased Religion.* The story about the Jews' metaphysical supremacy was compensation for the Jews' political inferiority.[7]

The idea of the Chosen People was born in the Diaspora. Before the Exile, during the biblical times of power and sovereignty, the Hebrews were told that God had chosen them from all the nations. But they were not told that they were better than the other nations. On the contrary: Moses used God's love for the Israelites to emphasize that they were no different from other nations. God's love, as Moses stressed in his last speech, was independent of any particular attributes of the beloved. This is an important biblical lesson: God's love for Israel highlights the fact that the People of Israel are not superior.[8] The Torah promulgated the notion that the Hebrew nation was chosen over others but was no better than them. The Diaspora promulgated the idea that this chosenness also attested to the Jews' superiority. Paradoxically, the transition from the belief that the Jews were chosen to the belief that they were superior happened precisely when the Jews felt inferior.

Even in the Diaspora, not all Jews believed that their people's chosenness was proof of their superiority. Maimonides, for example, believed that all people were equal. The image of God was the human mind, and the human mind was universal. God, therefore, resided equally among all of humanity.[9] But the position promoted by Maimonides and his disciples was pushed to the margins of Jewish consciousness. The Jews in exile needed a faith that would compensate for their humiliation. Under these conditions, Maimonides had no chance of persuading the masses. The *Kuzari* and the *Zohar* told their readers what they needed to hear: they were better and holier than their oppressors.

In the mid-twentieth century, the Jews returned to power. Thanks to the dramatic achievement of the Zionist movement, the predicament of nearly half the world's Jews was turned upside down. They no longer lived as minorities in non-Jewish societies but as a majority in a society that contained non-Jewish minorities. This change in their condition enabled and required Jews to change their interpretation of Judaism. If after Israel's establishment, the strong and powerful Jews were to be told the same stories as when they were weak and governed by others, the result would be an imbalance. Previously, stories of metaphysical superiority created balance; now these stories would throw the Jews *off* balance.

The establishment of the State of Israel allowed Judaism to be freed from its diasporic role of cultivating self-confidence in a weak nation and to return to its prophetic role of nurturing sensitivity in a strong nation. Maimonides' universalist worldview, marginalized in the Middle Ages, can return to the forefront of the Zionist Jewish mind.

What, then, is the purpose of Religious Zionism? Here is one possible answer: if secular Zionism took the Jews out of Exile, Religious Zionism can take the Exile out of the Jews.

ZIONISM AND HALAKHA

During the Exile, the Jews lived in autonomous communities. These communities were akin to limited, demilitarized states. They had their own taxation systems, and their courts had powers of enforcement. This was the situation until the modern, administrative state came into being in the nineteenth century and dismantled the systems of Jewish autonomy.[10]

In the past two thousand years, the Jews have effectively experienced two exiles: the first when the Romans dismantled the ancient Jewish kingdom, the second when modernity dismantled autonomous Jewish communities. The first exile was the more painful and dramatic, but it was the second that exposed the Jews to the greater threat to their survival. The dissolution of Jewish autonomy raised fears that without Jewish political communities Judaism would not survive, and the migration of its members to the modern societies of Western nation-states would bring Judaism to an end. The fear was that the elision of the political distinction between Jews and gentiles would also elide the differences between their identities.

How did the Jews nevertheless remain distinct? Halakha, their code of religious law, helped them to do so.[11] An increasingly stringent approach to halakha entrenched the Jews' cultural seclusion and protected their Jewish identity. Once halakha was treated primarily as a defense against assimilation, however, it lost its focus, because, among other reasons, it had abandoned the priorities of the prophets.

For the Hebrew prophets, moral sensitivity was more important than ritual exactitude. "For I desire goodness, not sacrifice," implored the prophet Hosea.[12] One of the essential differences between Judaism's moral and ritual commandments is that morality is universal while rituals are particular. Rituals set people apart; morality does not. Morality is not specifically Jewish; it is human. If a young Jew gives up a seat on the bus to an elderly person, that does not set him or her apart as specifically Jewish. Good Buddhists and good Muslims would do the same. But when Jews don tefillin in the morning or make kiddush on a Friday night, they are performing acts that are unique to Jews. From this distinction, it follows that the biblical prophets' call to place morality above ritual is effectively a call to highlight Judaism's universalist side over its own particularities. If "goodness" is more important than sacrifices, then universal acts are more important than uniquely Jewish ones. Yet in the reality that emerged after the dismantling of Jewish communal autonomy, the priorities of the ancient prophets could not become the priorities of modern Jews. In an era when the Jews needed halakha to distinguish themselves and set themselves apart, it became difficult to give prominence to the *moral* commandments, which did not specifically do so.

When the Jewish people were haunted by the danger of assimilation, could their rabbis, authors, and leaders have preached to their communities that the most important part of Judaism was not the part that was unique to Judaism? For an answer, consider what is currently happening to American Jewry. The statistics show that American Jews who are brought up believing that the most important part of their Jewishness is not exclusive to Jews tend not to insist on remaining Jewish.[13] In order to create a strong commitment to Judaism and the Jewish people, and overcome the temptation to assimilate into wider society, Diaspora Jews must teach their children that the center of Jewish life is a uniquely Jewish religious practice. In other words, the confluence of the Diaspora and modernity is a catastrophe for Jews who wish to focus on the prophetic priorities. It is a spiritual tragedy that in the Diaspora, Judaism must be changed to be protected.

The State of Israel is the place where a new Jewish religiosity can flourish, elevating morals above rituals without threatening Jewish continuity. Precisely because Israel is the nation-state of the Jewish people, its society can afford to highlight the nonnational aspects of Judaism. It is precisely because the State of Israel is politically distinct from the rest of humanity that the Jewish religion can rediscover its humanity.

Now that we have dealt with the hierarchical relationship between Judaism's ritual and moral commandments, let us consider a much more sensitive question: What if a ritual commandment runs counter to our understanding of morality? A growing number of Jewish men and women, for example, now feel that the Jewish legal code's attitude toward women is morally jarring. According to a poll conducted by the Israel Democracy Institute, over a third of religious Jews in Israel expect the status of women in the halakha to undergo a change.[14]

The prophets were concerned with changing halakha's order of priorities but not halakha itself. To find traces of efforts to reform the Jewish legal code, we need to move from the world of the biblical prophets to that of the Talmudic sages. Although these rabbis demanded full obedience to halakha, they also strove to reshape it. In interpreting halakha, they often made mighty efforts to strip away aspects that contradicted their own sense of morality.[15] They took explicit commandments, such as that Jews must destroy pagan towns and stone rebellious sons, and reinterpreted them in ways that neutralized their violent content. Like the patriarch Abraham, who was unafraid to challenge God in arguments about morality, the Talmudic sages were unafraid to reinterpret the Torah in a more egalitarian light. The halakhic tradition was dynamic and changeable, and the desire to live an ethical life was a part of its process of change until it veered off course. Ironically it was in the modern era, when the world started changing, that halakha stopped changing. As mentioned earlier, the historian Jacob Katz concluded that the opposition to innovations in halakha was itself an innovation. Judaism had never fostered an ideology of resistance to change, so the closing off of halakha was itself a change.

Jewish law began to fossilize because the Jewish autonomous communities began to disintegrate. This new halakhic conservatism emerged from an impression that in the absence of political barriers between Jews and gentiles cultural barriers were necessary. Orthodox rabbis who took this approach believed that the Jewish emancipation was creating a world that was accommodating to Jews but devastating for Judaism. The more the world opened up to the Jews, therefore, the greater the need to close Judaism off from the world. The Jewish political defensive barriers against assimilation—the autonomous community structures— were replaced with halakhic defensive barriers. As Rabbi Moses Sofer, known as the Chatam Sofer, wrote, "Anything new is forbidden on the authority of the Torah in every place and at every time, and now increasingly so."[16]

Was the Orthodox Jews' fear justified? It seems so. In 2013, a comprehensive Pew Research Center study of American Jewry discovered that the intermarriage rate among young American Jews had reached over 70 percent.[17] But the most important finding for our purposes is that not all American Jews assimilate at the same rate. The more conservative and reclusive their form of Judaism, the less they assimilate; the more open and flexible their form of Judaism, the more they assimilate.[18] Truth be told, this was expected. The most reactionary, reclusive Jews had the most accurate forecast. They were arguably right when they insisted that there was no sustainable future for attempts to craft a different Judaism from that of the past. They were right when they observed that the combination of the Diaspora and modernity would create a dangerous reality in which the only Jewish forces to survive and grow would be those that had internalized the two main elements of ultra-Orthodoxy: self-segregated communities and a static code of law. They alone would have a future, continuity, and growth.

But Jewish history offered another way, an alternative to cultural self-seclusion and a static code of Jewish law. The alternative of Zionism.

Consider another way of understanding the Zionist project: Zionism is an attempt to rehabilitate the Jewish political communities that were lost when Jewish autonomy in the Diaspora disappeared. Instead of reconstituting past Jewish communities, Zionism established a new state of the Jews. Put differently, if the second exile (from autonomous Jewish communities) could not be reversed, then the first exile (from the Land of Israel) would be reversed instead. Instead of going back to the Jewish communities of the Middle Ages, the Jews would go back a few hundred years more to the Jewish kingdom of ancient times.

In short: After the collapse of the Jewish communities, two effective responses emerged to protect Jewish identity. The first, Orthodox Judaism, proposed building cultural barriers; the second, Zionism, proposed erecting political barriers. The Orthodox answer has been effective. The Zionist answer has been no less effective. Compared to the situation of Jews in the United States and other Western nations, in Israel assimilation is not a threat to Jewish identity. It is almost nonexistent.

Jewish defense mechanisms in the Diaspora included nurturing a belief in Jewish supremacy over the gentiles, blurring the precedence of morals over rituals, and arresting the process of halakhic change. Since these mechanisms are indeed effective, we can conclude that outside Israel, Judaism is in a bind, and the Jews must choose between two bad options: to change Judaism and preserve it, or not to change it and risk losing it. Will Diaspora Jews find a way to escape this trap? Will they summon the fortitude, resilience, and creativity to guarantee Jewish continuity without relinquishing their openness and dynamism? I certainly hope so. But this book is not about diasporic Judaism; it is about Israeli Judaism, and in Israel there is good news. Israel is the only place where Jews are not confronted with the choice to assimilate or segregate. Israel is the only place where Jews are not forced to make the choice between tradition and modernity. In Israel, Jews can cultivate an open and dynamic Judaism without risking its continuity. This is the spiritual significance of the State of Israel: only *in* Israel and *thanks to* Israel can Jewish law be reformed without Judaism being endangered.

The great national achievement of Zionism was the creation of new historical conditions in which many of the threats to Jewish identity have disappeared. Jews can now consider whether to shake off the mechanisms that they created to protect themselves from these threats.[19] From the moment of Israel's birth and resurrection, the Religious Zionist movement has been asking itself why Zionism has religious significance. In the previous chapter I explored the messianic answer: Zionism has religious significance because it must be understood as part of the Redemption.[20] In this chapter I have shown how the Religious Zionist model can be flipped on its head: instead of reinterpreting Zionism through the lens of the Jewish religion, we can reinterpret the Jewish religion through the lens of Zionism.

The messianic model of Religious Zionism is based on the philosophy of Rav Kook, his son, and his followers. The alternative model, by contrast, was formulated by the Sephardic rabbis.

9 SEPHARDIC RABBIS AND TRADITIONALIST JUDAISM

Here is one of the greatest differences between Israelis and Jews in the English-speaking Diaspora: 50 percent of Jews in Israel are Sephardic, whereas outside Israel, only 15 percent of Jews are Sephardic (including only 10 percent of American Jews). American Jewry is predominantly Ashkenazi; Israel society embodies an Ashkenazi-Sephardic fusion. In Israel, Sephardic Judaism offers a constructive way to Jewish religious renewal.

ASHKENAZI ORTHODOXY

Orthodox Jewish thinkers believe that demands to change religious law are rooted in a lack of faith. That is the conclusion that inevitably follows from these two premises: first, that inherent in any amendment to halakha is the presumption that halakha is imperfect; second, that inherent in the position that halakha is imperfect is a belief that its creators were also imperfect.

The Chazon Ish, for example, one of the towering figures of twentieth-century ultra-Orthodoxy, ruled that anyone who believes that human judgment can be brought to bear on shaping religious law as recorded in the Talmud is effectively disputing the eternality of the Talmud's teachings. He declared it strictly forbidden for Jews to exercise their own judgment and dispute the sages: the text of the Talmud remains eternal.[1] And if halakha is eternal, then whoever seeks to change it is denying its eternality. This conclusion challenges the development described in the previous chapter. The idea that Zionism's historic breakthrough also paves the way for a reinterpretation of Judaism hits an intellectual snag. Is halakha not supposed to be immune to historical changes? This admittedly poses a weighty theological question. It was traditionally believed that the Talmudic sages did not devise halakha by themselves but rather revealed or mediated the will of God. Disputing the perfection of halakha therefore means disputing its divine provenance.

As Rabbi Moses Sofer (also known as the Chatam Sofer, one of the founders of Orthodox Judaism) wrote in his last will and testament: "And you shall not say that the times have changed, for we have an Ancient Father, may His name be Blessed, Who has not changed and will not change."[2]

History changes and so do the times, but for Orthodox Jews, God is eternal and so are his laws. This argument draws inferences about the nature of the Torah from the nature of God: God does not change, and neither does his Torah. There is admittedly profound religious logic to the claim that religious law should not reflect a mutable history but an immutable God. How can Jews confront the theological challenge posed by the Chatam Sofer and Chazon Ish? The assumption that Zionism creates a conducive climate for changes to halakha is challenged by the argument that a perfect and eternal divinity must entail a perfect, eternal, and immutable code of religious law. We can find the answer to this challenge with the Sephardic thinkers and authorities of the modern age.

THE SEPHARDIC THEOLOGICAL INVERSION

Rabbi Ben-Zion Meir Hai Uziel, the Sephardic chief rabbi of Mandatory Palestine from 1939 to 1945, completely rejected the proposition that "anything new is forbidden on the authority of the Torah." As one of the greatest intellectuals and religious authorities in Sephardic Judaism in the Land of Israel, Rabbi Uziel was not opposed to changes in halakha. He was opposed to *preventing* changes in halakha: "Living conditions, changes in values, and technical and scientific discoveries are creating, generation after generation, new questions and problems that demand solutions. We cannot avert our eyes from these questions and say, 'Anything new is forbidden on the authority of the Torah.'"[3]

Times change, values change, technologies change, and the Torah cannot be blind to all these changes. Rabbi Uziel pointed out one of the problems stemming from the ruling that "anything new is forbidden on the authority of the Torah." The prohibition on making changes in halakha amounted to a denial of changes in the real world. It could not be denied that the world changes, but the halakhic innovations that follow also could not be avoided. How did Rabbi Uziel dare reject the fundamental principle of Orthodoxy, forbidding innovation? This theological question remains a live one. How can halakha be changed without denying the perfection of its divine creator? A powerful answer was provided for this religious quandary by another representative of Sephardic Jewry in Israel, Rabbi Hayim David HaLevi.

Rabbi HaLevi marveled at the power of the Torah. He wondered how the Torah, given to the world thousands of years ago, could have survived so many generations and tribulations. He wrote:

> But there is room for us to ask [this question], because it is most obvious that no law or regulation can last long because of changes in living conditions, and laws that were good for their time are unsuitable after a generation or more and require correction or change, etc., just as our holy Torah gave us righteous and honorable laws and judgments thousands of years ago and we have continued to follow them up to today, and we shall continue until the end of time. How could it be that these laws were good for their time and remain good to this day? Indeed, the Holy One, Blessed be He, was certainly the giver of the Torah, seeing and watching [us] until the end of time, and he gave us a Torah that would be suitable until the end of time — but it is certainly our duty to understand how.[4]

The Torah, which had guided the Jews through life in antiquity, had continued to guide them through the Middle Ages and into the present day. The changing times and changing world had not erased the Torah's power to chart the way forward. Rabbi HaLevi refused to explain this remarkable fact by appealing to wonders and miracles. He had a different and surprising explanation for the secret of the endurance of the Torah and halakha: "This was possible only because the authority was given to the sages of Israel down the generations to renew halakha according to the changes in times and events, and only because of this could the Torah exist in Israel, and [the Jews] walk in the way of Torah and mitzvot."[5]

The Torah retained its relevance because of the rabbis who interpreted it, gave it new life, and adapted it to changing times. This was a highly meaningful inversion. In contrast to the position that the Torah is eternal *and therefore* humans must neither change nor reshape it, Rabbi HaLevi believed that the Torah was eternal *because* humans had renewed and reshaped it:

> Anyone who thinks that halakha is fixed and one cannot deviate from it left or right is wrong. On the contrary, nothing is as flexible as halakha, since a teacher in Israel can rule on the same question, at the same time, to two different people, and give one permission and prohibit the other, as the teachers of permissions and prohibitions know. . . . And it is only thanks to the flexibility of halakha that the people of Israel, by virtue of the many useful innovations made by the sages of Israel throughout the generations, could walk in the way of Torah and mitzvot for thousands of years.[6]

Rabbi HaLevi challenged Ashkenazi Orthodoxy with a surprising twist: the eternality of the Torah did not preclude the flexibility of halakha; the eternality of the Torah was the *product* of the flexibility of halakha.

Rabbi HaLevi's model of faith and religious law was not only an answer to Orthodox Judaism in Europe—it was also an answer to the Reform movement there. The most fundamental justifications offered by the founders of the Reform movement for their dramatic changes to halakha were based on their rejection of faith in the absolute, divine provenance of the Torah.[7] As a result of the emergence of biblical criticism, scientific discoveries, and new philosophies, the leaders of the Reform movement came to see the Torah as a fundamentally human creation, with no higher metaphysical status than its students had. And if the Torah was at root a human creation, written for one generation in a specific historical context, then it was perfectly acceptable to adapt it for another generation, living in another historical context. It is precisely here that we find the profound difference between the Sephardic innovations of Rabbi HaLevi and the innovations of the Reform movement. The Reform Jews' innovations were rooted in their rejection of the divinity of the Torah, Rabbi HaLevi's in his faith in the divinity of the Torah.

THE MIZRAHI ALTERNATIVE TO RELIGIOUS ZIONISM

Rabbi HaLevi was expressing an intuition shared by rabbis of the Middle East, one that differed sharply from that of the rabbis of Europe. In contrast to the members of the Reform movement, he believed that halakha was divine; but in contrast to Orthodox Jews, he believed that its divinity was precisely why it needed to be continually renewed.

The differences between the halakhic approaches of the Sephardic rabbis, such as Rabbi Ben Zion Uziel and Rabbi HaLevi, and those of the Ashkenazi rabbis, such as the Chatam Sofer and the Chazon Ish, were rooted in their different theological outlooks, but they were probably also rooted in their different historical contexts. According to the historian Jacob Katz, the main difference comes from the way in which modernity came onto the scene in Europe compared to how it arrived in the Muslim world.

In Europe, the penetration of modernity into the Jewish communities was traumatic. The Jews experienced the advent of modernity as an upheaval that threatened to destroy the halakhic structures built by traditional Judaism over the years. As a result of modernity, European Jewry produced a plethora of innovators and thinkers who sought to prevent this collapse. We have already seen that one of the most prominent initiatives was the Reform movement, whose adherents asked how to save Judaism from modernity and answered, Change it so that it *is* modern.

But from the perspective of the Orthodox rabbis, changing Judaism would aggravate and deepen the crisis, not avert it. Orthodoxy arose in response to the Reform movement. To counter the effort of Reform Jews to change halakha, Orthodox Jews set a prohibition on change. Reform and Orthodox Judaism are two modern movements. One created an ideology of changing Judaism, the other of opposing changes to Judaism.[8]

In the Muslim world, however, modernity appeared at a slower, more moderate, and less threatening pace. It did not upend the Jews' traditional lifestyles but melded with them. The rabbis did not panic at the approach of modernity, nor did they fear that Judaism was on the brink of collapse. And since the advent of modernity was not felt to be an upheaval, no movement arose to save Judaism from ruin. The movements and countermovements that complicated Jewish identity in Europe barely touched Jews in the Muslim world.[9]

The traditionalist forces of European Jewry took shape in response to modernity; the traditionalist forces of Middle Eastern (Mizrahi) Jewry took shape mainly as a movement to continue Judaism in its premodern form. Since premodern Judaism permitted halakhic innovations, Mizrahi Judaism preserved the possibility of making innovations in halakha. And Mizrahi Judaism thus challenges the hardline Ashkenazi approach to halakha with the idea that "nothing is as flexible as halakha."

The dramatic changes wrought by modernity in its European guise threatened the authority of Jewish religious beliefs and traditions. It was practically imperative for Jews to protect themselves from the new social trends in Europe by suspending reforms to Judaism. But the spiritual price has been grave, since the freezing of a dynamic code of law was bound to lessen its vitality. There may have been times when it was necessary to restrict Judaism's dynamism in order to preserve and protect it. But these times have passed. Thanks to the historic change introduced by Zionism, the dangers from which ultraconservative forms of Judaism sought to protect themselves have almost disappeared. And with the passing of this threat, the Jews can also dismantle some of the defense mechanisms they built to confront this threat. This is where Zionism can intersect with Mizrahi Judaism.

Zionism, which negates the threat posed by modernity, finds itself engaged now with a form of Judaism that was never threatened by modernity. Jews who wish to shape a religious Zionism for reasons other than self-defense can learn from the groups for whom Judaism never needed to be a means of self-defense. The Mizrahi option, in which the flexibility of halakha does not follow from a lack of faith but from a *depth* of faith, can be a model for the renewal of Religious Zionism. The two in tandem represent an alternative to the binary Ashkenazi model of Jewish religiosity.

Mizrahi Judaism contains a wide variety of lifestyles, beliefs, and identities. Not all Jews in Muslim countries were religious, and not all of them observed halakha in its entirety. Some stopped considering themselves bound by halakha. But even many of those who were secularized did not become secular. Mizrahi Jews who are not subservient to halakha frequently identify as *masorti*, "traditionalist."

This is the second challenge posed by Mizrahi Judaism to its European counterpart. Just as the Sephardic approach to halakha challenges reactionary forms of Jewish religiosity, the Sephardic brand of traditionalism challenges reactionary forms of Jewish secularism. The Mizrahi style of religion presents an alternative to the hardline, legalistic form of Judaism; the Mizrahi approach to tradition can offer an alternative to the rebellious version of secularism.

THE ANOMALY AT THE HEART OF TRADITIONALISM

Meir Buzaglo, a philosopher and scholar of traditionalist Judaism, likes to recall how in the golden days of Moroccan Jewry, one Jewish community held a special minyan very early on Saturday morning. The reason? Some of the congregants had to go to work.

This story must sound odd to many. Jews were waking up early in the morning for Sabbath prayers, thanking God for this day of rest, and then going to work. Yet the arrangement must have sounded reasonable to the rabbi of this particular community. Out of all the services held by this congregation, the rabbi chose to pray at the early-morning Sabbath minyan.[10]

This story reflects an important characteristic of traditionalist Judaism: its refusal to accept the premise that the Jewish religion is a matter of all or nothing. For European Jews, the halakhic system is a package deal. Either one endeavors to obey it in its entirety, or one ignores it. Just as there is no such thing as a partial pregnancy, there is no such thing as partial commitment to halakha. But the traditionalist approach disputes this sentiment. The lifestyle of traditionalist Jews is one of *selective* halakha.[11]

The selective nature of traditionalist Judaism raises tough questions, however. The halakhic system has a hierarchy. It contains commandments that are considered relatively trivial and others that are considered more severe. Part of the Talmud's undertaking is to rank the commandments by their importance. But the traditionalist Jews' selective approach to halakha takes no account of the halakhic order of priorities. Traditionalist Jews' behavior is not determined by the degree of a particular law's importance. Consider, for example, that many traditionalist Jews tend to ignore the conventional treatment of "thou shalt not" commandments as being more severe than "thou shalt" injunctions. From a halakhic perspective, it is more important not to drive on the Sabbath ("thou shalt not") than to make kiddush over wine on a Friday night ("thou shalt")—but many traditionalist Jews make kiddush *and* drive on the Sabbath. They choose to observe the "thou shalt" injunction and ignore the "thou shalt not" prohibition. Halakha, in short, is not what guides their halakhic choices.[12]

Such partial observance of halakha might point to a choice to relocate the source of authority from the past to the present, and from halakha to its adherents. In other words, it might be proof that traditionalist Jews are simply secular. But this would be incorrect: traditionalist Jews do not dispute halakha at all. They believe that halakha involves absolute obligations, but they do not feel obligated by them at all. This contradiction is evident from the attitude of many traditionalist Jews to their rabbis. For the most part, traditionalist Israeli Jews feel enormous respect and often even admiration for rabbis. They do not, however, feel subject to them or bound by their religious rulings.[13] This is the anomaly at the heart of traditionalist Judaism: traditionalist Jews believe halakha comprises *commandments* but nevertheless do not personally feel *commanded*.

Traditionalist Jews are poorly understood by many European Jews. Religious Jews see traditionalists as unwilling to devote themselves to the tradition and subject themselves to God. Secular Jews see them as unwilling to free themselves from the shadow of the past. Both perspectives are based on a fallacy: the imposition of European categories on an identity of non-European origin. Traditionalist Jews do not conceive of themselves as being located on a spectrum between liberation and subordination, religion and secularism. They belong to a different category altogether.[14]

This other category to which traditionalist Jews belong is one of *faithfulness*. Traditionalist Jews do not obey the past, but they are faithful to it. This is Meir Buzaglo's illuminating distinction: faithfulness is the traditionalist Jew's alternative to the religious Jew's obedience.[15] Traditionalist Jews conduct an intimate relationship with the past without being controlled by it. They are attached to their past and connected to their tradition without enslaving themselves to past generations. Their relationship is one of fidelity and proximity, rather than power and control.

Obedience to tradition means subordinating oneself to the various elements of that tradition; faithfulness does not demand such self-abasement. To demonstrate fidelity, it is enough to make a gesture expressing one's connection to the past. Thus the concept of loyalty explains the anomaly of the traditionalists' selective approach to halakha. Traditionalism cannot be placed on a spectrum between rebellious secularism and obedient orthodoxy. It is a Judaism with intimacy but without hierarchy. Tradition is not a tough-talking commander but a wise teacher.[16] It is a reservoir of ideas and lifestyle habits, not of strict commands.

TRADITIONALISM AS A CHALLENGE TO SECULARISM

Secularization is a primarily modern and European phenomenon. We have already seen that, unlike their European peers, Mizrahi Jews did not make an ideology of reforming Judaism, just as they did not make an ideology of prohibiting changes to Judaism. To this we must add that neither did they make an ideology of disconnecting themselves from Judaism. Jewish traditionalism is more a way of life than a formalized, systematic ideology. In Buzaglo's words, traditionalism is a "praxis in search of a worldview."[17] Over the years the absence of a worldview within traditionalist Judaism has allowed European Jews, both secular and religious, to attract and recruit groups of traditionalist Jews.[18] European Jews had clear, hardline, thought-out ideologies, and they entrenched a consensus in Israel that the only possible relationship with history is one of power and authority. Books above people. The past above the present. Thus Israeli Jews were confronted with a brutal choice: be enslaved by the past or rise in rebellion. Traditionalist Mizrahi Jews had to force their Judaism into the European hierarchies. Religious Jews tried to subject them to the past; secular Jews tried to free them. But for their own part, traditionalist Mizrahi Jews did not try to change their Ashkenazi peers. Since they never made an ideology of their traditionalism, they had nothing to preach or promote.[19]

Of course, Mizrahi Judaism is not identical to traditionalist Judaism. As we have seen, some Mizrahim are not "traditionalist" but "religious" and demand complete subservience to halakha. But we have also seen that rabbis of the Middle East had a different approach to halakha from the rabbis of Europe. In their understanding, believing in the eternality of the Torah does not *preclude* innovation—it demands it. This is why I argued earlier that the Mizrahi approach to religion might appeal to Religious Zionists who are looking for a path to renewal. Let us now add another layer to this argument: just as the Mizrahi approach to halakha might challenge Religious Zionism, the Mizrahi approach to *tradition* might challenge secular Zionism.

We saw earlier that the secular State of Israel is currently enjoying a kind of Jewish revival. Many of the descendants and successors of the members of the Second and Third Aliyah—who rebelled against the past—want to reconnect with the past but are afraid it might swallow them up, and now they see the traditionalist model as more attractive than ever. There is a glaring irony here: Israel's founding generation tried to change the Mizrahi Jews, who for their own part were not looking to change anyone else. Could the dynamic now have reversed, with the descendants of those who tried to change the Mizrahi Jews now changing, inspired by the Mizrahi way of life?[20]

If the traditionalist option is to be relevant, it will need to be articulated, and the path it offers will need to be conceptualized. It will probably also need to be updated. Traditionalists need to show the *answer* traditionalism can give to the challenges of Western life, such as the onslaught of digital stimuli, which inundate people's minds and have the potential to warp their personalities. What answer does it offer for the challenges of halakha, such as inequality between men and women in synagogues? In this sense,

Jewish traditionalism finds itself facing the same challenges as the other "alternative" identities. Any alternative secularism must gain confidence in its own identity to reconnect with Judaism. Religious Zionism must gain confidence in its own identity to reconnect with the world, and Mizrahi traditionalism must gain the self-confidence to update itself and offer Israeli society a way forward.

These three paths demand modern answers to Jewish questions, and Jewish answers to modern questions. All three enable Jews to repair their relationship with the past and thereby enhance their own lives in the present. All three meet the test of continuity: they are neither trapped in the past nor disconnected from it. They take it forward. All three paths represent different shades of Israeli identity, breaking the conventional sectarian dichotomy and making it possible to return to tradition without turning to religion.[21]

PART IV TOWARD A REVITALIZED JUDAISM

INTRODUCTION

The original sin of religious society in Israel, if I may generalize, is the sin of dogmatism. Religious Jews tend to latch onto rigid
positions and dismiss any nonconforming beliefs. People who believe that their personal opinions are shared by God (itself a remarkable coincidence) find it difficult to listen to others, for to
differ is not to disagree with an individual—it is to dissent from
God. The original sin of secular society in Israel, if I may generalize
again, is the sin of ignorance. Secular Jews, the product of Israel's
secular mainstream education system, know little about Jewish
tradition, have little or no familiarity with Jewish liturgy, and may
never have seen a page of Talmud. Israel's tragedy has always been
that the interaction between religious and secular Jews over Judaism is a clash of dogmatism and ignorance, and whenever dogmatism and ignorance collide, there can be no room for conversation.

But something big is changing in Israel. It is a change that I am
personally familiar with from my own students, who are at a stage
of life that in Israel we call "post-army." It is a chapter of life that is
unique to Israelis; Diaspora Jews have nothing comparable. Post-

army life is a period lasting two to three years in which Israelis who finish their mandatory military service take some time out before beginning their academic studies and professional careers. Many go on long backpacking adventures through South America or Asia. It is a time of discovery, curiosity, and openness. One institution, Beit Prat, invites Israelis embarking on the post-army chapter of their lives to take a trek deep into their own Jewish identity.

Its students come from both religious and secular quarters of Israeli society. The student body is diverse, and so is the curriculum. It includes masterpieces of Western civilization alongside the great works of the Jewish tradition. Plato and the Hebrew Bible, Shakespeare and Kabbalah. I have been honored to be involved in this project and to meet thousands of young Israelis. When I ask graduates what the program did for them, religious and secular students give me completely different answers. Secular students tend to say, "I connected." Through their studies, they connect to the accumulated wisdom of the past, to a rich and transcendent tradition, and to inspiring ideas. Religious students tend to say, "I opened up." Studying other perspectives, they open up to concepts that are different from the ones on which they were raised, to different people, and to different ways of life. Religious Israelis open up, secular Israelis connect, and all grapple with the original sins of their respective societies: they obliterate dogmatism, extinguish ignorance, and together create something new and wonderful.

Indeed, something new is happening throughout Israel. A new, centrist stream of Jewish life is emerging. One of the most intriguing characteristics of its members is that they all manage to overcome what I call the "trap of moderation." One of the advantages of extremists is that for the most part they are extremely enthusiastic.

The weakness of moderates is that their enthusiasm is also, by and large, moderate. So although extremists are a minority, they *sound* like they are the majority. Can this pattern be broken? Can Israelis overcome the problem that moderates are only moderately enthusiastic? My sense is that there is a growing middle ground in Israel, formed of moderate people with immoderate amounts of energy. This middle ground offers the hope for Israel's future.

10 PARALLEL WORLDS, PARALLEL DIVISIONS

The debate between Micha Josef Berdyczewski and Ahad Ha'am was an argument over the soul of Jewish secularism. They espoused two contradictory ways of thinking. Berdyczewski argued that the new secularism must sever itself from the tradition, Ahad Ha'am that the role of secularism was to revitalize the tradition. This debate runs parallel to a debate over the soul of Jewish religiosity. Some say that the Jewish religion must withdraw from the outside world, others that a genuinely profound religiosity should be open to the world and engaged in it. These two positions represent different interpretations of the foundational idea of Religious Zionism. But this debate is much greater than Religious Zionism. In reality, these are two ways of thinking that have clashed throughout the whole history of Jewish thought. To truly understand their depth, we need to put aside the modern frame of reference used in earlier chapters and return to the Middle Ages.

I first read Maimonides' *Eight Chapters* when I was eighteen, as I was beginning to develop an interest in Jewish thought. The book, I found, contained profound ideas about human nature and a wealth of intelligent, helpful, even illuminating psychological insights. Five years later, when I was a philosophy student at the Hebrew University of Jerusalem, I delved into a different book, Aristotle's *Nicomachean Ethics*. It was an enjoyable and edifying read, but the concepts that Aristotle laid out were familiar to me—too familiar. To my astonishment, I found that almost all the psychology I had learned from Maimonides was already present in Aristotle. This surprised and troubled me greatly. It was obvious that Maimonides had taken the ideas he presented in *Eight Chapters* from Aristotle's *Nicomachean Ethics*, but why had he not attributed them to their proper author? Why had he not mentioned Aristotle by name? I reread *Eight Chapters* and noticed something in the introduction that I had failed to spot the first time. Maimonides admits to his readers that the ideas he presents are not his own:

> Know, however, that the ideas presented in these chapters and in the following commentary are not of my own invention; neither did I think out the explanations contained therein, but I have gleaned them from the words of the wise occurring in the *Midrashim*, in the *Talmud*, and in other of their works, as well as from the words of the philosophers, ancient and recent, and also from the works of various authors, as one should accept the truth from whatever source it proceeds.[1]

Maimonides knew what would happen if he told his conservative readers that the wisdom he was imparting to them came from Aristotle, a Greek. He knew they would probably reject it. The sad irony was that in order to introduce Jews to Aristotle's thought, Maimonides had to hide from them that it was Aristotle's. Maimonides was not like his readers. He did not believe that a person's attitude to ideas should be affected by their provenance. The truth must be heard, he wrote, "from whatever source it proceeds"—no matter who said it. Rabbi Shem-Tov ibn Falaquera, one of his most eminent students, put it even more strongly:

> For many of the simple folk who are empty or light on wisdom, it would make things very difficult if the author brought evidence from the words of the sages of [foreign] nations, [since] they say their words are null and void and say that it is improper to accept them. These naive, mindless people will not understand that it is right to accept wisdom from anyone, even from a lower class or different nation.... And it is improper to look at the speaker rather than the spoken.[2]

Anyone who believes that fidelity to Judaism requires intellectual isolation is devoid of wisdom; the source of a piece of wisdom should not affect our acceptance of it. So believed ibn Falaquera, who summarized his position with that brilliant aphorism: "it is improper to look at the speaker rather than the spoken."

Maimonides' and ibn Falaquera's openness to foreign ideas was rooted in a broader worldview. They both believed that the mind was the most divine part of the human soul. It was impossible, therefore, to approach God while ignoring reason. And this position challenges anyone who believes there is religious virtue in anti-intellectual spirituality. If the human mind is the divine spark in humanity, then closing one's own mind means extinguishing the divine spark inside oneself. Rabbi Abraham ibn Ezra was a powerful proponent of this position and fiercely criticized those who were inclined to interpret the Torah contrary to healthy logic and human judgment: "Pure reason is the foundation, because the

Torah was not given to those who have no reason, and the angel who connects human beings and God is one's intelligence."[3]

In this short sentence, ibn Ezra plants a surprising image. He directs his readers to make an association with angels, the heavenly beings who mediate between God and humans. Even the rationalistic ibn Ezra believed in the existence of an angel who connects human beings to God, but for him, this angel was the human mind! *Reason* is the angel that connects human beings to God. Moreover, attaching religious value to reason entails a non-isolationist approach to religion. Reason, after all, is not a Jewish quality but a human one, and the glorification of reason is the glorification of something shared with the rest of humanity. Since the Jews have no monopoly on reason, anyone who seeks the truth must seek it wherever it is found, even beyond the cultural frontiers of Judaism.

Maimonides, ibn Falaquera, and ibn Ezra were Jewish thinkers of the twelfth and thirteenth centuries. They developed the Jewish tradition, broadened it, and enriched it. But theirs is not the only version of Judaism. The rival version is the more familiar: an irrational, reclusive Judaism. Ibn Ezra declared that "pure reason is the foundation," but the sixteenth-century Kabbalist rabbi Meir ibn Gabbai declared that "we are forbidden to contemplate anything the Torah says and then continue to intellectual matters."[4] Maimonides stated that Jews should not be afraid of exposure to non-Jewish wisdom and thought, but the German-born thirteenth-century rabbi Asher ben Jehiel warned that Greek philosophy was dangerous and threatening, since nobody can read it and remain unswayed. "Those who come do not return, that is, nobody who comes and enters this wisdom from the beginning can get out of it."[5]

The thirteenth and fourteenth centuries witnessed a cultural collision between these two schools, between those who attached religious value to reason and those who attached religious value to ignoring reason, between those who searched for the truth across the whole of human culture and those who insisted that the transcendent truth existed only in the Jewish Torah.[6]

But the battle over the soul of Judaism did not begin in the Middle Ages. The roots of this tension go back even farther. In classical times, it took the form of the debate between the two rival schools of thought in Second Temple-era Judea—Beit Shammai and Beit Hillel. To understand it, we shall have to return to antiquity.

BEIT HILLEL VERSUS BEIT SHAMMAI

"How does one dance before the bride, i.e., what does one recite while dancing at her wedding? Beit Shammai say: One recites praise of the bride as she is, emphasizing her good qualities. And Beit Hillel say: One recites: A fair and attractive bride."[7] Here is a difficult halakhic dilemma. Consider the situation: A man arrives at a friend's wedding, and the emotional groom asks him what he thinks of the bride. The groom needs reassurance. Like many, he seeks external validation of his choice, asking whether his friend thinks his new wife is attractive.

The situation becomes even more complicated if, in the friend's opinion, the bride is unattractive. What should he do? What should a good friend tell his concerned friend? If he speaks honestly, he might damage the groom's self-confidence on his wedding day and thereby imperil his friend's fresh and blossoming romance. Should he lie, in order not to harm the couple's new relationship?

Or should he risk injuring the groom's self-confidence, if only to avoid having to tell a lie? It is a question of one value against another—truth against domestic peace. Beit Hillel's position is decisive: the man should lie. He should sacrifice the truth for peace. Beit Shammai believes the opposite: no matter how painful, the man must not lie.

That is their argument. Now let's follow its structure:

> Beit Shammai said to Beit Hillel: In a case where the bride was lame or blind, does one say with regard to her: A fair and attractive bride? But the Torah states: "Keep you from a false matter" (Exodus 23:7).[8]

Beit Shammai enters the debate with a strong piece of evidence: an unequivocal injunction from the Torah. The book of Exodus is unambiguous: "Keep you from a false matter." How should Beit Hillel respond to Beit Shammai? How should it react to such clear textual proof? Usually in the Jewish tradition, when one side proves its point with a biblical source, the other side can be expected to defend its position with a biblical quote of its own. But Beit Hillel defies this convention:

> Beit Hillel said to Beit Shammai: According to your statement, with regard to one who acquired an inferior acquisition from the market, should another praise it and enhance its value in his eyes or condemn it and diminish its value in his eyes? You must say that he should praise it and enhance its value in his eyes.[9]

In the case of someone who makes a bad deal and buys damaged goods, and then asks a friend what he thinks of the purchase, it is acceptable not to insult him. It is appropriate to tell him that he made a good deal. *That's just what people do.* They are kind to their friends and try to make them feel good about themselves. Debating Beit Shammai, Beit Hillel invokes normal and intuitive human behavior. And this creates an unexpected balance between the sides: Beit Shammai cites evidence from the Torah, and Beit Hillel cites evidence from life.[10]

Beit Hillel's position is surprising. How dare it counterbalance the unambiguous word of God with mere human intuition? The answer, it seems, is that Beit Hillel attaches religious value to people's inner feelings. Unlike Beit Shammai, it finds enormous worth in human experience. This is apparent, for example, from the two schools' debate about the value of human life:

> The Sages taught . . . For two and a half years, Beit Shammai and Beit Hillel disagreed. These say: It would have been preferable had man not been created than to have been created. And those said: It is preferable for man to have been created than had he not been created. Ultimately, they were counted and concluded: It would have been preferable had man not been created than to have been created. However, now that he has been created, he should examine his actions that he has performed and seek to correct them. And some say: He should scrutinize his planned actions and evaluate whether or not and in what manner those actions should be performed, so that he will not sin.[11]

To be or not to be? Beit Shammai puts forth a very pessimistic position. It says it would have been better never to have been born. Beit Hillel believes the opposite: "It is preferable for man to have been created than had he not been created." The debate ends with a vote among the sages, and Beit Shammai wins. It is announced that it would have been better if man had never been created. But the sages conclude: "Now that he has been created, he should examine his actions." Since man *was* created, to his own detriment, he must examine his actions, search out his own sins, and be aware of his own weaknesses. That is, Beit Shammai's pessimistic position on humanity's creation produces persistent pangs of conscience. It seems to me that from a psychological perspective, the logical relationship between the premise that "it would have been preferable had man not been created" and the conclusion that "now that he has been created, he should examine his actions" is backward. If you feel consumed by guilt about your sins, you might tend to think that it would have been better if you had never been born.

Hillel the Elder, the leader of the Beit Hillel faction, took a different position. It is said that whenever he went to the bathhouse, he told his students that he was going to fulfill a commandment. Is it a religious commandment to wash? Few acts are more physical than reveling at an ancient Roman bathhouse. But Hillel insisted that bathing was a commandment, and to prove his point, he drew an intriguing equivalence between personal hygiene and the buffing of public statues of Roman emperors: "Have you not observed . . . how the caretakers in the theatres and other public places always wash the statues and keep them clean? If then such care is bestowed on inanimate sculptures, the works of man, it must surely be a holy duty scrupulously to clean the handiwork and masterpiece of God."[12]

Human beings are living statues of God, and therefore nurturing the body is a religious act. Beit Shammai sees humans as innately sinful creatures; Beit Hillel emphasizes that they are created in the image of God.[13] The differences between the two schools' conceptions of humanity ground their different approaches to textual interpretation. Beit Shammai sees humans as lowly creatures, and believes that sages should not consider their feelings when interpreting holy texts, whereas for Beit Hillel, humans contain a divine spark and so their intuitions have religious significance. That is why Beit Hillel, drawing on what was common sense at the time, proclaims that one must tell a white lie and say that every bride is "fair and attractive."[14]

Consider a further example: One of the most important interpretative changes that Hillel the Elder made as *nasi* (president) of the Sanhedrin during Second Temple times was to introduce the *prozbul* in Sabbatical years. Hillel devised a complicated halakhic system that effectively scrapped the Torah's commandment that all debts be canceled every seven years.[15] The biblical verses commanding debt relief were written in order to help the poor and to narrow socioeconomic gaps. But the result had been the opposite. People refrained from lending to the poor for fear they would never get their money back. The divine law that was supposed to help the poor ended up hurting them. In response, Hillel created a legal structure that would enable the rich to continue lending money to the poor without fearing that these debts would be canceled in the seventh year. Hillel permitted himself to interpret the Torah in a way that nullified a law that was clearly and explicitly enumerated. Once again, according to Hillel, moral intuition should be brought to bear on interpreting the word of God.

Beit Hillel and Beit Shammai represent two different Jewish ways of thinking, and both currents can be found pulsating throughout the history of Jewish thought.[16] For Beit Shammai, humans are sinful creatures whose feelings must be overridden by the word of the Bible. But for Beit Hillel, humans are transcendental creatures who must listen to their own senses and understand, through them, the verses of the Bible.[17]

"For three years Beit Shammai and Beit Hillel disagreed," records the Talmud. "These said: The *halakha* is in accordance with our opinion, and these said: The *halakha* is in accordance with our opinion. Ultimately, a Divine Voice emerged and proclaimed: Both these and those are the words of the living God. However, the *halakha* is in accordance with the opinion of Beit Hillel."[18] Why did the Divine Voice choose Beit Hillel?

> Since both these and those are the words of the living God, why were Beit Hillel privileged to have the *halakha* established in accordance with their opinion? The reason is that they were agreeable and forbearing, showing restraint when affronted, and when they taught the *halakha* they would teach both their own statements and the statements of Beit Shammai. Moreover, when they formulated their teachings and cited a dispute, they prioritized the statements of Beit Shammai to their own statements, in deference to Beit Shammai.[19]

Beit Shammai would study only its own positions and acted as its own echo chamber. Beit Hillel behaved otherwise. Beit Hillel also taught about the positions of Beit Shammai. Beit Hillel ultimately determined halakha because its sages listened to wisdom other than their own.[20]

But Beit Hillel went even farther. Not only was it willing to introduce into the academy positions that dissented from those accepted in the academy, it was also willing to introduce into the Hebrew Bible voices that dissented from those accepted in the Hebrew Bible! This much is apparent from the polemic between the rival schools over the canonization of the Hebrew Bible.

The debate centered, among other issues, on the book of Ecclesiastes, which represented a unique addition to the Hebrew Bible. It has a different conception of humans, who have no free choice; it has a different conception of time, which is circular rather than linear; and its general spirit is not particularly biblical. This change is palpable for many of Ecclesiastes' readers, which is why it is unsurprising that an argument arose over whether it should be included in the biblical canon. Beit Shammai demanded that Ecclesiastes be excised from the Hebrew Bible. Beit Hillel, however, argued that Ecclesiastes was a holy text and should be incorporated in the biblical canon.[21] The debate over the canonization of the Hebrew Bible was a debate over the boundaries of Judaism: Is the Jewish tradition its own echo chamber, or can it make room for dissenting voices?[22] Beit Hillel, it seems, was consistent. It not only fought for an academy containing multiple voices, it also extended this plurality of voices to the Hebrew Bible.

There are two well-known, celebrated stories featuring Hillel the Elder as the hero. In one, a young Hillel seeks to enter the academy to study Torah, but the gatekeeper bars him entry. Hillel does not despair. Despite the snowy, wintry weather, he climbs onto the roof and listens to the debates through the chimney.[23] In the other, a non-Jew asks to hear the whole Torah while standing on one foot as a way of converting to Judaism. Shammai turns him away, but Hillel obliges him, tells him what he wants to hear, and welcomes him into the Jewish people.[24] The first story presents

Hillel as having been left outside, the second as refusing to leave anyone else outside. The openness that typified Hillel and the school he founded can be explained psychologically: having suffered exclusion at the academy gates as a child, Hillel built an open and inclusive academy in his adulthood. But consider a theological explanation instead. A worldview that exalts the individual encourages us to listen not only to our own moral intuitions but also to positions that contradict our private sense of morality. Humans were created in the image of God, so all humans deserve to be listened to.

Beit Hillel's philosophical approach would crop up again and again throughout the history of Jewish thought. Earlier we met some of the medieval rationalists who believed that the human mind was divine and were therefore willing to hear the truth from any source. The philosophical model of Beit Shammai also repeated itself over the generations. Thinking poorly of reason, some of the Kabbalists, for example, did not seek truth from other sources of wisdom. Truth, they believed, should be sought only within the confines of Judaism. As a rule, different conceptions of humanity beget different conceptions of Judaism.

FALLACIES

Cultural isolationism is conventionally associated with a commitment to religion, just as religious openness is conventionally identified with a tendency to compromise on religion. But this is a fallacy. In Beit Hillel's approach, openness was not a form of religious compromise but of religious excellence. And for Maimonides, it was cultural isolationism that was considered a religious compromise. The difference between openness and conservatism, therefore, should be considered a difference not between weak and strong approaches to Judaism but between two different conceptions of the Jewish faith.

The tension between the two schools of thought in the Jewish religion is the mirror image of the tension between the two schools of thought of Jewish secularism. Micha Josef Berdyczewski and Yosef Haim Brenner conceived of secularism as a rebellion by the Jews against Judaism. Secularism, in this view, is an act of liberation because it is an act of disconnection. Jews are constricted by the chains of tradition, and liberation from these chains will enable a new, liberated Jew to flourish.

Ahad Ha'am and Hayim Nahman Bialik thought otherwise. Secularism, in their view, is not an attempt by Jews to rebel against Judaism but one to revitalize it. Like so many movements throughout Jewish history, secularism offers a path toward a new understanding of an ancient tradition, and it too constitutes a stream within Judaism. In this view, secularism is a force for liberation because it creates a new, free connection to the past. But here too is a common fallacy. Secular Jews who study Judaism and seek a connection to the ancient Jewish culture are considered lapsed. "Genuine" secularism, many Israeli Jews believe, severs itself from Judaism. Ahad Ha'am would have asked of these Jews: Who is freer—those who free themselves from the absolute authority of tradition, or those who extend their personal authority over the tradition?

In one conception of Judaism, religious isolationism amounts to religious excellence; in another, religious excellence means religious openness. One conception of Jewish secularism considers disengagement from Judaism the fulfillment of the secular ethos;

another sees free engagement with Judaism as the realization of secular freedom. These are parallel worlds, with parallel debates. There is one debate over the soul of Jewish secularism, and another over the soul of the Jewish religion. And they are both destined to continue.

11 SELF-CONFIDENCE AND FEARS ABOUT IDENTITY

The history of ideas is also the history of battles between ideas. And the fallacies described earlier play an important role in our attempt to understand two of these battles of ideas. They help us understand, at least at this point in time, which side has won the intrareligious Jewish battle and which has won the intrasecular Jewish battle.

The debate between Beit Shammai and Beit Hillel ended with a victory for the latter. A Divine Voice emerged and declared that halakha would be determined in accordance with the positions of the side that was also attentive to the other side's positions. But this decision was made at the time of the Mishnah, during the Second Temple era. Does the spirit of Beit Hillel still animate the religious world of the State of Israel in the twenty-first century? It does not. Instead, the prevailing approach of Israel's rabbinic leadership grossly undervalues human beings. It views the present generation as degenerate, distant from truth, and possessing untrustworthy independent judgment. The Chazon Ish wondered how people might base their actions on their independent reason when they know their reason is limited and the truth beyond their grasp, and Israel's rabbinate has adopted this pessimism.[1]

This doctrine was the result of the propagation of the concept of "the diminution of the generations." This is an idea with ancient roots that has assumed a central role in the culture of modern religious Jewish society in Israel.[2] It is a theory that proposes that humanity is steadily degenerating. And in the present day, the conviction that the intellectual and spiritual quality of humanity has been declining over the generations has turned into a powerful inferiority complex that limits religious Jews' freedom to creatively interpret their traditions and laws. Commentators who read the Talmudic sages and feel spiritually and intellectually inferior to the people they are studying cannot but subordinate themselves to them. Confronted with the giants of the past, Orthodoxy demands that its adherents ignore their private sense of morality. The result is ironic: halakha was decided according to Beit Hillel—but it is now interpreted according to Beit Shammai.[3]

This ultraconservative approach to textual interpretation came from the same source as the cultural isolationism. The rabbinic leadership in twenty-first-century Israel is strongly inclined to silence dissenting voices. Some rabbis do not seem to consider that in excluding other voices they are compromising the values of their own religion. On the contrary, they are adamant that they are faithfully fulfilling those values.

Many religious Jews are tolerant, open-minded, and attuned to their own sense of morality; they do not reject positions that differ from their own out of hand. But for the most part, the impulse that guides this openness is not a religious impulse. In fact, the prevailing perception in religious Jewish society in Israel is that genuine open-mindedness necessarily compromises one's faith. When the only position considered "authentically" religious is one of isolationism, Beit Shammai can be crowned the decisive victor. Beit Hillel's position was accepted in the days of the Talmud—and it has been sidelined in modern Israel. On what basis do I make these sociological observations? Primarily, life experience.

Beit Prat, the intellectual institution geared mainly at Israeli post-army university students, brings together men and women in their twenties. In Israel, one's twenties are years of discovery, and these students come to Beit Prat to make discoveries about themselves and the world. The curriculum is diverse: the Hebrew Bible, the Talmud, and Jewish thought are taught alongside Plato, Spinoza, and the masterpieces of Western culture. Moreover, the faculty and student body are as diverse as the curriculum: men and women, religious and secular, study side by side at the Beit Prat academies.

As a teacher at this institution, I myself have learned much about the renewal of Israeli identity by observing the student body. There is one phenomenon that keeps cropping up. The religious students find themselves forced to contend with judgmental attitudes from their own religious societies. Their communities think that their willingness to study alongside secular peers and to be open to Western thought is evidence that their religious commitment is waning. Cultural openness, their friends and families fear, is a form of religious compromise.

The fallacy about religious Jews is the mirror image of the fallacy about secular Jews. I have seen so many secular Israelis take their first steps into the fields of biblical and Talmudic wisdom and be forced to fend off judgmental attitudes from *their* own societies. Their friends and families fear that studying Jewish texts will fatally undermine their secularism. In the modern social climate in Israel, it is difficult to embrace Ahad Ha'am and Bialik's position that studying Judaism does not constrain a Jew's secular freedom but amplifies it.

Conservatives tend to erect barriers. Conservative forms of the Jewish religion erect barriers to keep Jews away from the modern world; conservative forms of Jewish secularism build barriers to keep Jews away from their ancient tradition. The persistence of the fallacy that conservative secularism is the only authentic manifestation of secularism and that religious conservatism is the only authentic manifestation of religion is proof that, for now, conservatism has won the intra-Jewish debate in Israel. Just as Beit Shammai ultimately trumped Beit Hillel in the religious world, Berdyczewski has beaten Ahad Ha'am in the world of secularism.

There exists a profound relationship between fear and conservatism. Just as physical fears lead to physical aggression, fears relating to a person's identity can induce aggression on questions of identity. This is the reason for the similarity between the aggressive, conservative forms of secularism and religion. Both are nurtured by fears about identity.

The most reactionary form of the Jewish religion emerged in the nineteenth century, when fears about the new and enticing world threatened the stability of Jewish identity. As the world opened up, Judaism closed up. But a parallel process also took place in the secular Jewish world, where a reactionary form of secularism was born as a result of fear.

For segments of the secular public in Israel, the Jewish religion is a frightening, even ominous force, which threatens their secular freedoms. And like those of religious Jews, secular Jews' fears are grounded in reality. The object of their anxieties can be found in two domains: the public-political sphere and the personal-emotional sphere.

Politically, there is a widespread fear in secular Israeli society of religious coercion at the hands of the country's growing and increasingly assertive religious minority. Many secular Israelis fear that Israel's secular and enlightened character is under threat from powerful forces bent on transforming it.[4]

But there is another, perhaps more profound, fear in the minds of many secular Israelis—rooted in the perceived fragility of their secular identity. Secular artists and thinkers sense that their identity is brittle enough to be easily shattered by the temptation of religion. "There is a law of gravity of sorts that applies to nationalist secular Israelis or humanistic Jews," observed the scholar Menachem Brinker, "which keeps pulling them back to their ancient Jewish identity." And this attraction to religion also generates tremendous aversion to it.[5]

Theodor Herzl expounded an almost prophetic literary representation of this phenomenon. In his magnum opus, *Altneuland* (*Old New Land*), the character Friedrich Löwenberg is a thoroughly assimilated Jew, completely devoid of any Jewish characteristics. But during his travels in the Land of Israel, Löwenberg sees the walls of the Old City of Jerusalem and is suddenly filled with a strange emotion. He finds himself assailed by religious sentiments as he beholds the holy city's ancient glory.[6] When we experience unfamiliar sentiments, whether religious or spiritual, we often take fright. Where is this religious emotional energy coming from? Where has it been hiding? The unexpected onslaught of feelings that Herzl's hero experiences as he faces the walls of Jerusalem is a fictional episode, but in the Six-Day War these emotions became reality when Israel's secular paratroopers were overcome with religious awe as they faced the Western Wall. Israeli history is full of examples and precedents of enlightened, secular citizens who enter a sudden religious frenzy and metamorphose in front of their anxious friends' eyes. Many Israelis presume that the primordial religious energy lurking in the recesses of the Jewish soul might awake from its slumber at any moment—and therefore believe that they must constantly be on their guard to stop it.

The emotional fear shared by secular Jews is arguably deeper than their political fear. Their concern that religious Jews will take over their country is dwarfed by their concern that an unchained, primitive, subconscious religious energy will seize control of their minds.

Naturally, fear begets struggle. In this case, it is a struggle to protect one's country from religious control and one's mind from its latent religious energies. Secular Israelis who fear the resurgence of historical forces might use bellicose rhetoric, but their impulse is defensive, and the readiest form of self-defense is withdrawal: they close themselves off from Jewish ideas and from Jewish books, religious rituals, and traditional symbols.

Fears about one's identity can lead to cultural isolationism. Religious Jews have closed themselves off to the outside world, fearing its influence; secular Jews have closed themselves off to tradition, fearing its influence too.[7] The common denominator of these two conservative tendencies is that they are both nourished by fears about identity. And such fears are most potent when people lack confidence in their own identities. Insecure religious societies take fright and withdraw; insecure secular societies do the same. The challenge for Israel's next generation is to feel sufficiently self-confident that secular Israelis can return to the vision of Ahad Ha'am and religious Jews to the openness of Beit Hillel.

12 THE ISRAELI MIDDLE GROUND

A MEETING OF MINDS

This book, which is nearing its end, has been about alternative forms of Jewish secularism and religiosity. In the first part, I outlined the collision of identities that fed the most reactionary form of Judaism and the most rebellious form of secularism in Israel. In the second, I articulated and analyzed the ideas that characterize secular Jewish philosophies that are unconstrained by fears about identity and seek to reconnect with Judaism. In the third, I dove into Religious Zionist thought and tried to show how here, too, a way can be found out of fears about one's identity—an opening to shape a non-isolationist form of Jewish religiosity.

The ideas explored in this book are my attempts to continue the Jewish tradition. Not to seek liberation from it or become locked inside it but to carry it forward. And these ideas are not merely theoretical. They are clearly in action in both secular and religious Israeli society. Together, these movements are challenging the homogeneous structures of the social sectors from which they emerged.

Secular Israelis who are party to the Jewish renewal are challenging the homogeneous model of secular Israeli society. In effect, one can no longer speak of secular Jews in Israel as a single group. As the scholar Gideon Katz has explained, modern Israel contains two streams of secularism: secularists who choose to sever themselves from Judaism, and those for whom Judaism is increasingly absorbed into their secular identity. The tension between them is causing a fissure within Israel's secular society. These are two distinct groups, which are growing farther apart from each other, and it is a mistake to view them as a single collective.[1]

A similar development is happening within Religious Zionism. The journalist and researcher Yair Ettinger has noted that while outside observers might think Religious Zionism is growing more extreme, a closer look shows it is not radicalizing but fraying. The ultraconservative strain of religion is getting stronger, but this is in reaction to another development within Religious Zionist society. A growing number of religious Jews are overcoming their fears about their identity and opening up to the world. They are not afraid that the slow, incremental revival of a tradition of openness will fatally undercut their religious identity.[2] The growing gulf between these two groups makes it difficult to view them both as part of a single Religious Zionist collective.

Observers commonly point to a culture war between the religious and secular worlds in Israel but seldom notice that the deeper fissure is actually *within* religious and secular societies. These are rapidly changing times. The secular and Religious Zionist worlds are fracturing at the same time. And these parallel divisions give Israelis an opportunity to make a new connection, one that I have personally witnessed in recent years. Meeting readers, students, and friends, I see a fascinating social trend. When secular Jews in search of inspiration meet religious Jews who dare to open up to the world, they frequently discover that they have more in common with *each other* than with their original societies. Together, these secular and religious Israelis are paving an Israeli middle way.

This is not a middle point *within* different societies but *between* them. A Jewish religiosity that is open to the world is another kind of religiosity; diverging from conventional religious norms, it cannot be said to be a middle way within religious society. Similarly, a secularism that is tied to Judaism is another kind of secularism; it diverges from the classical conception of secularism, so it cannot be said to be a middle way within secular society. But together, these paths constitute a middle way in the culture of Israeli society as a whole.

A MEETING OF IDEAS

Many of us feel both a longing for independence and a fear of loneliness. We are torn between two strong desires: to be free of frameworks that are greater than ourselves and limit us, and to be part of a story that is greater than ourselves and uplifts us. Is there a middle way between liberty and belonging? Is there a way out of the twenty-first-century identity trap?

The historian Yuval Noah Harari has observed that at the heart of every dynamic, developing culture is a latent tension between contradictory values. Tension between values is the source of any civilization's energy and growth.[3] But not all examples of tension are fruitful. Sometimes tension between ideas does not nourish cultural growth but stunts it.

In this book I have not sought to resolve the tension between liberty and belonging. Hillel the Elder and Maimonides do not offer perfect liberty, nor do Bialik and Ahad Ha'am offer perfect belonging. We have not discovered among the various thinkers a way to realize full liberty alongside full belonging, nor have we discovered a harmonic, redemptive, and perfect synthesis. But although none of the different approaches resolves or dissipates the tension, they all change it. The alternative forms of Jewish secularism and religiosity described here transform a debilitating tension into an empowering, growth-inducing dilemma. Or rather, into two parallel dilemmas.

The secular dilemma: Modernity has caused religion to appear antiquated and irrelevant. But as the anthropologist Tanya Marie Luhrmann of Stanford University explains, now more than ever people need intimate, nonjudgmental spaces as sanctuaries from alienation, competition, and loneliness. This need is why people are increasingly drawn to religion. Participation in religious rituals creates balance in our intense Western lives. It provides intimacy in a world that has lost its intimacy, and community in a world that has eroded community.[4] In other words, contrary to conventional wisdom, the West's progress has rendered traditional spaces not irrelevant but *vital.*

In the history of philosophy, some figures have believed that human beings are thinking creatures defined by their quest for truth; for them it follows that, if religion fails the test of science, as atheists believe, a religious life is an impediment to self-actualization as humans. But the quest for the truth is not the only definition of our humanity. According to the psychologist Stephen Mitchell, humans are first and foremost beings who crave connections. We need healthy and empowering relationships with other people in order to realize our own humanity.[5] And as stated in the introduction to this book, severing connections to a religious tradition leads to loosening community bonds, weakening family ties, and a decline in happiness for many secular people. The conclusion is thus that renouncing religion for reasons of rationality will invariably cause emotional damage.

In the film *The Matrix*, there is a scene in which the hero must choose to swallow one of two pills. The red pill will open his eyes and expose him to the truth, but this is a painful truth and will cause him grief. The blue pill will keep him in his sweet illusions, which guarantee him a modicum of happiness. This existential dilemma between truth and happiness is not just a movie plot. Many face it in their own lives. In the nineteenth century, natural science challenged the foundations of religion. It undermined the certainty that many religious people had in their faith. But now in the twenty-first century, the relationship between religion and science is experiencing another shift, as *social* science starts challenging secularism. It undermines the belief that secular freedom enhances human happiness. And so those who believe that religion has no response to the challenge of natural sciences but also suffer from the alienation and loneliness induced by modern secularism are faced with a dilemma. What should they choose: truth or happiness? The blue or the red pill? An illusory religious life, with its greater prospects for happiness, or sober secularism, with its heightened risk of misery?

But by reviewing the philosophies of Ahad Ha'am, Hayim Nahman Bialik, and A. D. Gordon, we learn that this dilemma is not irresolvable. Victory for secularism does not require the banishment of tradition. In this book, we have seen how these thinkers developed secular paradigms that accommodated the past and tradition as inseparable parts of a secular life. Jews can be part of the Jewish story without committing to the Jewish God. They can belong to an ancient tradition without giving up on modern rationalism.

I have called this path alternative secularism, but it is only "alternative" in terms of contemporary understandings of secularism. Viewed from the perspective of the early days of Jewish secularism, this path is not alternative but definitive. Ahad Ha'am, Bialik, and Gordon were the founding fathers of the Israeli secular enterprise, and they were the ones who nurtured the option of belonging to the Jewish tradition without being controlled by that tradition.

The religious dilemma: The Jewish religious tradition creates a welcoming environment for family and community, but it is not always welcoming to outsiders, nor does it encourage openness and tolerance. This is a generalization that permits many exceptions, but it is difficult to ignore the fact that many religious Jewish communities discriminate against women and are frequently intolerant of homosexuals and others. Religious Jewish communities in Israel also tend to encourage a closed-off and often xenophobic nationalist mindset. The Jewish religion, it seems, is enormously efficient in cultivating a strong sense of "us" but too often excels at excluding and negating "them."

The Western world is full of challenges but also rich in treasures. Life in the West has enhanced people's sensitivities to such transcendent values as freedom and equality. And this way of life puts religious Jews in a difficult position: their religion, which as we have seen protects them from some of modernity's worst problems, also deprives them of some of modernity's loftiest values. In the Introduction I asked, concerning the failure of religion, Must religious Jews sacrifice their values for their faith? Does the Jewish religion necessarily require an attitude in which a strong sense of "us" erodes the worth of "them"?

Hillel the Elder's answer was no. Beit Hillel believed that openness did not contradict the values of the Jewish tradition but realized them. Beit Hillel insisted that different voices must be heard in the beit midrash, and that ideas from beyond the Jewish tradition were not an existential threat. And in modern times, some Sephardic rabbis believe that closing off Judaism will not protect it; rather, revitalizing the tradition will keep it going. I call this approach alternative religiosity, but again, it applies only in terms of modern conceptions of religion. The paths of Beit Hillel in antiquity, Maimonides in the Middle Ages, and Sephardic rabbis in modern times are not alternative forms of Jewish religiosity.[6] They represent central currents in the history of Jewish ideas.

Bialik searched for a way to combine halakha with secular freedom; Maimonides sought to combine a universalistic worldview with the religious tradition. The leaders of the alternative Jewish secularism and religiosity discussed in this book have found a way to take the middle road, a midpoint not between different groups but between different ideas. But I must stress that the middle is not a synthesis. Synthesis is an attempt to take two different and perhaps contradictory ideas, combine them, and create a completely new idea. In a synthesis, both original ideas are canceled out. But the middle road I have outlined does not cancel out the ideas it causes to meet. On the middle road, different ideas do not merge with each other but *balance* each other.

The alternative secularism counterbalances the modern experience with Jewish inspiration. The dangers of the modern world include extreme individualism, addictive consumerism, and excessive exposure to digital technology—and together these forces threaten to make people retreat inward. But for Jews, these factors can all be confronted by cultivating a sense of belonging to their ancient tradition, studying ancient Jewish wisdom, and selectively participating in traditional rituals. Judaism thus acts as a balance against modern threats.

The alternative religiosity also offers a balance, but in the other direction. The xenophobia and nationalistic chauvinism that are often evident in the Jewish tradition are balanced by the modern values of tolerance and openness. Modern values can serve as a source of inspiration for religious interpreters who seek the more egalitarian voices in the Jewish tradition and give them greater emphasis.

The alternative religiosity illustrates how Judaism can be modernized; alternative secularism illustrates how tradition can help Jews cope with the threats of modernity. One seeks to heal Judaism through modernity, the other to heal modernity through Judaism. Returning to tradition without turning to religion.

In my previous book, *Catch-67*, I sketched out the features of a middle way for Israeli politics. In this book I have outlined the features of a middle way for Israeli Judaism. Those who live in a binary world—of sacred and profane, good and evil, religious and secular—might recoil from the idea of the middle as something mediocre, excessively conciliatory, indulgent. Human beings are used to dichotomous thinking, but human feelings are not dichotomous. Words can easily express black and white, good guys and bad guys, but spiritual feelings cannot be captured in binary categories.

In the commonly accepted dichotomy in Israel, Jews who seek to reconnect with the Jewish tradition are immediately assumed to be turning religious. In Hebrew, the process of becoming newly religious is called *teshuva*, "return." But the word *teshuva* also means "answer." And so the wordplay gives rise to the common impression that Jews who return to religion are "returning with an answer," while those who sever their connection to tradition are "leaving with a question." The illusion here is that the religious tradition contains answers, whereas modern secularism has only questions; tradition means certainty, but secularism promotes skepticism. These faulty generalizations were born in the original sin of binary thought. Jews can return to their tradition without finding God, just as they can search for God without subordinating themselves to halakha, or revitalize halakha without denying its eternality. It is possible to return to tradition without turning to religion.

The search for a middle ground is an ancient quest. One ancient midrash halakha says that the path of moderation, keeping away from extremes, is not a compromise but an aspiration: "'And the whole of Mount Sinai smoked ... for the Lord had come down upon it in fire' (Exodus 19:18): We are hereby apprised that the Torah is fire, that it was given from fire, and that it is comparable to fire, i.e., just as with fire, if one gets (too) close to it, he is burned, and if he is (too) far from it, he is chilled, so, (with Torah) one must 'heat' himself only by its light, (and not in its 'flames')."[7]

Such clarity! Move too far from the Torah and freeze; move

too close and burn. According to the midrash, it is just as dangerous to get too close to the Torah as too distant from it. The modern world suffers from both the cold of secular skepticism and the
burning fire of religious fundamentalism. How can we find the correct Jewish temperature? The Jerusalem Talmud contains a hint:
"This Torah is like two paths—one of fire, the other of snow. If he
steers on one, he dies in the fire; if he steers on the other, he dies in
the snow. What will be do? He will walk in the middle."[8]

Secular skepticism, which disrupted the line of tradition between the Jews and their past, is a threat to the Jewish future. It is
a threat to the whole of Western society, which is suffering from
aging populations, deepening melancholy, and the loss of meaning. The cold is fatal. At the same time, the flame of isolationist
forms of religion denies the world, and fanatical forms threaten to
consume it in flames. Fundamentalism sows destruction and dev-
astation wherever it goes. The heat is fatal.

Between the path of doubt, which empties the world of meaning, and the path of fanaticism, which lays the world to waste,
there is a middle ground. It contains room for more than one idea
and more than one path. In the Israeli context, this space can accommodate Religious Zionists whose Zionism opens fresh opportunities for the Jewish religion, as well as secular Zionists whose
secularism permits a reconnection to the past. Together, they are
paving a new path to a way of life that contains tradition but no
certainty—a path of returning to tradition, without necessarily
turning to religion.

AFTERWORD

A Digital-Free Sabbath

Western civilization has fundamentally transformed the relationship between humanity and nature. Premodern humans looked at the world and understood that their lives depended on forces of nature. They also understood that they could not control these forces. These two understandings instilled fear and anxiety: people experienced nature as a mighty and threatening force.

Modern science and technology have radically changed our relationship with our environment. Science is an attempt to understand the world; technology is an attempt to control it. The advance from science to technology is the most elegant expression of the advance from knowledge to power. The more science developed, the more technology developed; and the more technology developed, the more control humans exerted over their surroundings—until they hubristically believed themselves to be the masters of the natural world. Technology enabled humanity to control many aspects of the environment, with advances in travel, communications, and medicine. It reached its apex with the advent of the internet and digital technology. But then something unforeseen happened: technology started to affect the personalities of its users.

Some people develop obsessions with other people. They need perpetual contact with them and cannot be calm when they are not together. People who suffer from such obsessive dependency are for the most part emotionally disturbed. The social psychologist Adam Alter argues that this is precisely the same relationship that many of us have with digital technology. In his book *Irresistible*, Alter demonstrates how people develop obsessive relationships with their technology. He claims that 40 percent of Americans, for example, have developed a serious addiction to technology.[1]

One of the hallmarks of addiction is an inability to predict one's own behavior. Technology addicts cannot know in advance how long they will spend plugged in at a given time. People might log in "just to check something on Facebook" and remain there on average for over twenty minutes. Studies in the United States show that many Americans report needing to check email or Facebook at least once an hour, and many struggle to concentrate or continue their daily routine. And similar situations can be found worldwide.

Addicts are people who have lost control of their own behavior. Their behavior controls *them*, not the other way around. The addiction to technology represents a dramatic shift in the history of our relationship to nature. Technology, which humans created to enhance their control over nature, threatens to control humans. History has come full circle: if our premodern forebears were controlled by nature, we postmoderns are in danger of being controlled by our own means of control over nature.

TECHNOLOGY AND EMOTIONS

The researcher Sherry Turkle has shown that high technological aptitude can lead to low emotional aptitude. We invent technology, then technology reshapes us. Turkle illustrates this with a diagnosis of the difference between online and face-to-face conversations. Online conversations are conversations over which we have some control. In contrast, in conversations unmediated by technology, we have less control over the messages we convey because our bodies tend to give us away. Facial expressions, body language, and tone all reveal to our interlocutors what our words try to hide. When we talk face-to-face, we are exposed. Our feelings can be betrayed through involuntary blushes or an unplanned quiver in the voice.[2]

We can hide our emotions when we communicate via text messages—a medium without body language, and no fear of blushing cheeks or trembling voices. Digital communications platforms give people a measure of control over the messages they convey. With these media, we cannot get an accurate sense of other people—and they cannot get a sense of us. Turkle concludes that this is why we prefer to have our most difficult conversations by email. Bosses might criticize employees by text, and families hold sensitive consultations on WhatsApp. It is easier, less threatening, and less embarrassing. But there is a heavy emotional cost to such distancing. Turkle explains that the more accustomed we become to digital communications, the more difficult it becomes for us to talk face-to-face. Our retreat to technology is rooted in our social anxieties, but the technology nourishes and aggravates them.[3]

This problem is compounded by the fact that it is harder than ever for us to spend time alone. We no longer spend time letting our imaginations roam. We whip out our smartphones as a solution to not just socially awkward situations but also boredom. This is, of course, a self-perpetuating dynamic: the more frequently people avoid spending time alone, the harder they find it to feel comfortable in their own company. They lose the ability to be bored. Turkle's conclusion is that people who cannot be alone cannot be together either.

In recent years, our technological abilities have developed while our emotional abilities have worn thin. One of the most serious expressions of this has been the collapse in levels of empathy. Empathy is an acquired ability. The capacity to feel what somebody else is feeling is a skill that can be developed and cultivated. But digital technology strikes a blow at this skill, as evident, for example, from the 40 percent fall in empathy among young Americans in the past two decades.[4] This damage to our ability to feel for other people is happening at the same time as the erosion of our sense of self-worth. In the twenty-first century a new need has been created, one that never existed before, to constantly and unceasingly record ourselves. For some, each passing moment that is not photographed and shared with everyone might as well never have happened. We have always needed to feel that we are seen by others, but our digital reality has increased this need and turned it into a kind of obsession.

This digital culture strengthens our need for external validation. People sit facing their screens and wait for "likes" and favorable comments to their posts. Their sense of self-worth depends on such reactions.[5] And this phenomenon is unrelenting. If children were once able to take a break from popularity contests when they came home from school, now they find themselves lying on the sofa at 8 p.m., still in the middle of a conflict-ridden class party. A life dedicated to technology is an unceasing race for validation. It permits no pauses. The same technology that weakens our empathy also strengthens our narcissism. The means that were invented to help us communicate are disrupting our ability to communicate.

FROM AN ECOLOGICAL TO A
TECHNOLOGICAL CONVERSATION

Technology is a human success story. Technology was supposed to liberate humankind from our dependence on nature, and to a large extent it has succeeded in doing so. But this liberating technology is also enslaving us. It remolds our personalities and emotions.

Recent years have witnessed the emergence of a global environmental awareness, rooted in a debate over the relationship between humanity and nature. This ecological discourse is based on the recognition that our unrestrained domination of nature is polluting our environment and will, as experts warn, lead to its destruction. We require an analogous discourse about our relationship with the means we have developed to dominate our environment. While our unhealthy relationship with nature is polluting our environment, our unhealthy relationship with technology is polluting our minds. The ecological movement, which has existed for decades, has succeeded to some degree in changing our habits. People now sort their waste, recycle bottles, switch energy sources, and support the signing of international treaties to reduce harmful emissions. This movement is gathering momentum. Its aim is to protect the environment from the effects of the Industrial Revolution. But the movement to protect people from the effects of the Digital Revolution has barely begun.

Just as citizens of the modern world have developed an awareness about the human-nature relationship, they need to rethink the human-technology relationship. A technological awareness would address the collapse in empathy and rise in narcissism as well as other threats to the human personality, including the toxic influence of the increased availability of pornography on our sex lives; our addiction to hypnotic video games, which make the non-virtual world feel dull and slow; our constant exposure to digital stimuli, which sabotages our ability to concentrate and focus; and the loss of eye contact between parents who are absorbed in their screens and children who crave their attention. These phenomena compound one another and create one of the most complicated challenges of the modern day. In the next few years, we are told, virtual- and augmented-reality glasses will enter our lives, greatly increasing the challenge posed by technology to our personalities.[6]

EXCELLENT SERVANT, TERRIBLE MASTER

Technology cannot be stopped. It is developing at a fast and unstoppable pace. Neil Postman, a theorist in the field of mass media, has proposed the following distinction. It is foolish to be against technology. Being against technology, Postman says, is like being against food. But although it would be foolish to be against food, it is entirely reasonable to ask "How much should I eat?" or "What should I eat?" or "When should I eat?" It would similarly be foolish to be against technology, but likewise it would be reasonable to ask questions about how we consume it: how much and what we eat, and when. Turkle put it most eloquently: smartphones make excellent servants and terrible masters. As a servant, a smartphone saves us time; as a master, it swallows up our time. As a servant, it strengthens our relationships; as a master, it disrupts our relationships.

Not so long ago, smoking was pervasive throughout society. Science had not yet discovered the dangers smoking posed to humans' physical health; but even after they became known, it took decades for people to internalize those dangers and change their behavior. Now in many countries smoking is frowned upon or banned entirely in public places, and far fewer people smoke. Similarly, when digital technology was born, it took time for science to discover the dangers that excessive use posed to our mental health. But that era is over. It is now clear that the increased use of technology is a danger to our emotional prosperity and our children's mental health. The problem is that the scientific knowledge exists but has not yet been internalized; the findings are known, but the behavioral habits to protect our mental health have not yet been developed.

We are living in an "in between" period, between the science and its internalization. We have not yet developed a far-reaching conversation about our relationship with technology, and therefore we have not yet developed the means to cope with it. Coping with technology does not entail abstaining from it. Technology can be a blessing and a curse. The question is what behavioral habits will prevent this new technology from controlling us and enable it to serve us instead. Social habits are the product of cultures—cultures of expectations and patterns of behavior. And these can nurture a more refined and restrained approach to technology.

How can we take back control of the technology that was invented to serve us?

What could a culture that regulates our relationship with technology look like? Turkle has two suggestions:

1. Set aside times to be free of digital technology; for example, set times for keeping your cell phone and computer switched off. At these times, the digital noises will be silenced, the temptations of the virtual world cast aside, and our attention can be devoted to the place and moment we are in, and the people we are with.

2. Mark out a "digital technology-free zone." Like "no-smoking zones," we also need "no-screen zones." Every home, for example, should have one room—preferably a central room, such as the living room or the dining room—which is a "no-phone zone." Such signposted spaces are also needed at workplaces where employees take their breaks and in places of leisure. I am convinced that the first restaurant owner to mark out a seating area as a screen-free zone will quickly find it to be the most popular spot for couples and families.

In this new culture we would create "islands of time" for people to disconnect from digital technology and "islands of space" free of digital technology as well. These would give people opportunities to encounter themselves and others, free of screens and technological mediation.

Yet the pace of cultural development is naturally slow and incremental, whereas technology develops at an incredibly rapid, often dizzying, speed. This is the reason for the asymmetrical relationship between culture and technology, and we are living inside this gap. Technology is leaping ahead, while the cultural changes that could cope with it have not yet been developed.

But this lag between cultural and technological change offers an opportunity for ancient traditions. Perhaps ironically, an ancient culture contains the means to enable Jews and non-Jews alike to cope with this modern problem. The Jewish Sabbath—a day in which the use of technology is forbidden—can serve precisely this goal. The essence of the Sabbath is to take a break from technology. The Sabbath allows moments of communication uninterrupted by communications technology. It forces us to be *present* in our conversations with other people, without distractions and without the ability to disappear into our smartphones. The Sabbath creates moments that are not recorded, reminding us that our time has meaning even if it is not shared with virtual audiences. In brief: the Sabbath creates a space that allows our minds to be present where our bodies are. The greater our awareness of the vital need to repair the relationship between people and technology, the more relevant the Sabbath will become.

Of course, the Sabbath cannot be the only means for protecting humankind from the technology it has invented. The Sabbath alone cannot give our minds full protection from the damages of bombardment by digital stimuli. But it can be a first and meaningful step, indicating the way toward a more wide-reaching and comprehensive move. Switching off all digital noise once a week creates an unfamiliar silence, but it is a silence we need for relationship-building, family bonding, spiritual worship, and intellectual enrichment. Shutting down our digital lives for one day a week can empower our emotional lives for the rest of the week.

The pioneers of a revitalized Israeli Sabbath already walk

among us. They are the secular Israelis who have managed to over-come the trauma of the politicization of religion in Israel and have decided to switch off their smartphones on the Sabbath—much like Reboot initiative in the United States, which we have already discussed. They are not "Sabbath observant" in the accepted, reli-gious, sense of the term, but some of them define themselves as "screen observant." I have friends who travel and use electricity on the Sabbath but will not touch their computers or smartphones. By announcing a temporary break from digital technology, they liber-ate themselves from its tyranny.[7] In so doing, they illustrate a facet of Bialik's halakhic revitalization. "Screen-observant" Jews repre-sent the realization of all that Bialik foresaw: a code of Jewish law that is not a return to the *Shulchan Aruch* but the use of halakhic ideas from the past in order to reform the present.

Hayim Nahman Bialik focused his halakhic vision on the re-vitalization of the Sabbath. He believed that it had the power to uplift the entire Zionist enterprise. But Bialik might not have fully understood the regenerative potential of his vision. The Sabbath is something that not just Israeli Jews but all denizens of the modern world need. More than just improving life in Israel, the regenera-tion of the Sabbath can balance life across the modern world.

NOTES

Unless otherwise noted, all translations are by Eylon Levy.

INTRODUCTION

1. Yeshayahu Leibowitz, "Religious Praxis: The Meaning of Halakhah," in his *Judaism, Human Values, and the Jewish State* (Cambridge: Harvard University Press, 1995).

2. Karl Popper, *The Open Society and Its Enemies* (Princeton, N.J.: Princeton University Press, 1966). The historian Jacob Talmon has explored the way the seeds of totalitarianism were sown in the rebellion against tradition sparked by the French Revolution. The philosophers Hannah Arendt and Zygmunt Bauman have also demonstrated how the extreme rationalism of the modern era prepared the ground for the emergence of such atrocities as the Holocaust. See Jacob L. Talmon, *The Origins of Totalitarianism* (New York: Praeger, 1960); Jacob Talmon, *Political Messianism: The Romantic Phase* (New York: Praeger, 1961); Hannah Arendt, *Eichmann in Jerusalem: A Report on the Banality of Evil* (New York: Viking, 1963); Zygmunt Bauman, *Modernity and the Holocaust* (Ithaca: Cornell University Press, 1989).

3. Johann Hari, *Lost Connections: Uncovering the Real Causes of Depression and the Unexpected Solutions* (New York: Bloomsbury, 2018).

4. Many studies have been devoted to the question of happiness differentials between secular and religious people. One meta-review of 850 different studies that examined the relationship between religious activity and mental health concluded that there is clear evidence of a strong

correlation between a high emotional quality of life and religiosity. See Alexander Moreira-Almeida, Francisco Lotufo Neto, and Harold G. Koenig, "Religiousness and Mental Health: A Review," *Brazilian Journal of Psychiatry* 26, no. 3 (2006). See also Marilyn Baetz and John Toews, "Clinical Implications of Research on Religion, Spirituality, and Mental Health," *Revue Canadienne de Psychiatrie* 54, no. 5 (May 2009). See also Yoram Kirsh, *Roads to Happiness: The Philosophy, Psychology, and Mathematics of Happiness* (Tel Aviv: Am Oved, 2011), 58–60 [Hebrew].

For a more critical and detailed examination of the different studies, see Charles H. Hackney and Glenn S. Sanders, "Religiosity and Mental Health: A Meta-Analysis of Recent Studies," *Journal for the Scientific Study of Religion* 42, no. 1 (2003): 43–55.

5. For a clear and readable overview of the findings of studies on this question, see Pamela Paul, "The Power to Uplift," *Time* (9 January 2005), accessible at: http://content.time.com/time/magazine/article/0,9171 ,1015870,00.html.

6. These figures have led some conservative writers in recent years to make prophecies of doom with such chilling (or entertaining) titles as: Pat J. Buchanan, *The Death of the West: How Dying Populations and Immigrant Invasions Imperil Our Country and Civilization* (New York: St. Martin's, 2002); Walter Laqueur, *The Last Days of Europe: Epitaph for an Old Continent* (New York: Thomas Dunne Books, 2007); Jonathan V. Last, *What to Expect When No One's Expecting: America's Coming Demographic Disaster* (New York: Encounter, 2013).

Even if we decline to take this approach, these thought-provoking facts should raise concerns. On the other side, however, is criticism of the excessive dramatization of the statistics, saying that although the figures pose a challenge, the trends are not irreversible. Moreover, some researchers argue that the aging of Western societies is also a positive trait, inasmuch as the "maturity" of European societies allows for democratic stability and a developed civil society. See for example David Coleman and Stuart Basten, "The Death of the West: An Alternative View," *Population Studies* 69, no. S1 (2015): 107–118. The entire volume is devoted to a comprehensive discussion of this subject.

Note that besides the high divorce rates, marriage rates are dropping and the average age at marriage is rising. Note also that in many Western states, more than 40 percent of children are born out of wedlock. Elizabeth Thompson, "Family Complexity in Europe," *Annals of the American Academy of Political and Social Science* 654, no. 1 (July 2014): 245–258. For more research, see the other articles in this volume, which is dedicated to the issue of changing trends in the structure of the family in the United States.

7. Alexis de Tocqueville, *Democracy in America,* 2 vols., trans. Henry Reeve (2006), vol. 1, accessible at the Gutenberg Project: http://www.guten berg.org/files/815/815-h/815-h.htm. See also Charles Taylor, *The Malaise of Modernity* (Concord, Ont.: Anansi, 1991).

8. Robert D. Putnam, *Bowling Alone: The Collapse and Revival of American Community* (New York: Simon and Schuster, 2001).

9. Robert D. Putnam and David E. Campbell, *American Grace: How Religion Divides and Unites Us* (New York: Simon and Schuster, 2012), chap. 13. This study notes that religious and nonreligious Americans differ in their levels of charitable giving and volunteering not just with regard to "religious" beneficiaries (such as churches) but also secular ones. The study also demonstrates that measured in terms of political and community participation, religious people are better citizens. And indeed, the authors argue, religious faith in itself is not the main factor behind charitable giving; rather, religious people are motivated by membership in a religious community.

10. This interpretation is notably used by Abraham Joshua Heschel in *The Sabbath: Its Meaning for Modern Man* (New York: Farrar, Straus and Giroux, 2005).

11. Moses Maimonides, *The Guide of the Perplexed,* trans. M. Friedländer (New York: Dutton, 1885).

12. For a comprehensive and exhaustive summary of the history of the term "postmodernism," see Steven Best and Douglas Kellner, *The Postmodern Turn* (New York: Guildford, 1997); Steven Best and Douglas Kellner, *Postmodern Theory: Critical Interrogations* (New York: Guildford, 1992). For the main thinkers of postmodernism, see Michael Drolet, ed., *The Postmodernism Reader: Foundational Texts* (London: Routledge, 2004). For its philosophical roots, see Drolet's introduction (13–17).

PART I INTRODUCTION

1. David Ben-Gurion, "The Imperative of the Jewish Revolution," in *In the Campaign* [*Bama'archa*], vol. 3 (Tel Aviv: Am Oved, 1957), 197–211 [Hebrew].

2. Ehud Luz has shown that the Uganda debate was, among other things, about precisely this question. Was Zionism a revolt against the past or a return to the past? Ehud Luz, "The Uganda Controversy," *Kivunim* 1 (1979): 59–60 [Hebrew]. See also Michael Greenzweig, "The Hebrew Language in the Second Aliyah," in Israel Bartal, Zeev Tzachor, and Joshua Kaniel, eds., *The Second Aliyah* (Jerusalem: Yad Yitzhak Ben Zvi, 1997), 406–418 [Hebrew]; Margalit Shilo, "The Language Wars as a 'Popular Movement,'" *Cathedra* 74 (1994): 87–119 [Hebrew].

3. The Israeli philosophy professor Nathan Rotenstreich believed that these two criteria—language and land—were the lines that demarcated the Zionist forms of Jewish nationalism from its non-Zionist varieties (Jewish Autonomism, Jewish Territorialism, and the Bundist movement). Nathan Rotenstreich, *Jewish Philosophy in Modern Times: From Mendelssohn to Rosenzweig* (New York: Holt, Rinehart and Winston, 1968).

4. Many have commented on this dialectical tension in Zionism's approach to the Jewish tradition. See for example Gershom Scholem, "Zionism—Dialectic of Continuity and Rebellion" (1970), in Ehud Ben-Ezer, ed., *Unease in Zion* (New York: Quadrangle, 1974), 263–296. See also Muki Tzur, *Doing It the Hard Way* [*Le-lo Kutonet Passim*] (Tel Aviv: Am Oved, 1976), 95–122 [Hebrew]; Shlomo Avineri, "Zionism and the Jewish Religious Tradition: The Dialectics of Redemption and Secularization," in Shmuel Almog, Jehuda Reinharz, and Anita Shapira, eds., *Zionism and Religion* (Hanover, N.H.: University Press of New England, Brandeis University Press, 1998).

1 THE GREAT REVOLT

1. Cited in Anita Shapira, "The Origins of the Myth of the 'New Jew': The Zionist Variety," in Jonathan Frankel, ed., *The Fate of the European Jews, 1939–1945: Continuity or Contingency?* (New York: Oxford University Press, 1997), 257. See also Joachim Doron, *The Zionist Thought of Nathan Birnbaum* (Jerusalem: Ha-Sifriya Ha-Tzionit, 1968), 181 [Hebrew]. The

term is usually attributed to Birnbaum, but there is also a theory that it had been used in a similar sense before him. See Shmuel Almog, "Between Zionism and Antisemitism," *Patterns of Prejudice* 28, no. 2 (1994): 49-59.

2. Nachman Syrkin, "Out of the Tent," in *The Writings of Nachman Syrkin* (Tel Aviv: Davar, 1933), 170-171 [Hebrew]. See Yitzhak Conforti, "'The New Jew' in the Zionist Movement: Ideology and Historiography," *Australian Journal of Jewish Studies* 25 (2011). Syrkin was specifically addressing diasporic, Talmudic, Rabbinical Judaism, which he condemned, while praising the intrinsic values of the ancient Israelite Judaism.

3. Yosef Haim Brenner, "Our Self-Evaluation in Three Volumes," in *Writings,* vol. 3 (Tel Aviv: HaKibbutz HaMeuchad, 1976-1984), 1249 [Hebrew].

4. See Rachel Elboim-Dror, "He Comes and Goes: From Inside of Us Comes the New Hebrew Man," *Alpayim* 12 (1996): 123 [Hebrew].

5. See Joachim Doron, "Classic Zionism and Modern Anti-Semitism: Parallels and Influences (1883-1914)," *Studies in Zionism* 4, no. 2 (1983): 169-204. See also Rachel Elboim-Dror, *Hebrew Education in Palestine, 1854-1914,* 2 vols. (Jerusalem: Yad Yitzhak Ben-Zvi, 1986), 1:360-365 [Hebrew]; Oz Almog, *The Sabra: The Creation of the New Jew,* trans. Haim Watzman (Berkeley: University of California Press, 2009).

6. On this matter, see Almog, "Between Zionism and Antisemitism"; Doron, "Classic Zionism and Modern Anti-Semitism"; Moti Zeira, *Torn Apart We Are: The Affinity of the Labor Settlement in the 1920s to Jewish Culture* (Jerusalem: Yad Yitzhak Ben-Zvi, 2002), 35 [Hebrew]; Anita Shapira, "Antisemitism and Zionism," in Shapira, *New Jews, Old Jews* (Tel Aviv: Am Oved, 1997), 175-191 [Hebrew]; Shapira, *Land and Power: The Zionist Resort to Force, 1881-1948,* trans. William Templer (Stanford: Stanford University Press, 1992).

7. See Shmuel Almog, "Judaism as Illness: Antisemitic Stereotype and Self-Image," *History of European Ideas* 13, no. 6 (1991): 793-804.

8. In this sense, Zionism was a continuation of the Jewish Enlightenment movement. Zionists did not invent the rebellion against the past but carried it forward, intensified. Their ideal of the "new Hebrew" was a continuation of the previous generation's ideal of "the new Enlightened

Jew." But the new ideal also differed from that of its predecessor in one significant respect: the problem of liberation from the ghetto, tradition, and the old world could not be solved through adaptation to the tolerant, liberal societies of Europe, they reasoned—it could take place only in a uniquely national environment. See Shapira, "The Origins of the Myth of the 'New Jew.'"

Even Theodor Herzl, whose primary interest in Zionism was political, addressed its psychological aspects. In one essay he depicted Zionism as a new hospital that would cure the Jewish people "by means of a healthy life on their land, the land of our forefathers." Theodor Herzl, "The Family Patients," in *Herzl's Writings: In Ten Volumes,* vol. 8 (1959–1960), 292–295 [Hebrew]; see also Almog, "Judaism as Illness."

Much has been written about the myth of the "new Jew." See for example Shapira, "The Origins of the Myth of the 'New Jew'"; Conforti, "'The New Jew' in the Zionist Movement"; Elboim-Dror, *Hebrew Education in Palestine;* Zeira, *Torn Apart We Are,* 37–45 [Hebrew]; Ehud Luz, *Parallels Meet: Religion and Nationalism in the Early Zionist Movement (1882–1904),* trans. Lenn Schrem (Jerusalem: Sefrit-Aliya, 1991).

9. Jabotinsky phrased this powerfully in one of his early essays, contrasting the character of the new Hebrew and of the diasporic *zhid,* or "Yid": "The frightened and humiliated *zhid* ... is used to surrendering ... the *zhid* likes to hide, holding his breath, from the eyes of others." Ze'ev Jabotinsky, "Dr. Herzl" (1905), in *Collected Works,* 18 vols., ed. Eri Jabotinsky (Jerusalem: E. Jabotinsky Ltd., 1947–1959), vol. 8: *First Zionist Writings,* 99 [Hebrew]. See also Jabotinsky, "On the *Hadar* of Betar," *Collected Works,* vol. 11: *Speeches (1927–1940),* 347 [Hebrew]. For more on Jabotinsky's approach, see Raphaella Bilski Ben-Hur, *Every Individual, a King: The Social and Political Thought of Ze'ev Vladimir Jabotinsky* (Washington, D.C.: B'nai B'rith Books, 1993). Of course, not all Zionist thinkers felt this way, as will be discussed below.

10. Baruch Spinoza, *Theological-Political Treatise* (1677). As a rule, Spinoza considered it a good thing to educate the masses to obedience through religion, so long as this obedience led them to behave according to the principles of reason. See Ze'ev Levy, *Spinoza and the Concept of Judaism*

(Tel Aviv: Poalim, 1983), 11-43 [Hebrew]; Yirmiyahu Yovel, *Spinoza and Other Heretics* (Princeton, N.J.: Princeton University Press, 1989).

11. Shaul Tchernichovsky, "I Believe" [Hebrew]. A translation by Vivian Eden can be found in "Poem of the Week: This Is the Poem That Could Replace 'Hatikvah,'" *Haaretz*, 13 October 2013, available at https://www.haaretz.com/life/books/.premium-poem-this-could-replace-hatikvah-1.5272958. My understanding of the two types of hero is influenced by a distinction drawn by the Canadian philosopher Charles Taylor, who defined modernity as the ideal of self-realization on top of individualism and authenticity. Charles Taylor, *The Malaise of Modernity* (Toronto: House of Anansi Press, 1997); Charles Taylor, "Two Theories of Modernity," *Hastings Center Report* 25, no. 2 (March-April 1995): 24-33. Eyal Chowers has observed that Zionists took the Promethean aspect of modernity to its extreme, and in this sense they were not "exemplary moderns." Their sense of detachment and lack of history allowed them to create a world in their own image, which was not fettered to any predetermined reality. Eyal Chowers, "The End of Building: Zionism and the Politics of the Concrete," *Review of Politics* 64 (2002): 611.

12. Micha Josef Berdyczewski, "Old Age and Youth," in *Collected Works*, 13 vols., ed. Avner Holtzman and Yitzhak Kafkafi (Tel Aviv: HaKibbutz Ha-Meuchad, 1996-2015), 5:209 [Hebrew]; Berdyczewski, *"Harut ve-Herut,"* in *The Writings of Micha Josef Ben-Gorion (Berdyczewski)* (Tel Aviv: Dvir, 1964), 2:38 [Hebrew]. (I generally prefer Holzman and Kafkafi's new and more detailed anthology of Berdyczewki's writings, but in some instances the edition published by Dvir seems preferable.) Berdyczewski compares the Jewish people to a decrepit hunchback, his legs swollen from endless wanderings, buckling under the weight of the Jewish tradition. Micha Josef Berdyczewski, "Singular and Plural," in *Collected Works*, 2:93-94 [Hebrew]. See also Avner Holtzman, "Old Jews, New Hebrews," in *Literature and Life Essays on M. J. Berdyczewski* (Jerusalem: Carmel, 2003), 44-57 [Hebrew].

According to Nachmanides, outside the Land of Israel Judaism is incomplete; according to Ben-Gurion, outside the Land of Israel the Jews are incomplete. Shmuel Rosner has noted this similarity between one of the greatest Kabbalists (Nachmanides) and one of the greatest Zionists (Ben Gurion). Shmuel Rosner, *The Jews—Seven Common Questions* (Or Yehuda: Kinneret, Zemora, Dvir, 2016), 89 [Hebrew].

13. The poem, "In the City of Slaughter," was translated into Yiddish by I. L. Peretz and into Russian by Ze'ev Jabotinsky, and it quickly spread across the Jewish world. According to Avner Holtzman, a professor of Hebrew literature, the publication of "In the City of Slaughter" changed Jewish history. Avner Holtzman, *Hayim Nahman Bialik: Poet of Hebrew* (New Haven: Yale University Press, 2017). Anita Shapira concludes that Kishinev was a high-water mark in terms of the attitudes of young Jews to attempts to harm them: "The impotent rage was a kind of revolutionary explosive charge that demolished traditional Jewish responses, insisting on a new demonstration that the Jew was also a human being, whose blood would not be shed with impunity." Shapira, *Land and Power*, 36.

14. "Av HaRachamim," in the Metsudah Machzor (Machzor Yom Kippur Ashkenaz), translated by Rabbi Avraham Davis, available through the Sefaria Library at Sefaria.org.

15. Hayim Nahman Bialik, "The City of Slaughter [Version 1]," in A. M. Klein, *Complete Poems, Part II: Poems, 1937–1955 and Poetry Translations*, ed. Zailig Pollock (Toronto: University of Toronto Press, 1990), 735–736. On Bialik's blaming the victims, see for example the analysis of Hannan Hever, "Victims and Zionism," in Dan Miron, Hannan Hever, and Michael Gluzman, *In the City of Slaughter—A Later Visit: 100 Years since Bialik's Poem* (Tel Aviv: Resling, 2005) [Hebrew], 62–66. For the turn from the ethos of sanctifying God's name to a rhetoric of self-defense, see Ehud Luz, *Wrestling at Jabbok River: Power, Morality, Jewish Identity* (Jerusalem: Magnes, 1998) [Hebrew], 50–60; Alan Mintz, "The Russian Pogroms in Hebrew Literature and the Subversion of the Martyrological Ideal," *AJS Review* 7/8 (1982–1983): 263–300.

    Before leaving for Kishinev, Bialik wrote another poem that became famous, "On the Slaughter" (1903), in which he pointed an accusatory finger at the heavens. The fact that the literary, interpretative, and critical debate about this poem continues to create a lively intellectual discourse attests to its power and signal importance in the Zionist ethos. See for example Miron, Hever, and Gluzman, *In the City of Slaughter—A Later Visit*. See also Uzi Shavit and Ziva Shamir, eds., *At the Gates of the City of Slaughter: A Selection of Essays on Bialik's Poem* (Tel Aviv: HaKibbutz HaMeuchad, 1994) [Hebrew].

16. In one of the classics of Zionist literature, *The Sermon*, the novelist Haim Hazaz writes about a native Israeli man called Yudka who mounts an eloquent attack on the passivity of Diaspora Jews. "We never made our own history," he says; "the Gentiles always made it for us." Haim Hazaz, *The Sermon and Other Stories* (New Milford, Conn.: Toby Press, 2005), 236.

17. See. e.g., Zeira, *Torn Apart We Are*, 35-36 [Hebrew].

18. The Zionist essayist and activist Zalman Epstein expressed this view in his lament that the Jews cared only for "old, ancient, and obsolete books." Zalman Epstein, "Literature and Life," cited by M. J. Berdyczewski, "To Be or Not to Be," in Berdyczewski, *Collected Works*, 3:138 [Hebrew].

19. Berdyczewski wrote to the Hebrew author Mordecai Ehrenpreis that the Jews were "rotting" under the weight of their "cursed inheritance." Quoted in Avner Holtzman, *Toward the Tear in the Heart: M. J. Berdyczewski—The Formative Years (1887-1902)* (Jerusalem: Bialik Institute, 1995), 268-269 [Hebrew]. The combination of the Jews' outward oppression by the gentiles and internal oppression by the Bible is a running theme in Berdyczewski's works. He wrote that the Jews' transformation into Hebrews would release them from the slavery of their "abstract world" and into "human and national liberty." Berdyczewski, "Old Age and Youth," 195 [Hebrew]. In his comprehensive sociological study *The Sabra*, the sociologist Oz Almog outlines the profile of native Israelis ("Sabras") as reflected in Israeli literature and culture. See also "A Generation in Israel" and "The Myth of the New Jew," in *New Jews, Old Jews*, 122-174 [Hebrew]. Rachel Elboim-Dror presents a more comprehensive and complicated picture in "He Comes and Goes" [Hebrew].

2 THE NEW ORTHODOXY

1. Jerusalem Talmud, Sanhedrin, Chapter 4, Law 2. Translation adapted from David Golinkin, "Is Judaism Really in Favor of Pluralism and Tol-

erance?" *Responsa in a Moment* 9, no. 6 (2015), available online at https://
schechter.edu/is-judaism-really-in-favor-of-pluralism-and-tolerance/.

2. The German Jewish rabbi David Frankel explained the Talmudic sen-
    tence "there would be no room for the leg to stand" in his commentary
    on the Jerusalem Talmud, *Korban HaEdah* ("The Communal Sacrifice").
    He argues that halakha would not have been able to exist without
    changing views of it because at any point in time, historic conditions
    are mostly not like those in the Torah. Frankel's unequivocal remarks
    might seem surprising: reality is changeable, so halakha could not have
    survived if it were too "clear-cut."

    In his commentary on this Talmudic maxim, Rabbi Chaim
    Hirschensohn wrote that if the Torah were "clear-cut," there would
    not have been disagreements, and without disagreements, there would
    not have been the flexibility to adapt the Torah to a changing reality.
    See the introduction in Rabbi Chaim Hirschensohn, *The Institutions of
    the Oral Law* (Jerusalem: Hamechaber, 1889) [Hebrew]. Rabbi Nathan
    ben Jehiel of Rome explained the term "halakha" thus in his twelfth-
    century commentary, *HeArukh:* the word, which uses the Hebrew root
    for "to go," literally means something that is in constant movement, or
    within which the Jewish people move.

3. See Jacob Katz, *A House Divided: Orthodoxy and Schism in Nineteenth-
    Century Central European Jewry,* trans. Ziporah Brody (Hanover, N.H.:
    Brandeis University Press, 1998). See also Jacob Katz, *Out of the Ghetto:
    The Social Background of Jewish Emancipation, 1770–1870* (Syracuse, N.Y.:
    Syracuse University Press, 1998). For more on Orthodox Judaism and
    the figure of the Chatam Sofer, see Moshe Samet, *Anything New Is For-
    bidden on the Authority of the Torah* (Jerusalem: Dinur Center for Re-
    search in Jewish History, 2005) [Hebrew].

4. According to Jacob Katz, the claim by Orthodox Jews to be the de-
    fenders of the true, ancient Judaism is a fiction. Jacob Katz, "Orthodoxy
    in Historical Perspective," in Peter Medding, ed., *Studies in Contemporary
    Jewry II* (Bloomington: Indiana University Press, 1986).

5. My narrative is based on the commonly accepted history of how the
    status quo agreement emerged, but there are those who dispute it. For
    criticism of this narrative, see Menachem Friedman, "The Chronicle of

the Status-Quo: Religion and State in Israel," in V. Pilowsky, ed., *Transition from "Yishuv" to State, 1947–1949: Continuity and Change* (Haifa: University of Haifa, Herzl Institute for Research in Zionism, 1990), 47–80 [Hebrew]. See also Eliezer Don Yehiyeh, *The Politics of Accommodation: The Resolution of Religious Conflicts in Israel* (Jerusalem: Floersheimer Institute, 1997), esp. 28–32 [Hebrew]. Note further that Ben-Gurion inherited the rabbinate monopoly over Jewish religious affairs from the legal situation that existed prior to Israel's establishment. It was a continuation of sorts of Ottoman and Mandatory legislation, which treated the Jews as a religious group with autonomy over personal-status matters. See for example Friedman, "The Chronicle of the Status-Quo," 64 [Hebrew].

6. Alexis de Tocqueville, *Democracy in America*, trans. Henry Reeve (New York: Edward Walker, 1847).

7. Ibid., 337. See also Ofir Inbari's introduction to a Hebrew edition: Alexis de Tocqueville, *Democracy in America* (Jerusalem: Shalem Press, 2008).

8. According to the Israel Democracy Institute's 2014 Democracy Index, only 9.4 percent of secular Jewish Israelis have "very much" or "quite a lot" of trust in the Chief Rabbinate. See Tamar Hermann et al., *The Israeli Democracy Index 2014* (Jerusalem: Israel Democracy Institute, 2014), 117–124 [Hebrew]. An English translation is available at: https://en.idi.org .il/media/3666/democracy_index_2014_eng.pdf. See also Talia Sagiv and Edna Lomsky-Feder, "An Actualization of a Symbolic Conflict: The Arena of Secular 'Batei Midrash,'" *Israeli Sociology* 8, no. 2 (2006–2007): 269–299 [Hebrew]; Amos Oz and Fania Oz-Salzberger, *Jews and Words* (New Haven: Yale University Press, 2014), 3; Amos Oz, "Between Zionism and Hellenism: Amos Oz on the Meaning of Secular Judaism," *Haaretz*, 28 January 2019, available at https://www.haaretz.com/israel-news /culture/.premium.MAGAZINE-amos-oz-there-is-no-judaism-without -debate-over-the-meaning-of-judasim-1.6875342; Rabbi David Stav's remarks cited in Tomer Persico, "Degenerate Coercion: Give Us a Great Torah," *Makor Rishon*, 13 January 2012 [Hebrew]; Kobi Nachshoni, "Rabbi Bakshi-Doron: The Marriage Law Antagonizes Religion," *Ynet*, 14 June 2007 [Hebrew], available at https://www.ynet.co.il/articles /0,7340,L-3412925,00.html.

9. Empirical studies from Europe and the United States in recent decades point to a negative correlation between the establishment of official religions and citizens' participation in religious activities. See Laurence R. Iannaccone, "The Consequences of Religious Market Structure: Adam Smith and the Economics of Religion," *Rationality and Society* 3, no. 2 (1991): 156–177; Laurence R. Iannaccone, Roger Finke, and Rodney Starke, "Deregulating Religion: The Economics of Church and State," *Economic Inquiry* 35 (1997): 350–364. For the type of secularism that became more of a protest than a position or way of life, see Yaacov Yadgar, *Beyond Secularism: Traditionism and the Critique of Israeli Secularism* (Jerusalem: Van Leer Institute, HaKibbutz HaMeuchad, 2012) [Hebrew]. Yadgar focuses the discussion in the third chapter on the nature of secularism in Israel. He draws a distinction between a small group of ideological secularists and a large group he terms "secular by default." This latter group, he argues, contains many Israelis who call themselves secular in an institutional sense, as a symbolic social statement against the rabbinic and religious establishment (66–67). Yadgar shows that many of the Israelis who define themselves as secular report that they observe quite a few Jewish commandments, rituals, and customs (74–78). That is, Israel contains an enormous camp of "traditional" Jews who label themselves secular for political reasons, namely, their opposition to institutionalized religion. As for the "ideological secularists," Yadgar presents what he sees as "the authoritative formulation of positive secularism" (63). See also Asher Arian and Ayala Keissar-Sugarmen, *A Portrait of Israeli Jews: Beliefs, Observance, and Values of Israeli Jews, 2009* (Jerusalem: Israel Democracy Institute, 2012), available at: https://en.idi.org.il/media/5439/guttmanavichaireport2012_engfinal.pdf. See also Asher Cohen and Baruch Zisser, *From Accommodation to Escalation* (Tel Aviv: Schocken, 2003) [Hebrew].

10. Micha Josef Berdyczewski, "On the Question of the Past," in *The Writings of Micha Josef Ben-Gorion (Berdyczewski)* (Tel Aviv: Dvir, 1964), 2:42 [Hebrew].

11. Yaacov Yadgar surmises that the relationship between the authoritarian religiosity and secular rebellion is perhaps to some extent intentional. See *Beyond Secularism*, 10–11, 68–69, 78–82 [Hebrew].

12. For the critique of religion as a threat to democracy, as put forth by Israeli intellectuals, see Gideon Katz, "The Culture War in Israel," in Avriel Bar-Levav, Ran Margolin, and Shmuel Feiner, eds., *Secularization in Jewish Culture* (Raanana: Open University of Israel Press, 2012), esp. 2:903-908 [Hebrew].

13. Betty Mahmoody, *Not Without My Daughter* (New York: St. Martin's, 1987).

PART II INTRODUCTION

1. The historian David Biale, who has researched the traditionalist leanings of secular thinkers, argues that this type of secularism is not "alternative" at all, and he would no doubt disagree with my characterization of it. He argues that Yosef Haim Brenner's school of rebellious secularism, which seeks to cut itself off from the past, is the exception to other kinds of Jewish secularism. See David Biale, *Not in the Heavens: The Tradition of Jewish Secular Thought* (Princeton: Princeton University Press, 2010).

2. Gershom Scholem, "Zionism—Dialectic of Continuity and Rebellion" (1970), in Ehud Ben-Ezer, ed., *Unease in Zion* (New York: Quadrangle, 1974). See also Assaf Inbari, "The End of the Secular Majority," *Haaretz*, 3 February 2012, available at: https://www.haaretz.com/1.5181093.

3. Samuel Hugo Bergmann, "Dean's Speech at the Commencement of Academic Year 1935," in his *On the Trail* (Tel Aviv: Am Oved, 1976), 93 [Hebrew]. See also Tzvi Tzameret, "To Rebel and Continue: The Shaping of Shabbat According to Yosef Haim Brenner, Aharon David Gordon, Hugo Bergmann, Eli Schweid, and Meir Eyali," in Yehuda Friedlander, Uzi Shavit, and Uri Sagi, eds., *The Old Shall Be Renewed and the New Sanctified: Essays on Judaism, Identity, and Culture in Memory of Meir Eyali* (Tel Aviv: HaKibbutz HaMeuchad, 2005), 358-361 [Hebrew].

4. Martin Buber, "The Holy Way: A Word to the Jews and to the Nations," in Martin Buber, *On Judaism*, ed. Nahum N. Glatzer (New York: Schocken, 1972), 140-141.

5. See for example A. D. Gordon, "Nation-Building," in *The Works of A. D. Gordon*, 3 vols., ed. Samuel Hugo Bergmann and Eliezer Shochet (Jerusalem: Zionist Library, 1951-54), 1:251-257 [Hebrew]. Gordon calls on

Jews "to care for our people, who are not a living people, who have no ground beneath their feet, and do not sprout, from their natural soil," and protests the "borrowed perspectives" with which Jewish authors looked at their own people (252-253).

One of Katznelson's most celebrated essays is "Destruction and Uprooting," which he wrote in protest at plans by youth leaders to run activities on the eve of Tisha B'Av. See Berl Katznelson, *Writings of Berl Katznelson* (Tel Aviv: Workers' Party of the Land of Israel, 1945-1950), 6:365-367 [Hebrew]. For many further examples of Katznelson's approach see Berl Katznelson, *Revolution and Roots: Selected Works*, comp. and ed. Avinoam Barshai (Tel Aviv: Y. Golan, 1996) [Hebrew]; Avraham Tzivion, *The Jewish Portrait of Berl Katznelson* (Tel Aviv: Sifriat HaPoalim, 1984) [Hebrew].

In a letter to the members of Kibbutz Geva, Bialik protested the desecration of Shabbat by workers from the community: "The Land of Israel shall not be built without Shabbat. It will be destroyed, and all your work will be for naught. The Jewish people will never give up Shabbat, which is not only the keystone of Israel's existence but of human existence. Without Shabbat, there would be no image of God or semblance of humanity in the world.... I believe Shabbat is not just about keeping the 613 commandments of the Bible, as the Sages wrote, but keeping the Torah of all of humanity.... Without Shabbat there would be no Israel—no Land of Israel, and no Israeli culture. Shabbat *is* Israel's culture." Hayim Nachman Bialik, *Letters of Hayim Nahman Bialik*, ed. Fischel Lachower (Tel Aviv: Dvir, 1937-1939), 5:248-249 [Hebrew].

3 CULTURAL SECULARISM

1. For an understanding of Ahad Ha'am, his life, his political path, and his ideas, I recommend two biographies: Joseph Goldstein, *Ahad Ha'am: The Prophet of Zionism* (Brighton: Sussex Academic Press, 2001), and Steven Zipperstein, *Elusive Prophet: Ahad Ha'am and the Origins of Zionism* (London: Halban, 1993). Ahad Ha'am did not use the term "secular." In fact, secular Jews of the early twentieth century did not know that they were secular because the term was not used at the time. They called

themselves *hofshi*, "free," a term that aptly expressed their sense that they were free of the past and the religious authorities who had always governed them. For a discussion of the origins of the term "secular," see David Biale, *Not in the Heavens: The Tradition of Jewish Secular Thought* (Princeton: Princeton University Press, 2010).

2. See Yehiel Alfred Gottschalk, *Ahad Ha'am and the Jewish National Spirit* (Jerusalem: HaSifria HaZionit, 1992) [Hebrew]; Rina Hevlin, *Double Commitment: Jewish Identity Between Tradition and Secularization in the Thought of Ahad Ha'am* (Tel Aviv: HaKibbutz HaMeuchad, 2001) [Hebrew]; Eliezer Schweid, "The Sources of the Obligation to Tradition According to Ahad Ha'am," *Tura* 4 (1996): 18-31 [Hebrew]; Gideon Katz, "Ahad Ha'Am and the Concept of National Spirit," *Da'at* 54 (2004): 47-69 [Hebrew]; Laurence J. Silberstein, "Judaism as a Secular System of Meaning: The Writings of Ahad Ha'am," *Journal of the American Academy of Religion* 52 (1984): 3547-3568.

    This idea recurs in almost all of Ahad Ha'am's essays, even if it is not stated explicitly or directly. It comes up in the following essays in particular, all in Ahad Ha'am, *Complete Works* (Tel Aviv: Dvir, 1974) [Hebrew]: "Revival and Creation," 291-293; "On the Jewish Treasure in the Hebrew Language," 104-114; "National Morality," 159-164; "Resurrection of the Spirit," 173-186; "Torah from Zion," 401-409.

    In "Revival and Creation," for example, he writes: "The Jew who is free in his opinions, but who loves his nation and its literature and all its intellectual property," 292 [Hebrew]. And in "On the Jewish Treasure": "If our forefathers said, 'Study is greater as it leads to action,' here we are compelled to say, 'Study is great as it leads to love,'" 105. Ahad Ha'am was determined to increase Jews' understanding of the Torah, but not out of obedience.

3. In his essay "Torah from Zion," criticizing the approach of Yosef Haim Brenner and other radical secularists toward the Jewish tradition and holy texts, Ahad Ha'am writes: "The believer sees a 'Book of Books,' a divine revelation, which cannot be judged by the standards of literary criticism.... But even a nonbeliever, if he is a nationalist Jew, does not have an exclusively literary approach to the holy scriptures, but a literary and national approach rolled into one.... On the national side, this

[literary criticism] will not change one iota the internal feeling connecting him to the Hebrew Bible, a feeling of special closeness perme-
ated with national holiness, a feeling that a thousand narrow capillaries
leave his body and course through era and era to the depths of the distant past.... And there is no difference between him and the religious
Jew, except that one says 'I believe' and the other 'I feel'" (108 [He-
brew]). Ahad Ha'am even argued that secular, nationalist Jews are more
connected and loyal to their nation's cultural assets. See Ahad Ha'am,
"Revival and Creation," 292 [Hebrew].

4. Ahad Ha'am, "Torah from Zion," 407 [Hebrew].

5. Micha Josef Berdyczewski, "Feelings of the Heart," in *The Writings
   of Micha Josef Ben-Gorion (Berdyczewski)* (Tel Aviv: Dvir, 1964), 2:22
   [Hebrew].

6. I have slightly changed and reconfigured Oz's metaphor. The original
   metaphor appears in Amos Oz and Fania Oz-Salzberger, *Jews and Words*
   (New Haven: Yale University Press, 2012), 200. Oz brings it up in the
   context of a conversation he had with settlers from Ofra in 1982, recounted in full in his *In the Land of Israel* (New York: Mariner, 1993).
   Berdyczewski explicitly addressed the inheritance metaphor: "The
   wealth we have only saved since yesterday means poverty today and
   the impossibility of enriching ourselves tomorrow.... Let me hope that
   I may generate wealth myself, and do not make me a mere watchman
   of my ancestral estate." See "Feelings of the Heart," 91 [Hebrew]. Else-
   where, he wrote that instead of performing their national duties, the
   Jews were constantly held back by the burden of their inheritance. See
   "Old Age and Youth," 33 [Hebrew]).

7. I shall discuss this further in Part IV.

8. For the roots of this debate and its issues, see Asher Rivlin, *Ahad Ha'am
   and His Opponents and Their Views on the Hebrew Literature of Their Generation* (Tel Aviv: Dvir, 1956) [Hebrew]; Eliezer Schweid, "The Argument Between Ahad Ha'am and Micha Josef Ben-Gorion—Polemic or
   Dialogue? The First Debate Between Monism and Pluralism in Modern Jewish Culture," in Nahem Ilan, ed., *A Good Eye: Dialogue and
   Polemic in Jewish Culture—A Jubilee Book in Honor of Tova Ilan* (Tel Aviv:
   HaKibbutz HaMeuchad, 1999), 517-529 [Hebrew]; Yosef Oren, *Ahad*

Ha'am, Berdyczewski, and the Group of "Youth" (Rishon Lezion: Yachad, 1985) [Hebrew]; Ehud Luz, *Parallels Meet: Religion and Nationalism in the Early Zionist Movement (1882–1904)*, trans. Lenn Schrem (Jerusalem: Sefrit-Aliya, 1991); Arnold Band, "The Ahad Ha'am and Berdyczewski Polarity," in Jacques Kornberg, ed., *At the Crossroads: Essays on Ahad Ha'am* (Albany: State University of New York Press, 1983); Jacob Golomb, "On a 'Nietzschean' Dispute Between Ahad Ha'am and Berdichevski," in Simone Gigliotti, Jacob Golomb, and Caroline Sternberg Gould, eds., *Ethics, Art, and Representations of the Holocaust* (Lanham, Md.: Lexington Books, 2014). I do not know whether this debate shaped secular society in Israel. The Israeli secular character was undoubtedly shaped by many ideas and thinkers who remain unaddressed in this short book. Nevertheless, this debate helps us sketch out two basic models for secularism, which represent the different faces of Israeli secularism today quite well.

9. S. Yizhar, "One Decade of Statehood and Hebrew Literature: Remarks at the Eighteenth Writers' Convention," in Ornah Golan, ed., *Between Discussion and Reality: Tropes in Israeli Stories* (Tel Aviv: Open University of Israel Press, 1983–1985), 8:170 [Hebrew]. Originally published in the literature supplement of the Israeli Labor Party's newspaper *LaMerhav*, 10 April 1958, 1–2 [Hebrew].

10. Interview with Ari Shavit, "A Jewish Soul," *Haaretz*, 11 February 2004, available at https://www.haaretz.com/1.4714221.

11. Some writers have noted the paradox that this victory happened in the early days of Zionism. Ironically, it was the individualistic Berdyczewski—who lived in the Diaspora and was distant from the Zionist movement—who influenced the collectivist, belief-driven Jews of action who comprised the First, Second, and Third Aliyot. It was his belief that they needed to start anew, cut themselves off, and isolate themselves to create together. It was their despair, their sense of rift and rootlessness, that they sought to soften with their act of self-actualization. In this sense, Ahad Ha'am's harmonic Judaism was alien to them and reminiscent of the Diaspora, despite its Zionist nature. See Avner Holtzman, "M. J. Berdyczewski, Y. H. Brenner, and Eretz Yisrael of the Second Aliyah," in *The Land of Israel in Twentieth-Century Jewish Thought*, ed. Aviezer Ravitzky

(Jerusalem: Yad Ben-Zvi, 2004), 359–375 [Hebrew]; Avner Holtzman, "Between Micha Joseph Berdichevsky and David Ben-Gurion," *Iyunim Bitkumat Israel (Studies in Zionism, the Yishuv, and the State of Israel)* 3 (1993): 191–204; Arnold Band, "Micah Josef Ben-Gorion (Berdyczewski): The Rebellion and the Price," in Pinhas Ginossar, ed., *Hebrew Literature and the Labor Movement* (Beersheba: University of Ben-Gurion Press, 1989), 17–25 [Hebrew]; Nurit Govrin, *Alienation and Regeneration: Hebrew Fiction in the Diaspora and Eretz-Israel in the Early Twentieth Century* (Tel Aviv: Ministry of Defense Books, 1997).

12. Berdyczewski, "On the Question of the Past," in *Collected Works*, 13 vols., ed. Avner Holtzman and Yitzhak Kafkafi (Tel Aviv: HaKibbutz HaMeuchad, 1996–2015), 6:264 [Hebrew]. In a different place he writes that he cannot destroy what he wishes to destroy: "With my hands I destroy, and I take my shoes off my feet lest I touch our holy ground." Berdyczewski, "Gloom," in *Collected Works*, 5:183 [Hebrew].

Although he often expressed himself as a rebel against the past and Jewish tradition who only wanted upheaval, change, and renewal, Berdyczewski made a great intellectual effort to find heroes and inspiration in the Jewish tradition itself. His heroes were the rebels who refused to accept the crippling authority of the prophets or rabbis, and he drew inspiration from them for his own rebellion. Berdyczewski searched the Jewish tradition for agents of spontaneity and might, vitality and natural health, of the culture of the "sword" as he put it; leaders who characterized the Jewish people in earlier eras, and he compared them to the atrophy and excessive spirituality that had afflicted the Jews since the prophets and the culture of the "Book" took over. Berdyczewski thus rests on historical foundations when he rebels against history. He prefers the fanatics of Jerusalem to the leader from Yavne who escaped in a coffin, and prefers Shammai to Hillel. See, e.g., Berdyczewski, "Steps," in *The Writings of Micha Josef Ben-Gorion (Berdyczewski)*, 2:46 [Hebrew]. He draws an equivalence between the prophets of Baal and Elijah ("Questions and Observations," in *The Writings of Micha Josef Ben-Gorion (Berdyczewski)*, 2:54 [Hebrew]), takes the side of the Israelite mutineers against Moses, and praises such figures as the Edomite king Herod the Great, the heretical rabbi Elisheva Ben Abuya, and even the pagan gods

("On the Book," in *The Writings of Micha Josef Ben-Gorion [Berdyczew-ski]*, 2:19). In one characteristic passage, Berdyczewski calls the genera-tion of the prophets Ezra and Nehemiah, who returned to Judah from Babylon, "giants"—and the defeated rebels who fell on their swords at Masada "dwarfs." He praises Samson for bringing the Temple of Dagon down on the Philistines rather than "running away blind." Berdyczew-ski, "Crumbs," in *Collected Works*, 6:102-103 [Hebrew].

See also Golomb, "On a 'Nietzschean' Dispute Between Ahad Ha'am and Berdichevski"; Zafrira Dean, "Historical Consciousness in the Thought of Micha Josef Berdyczewski," in Avner Holtzman, ed., *Micha Josef Berdyczewski: Studies and Certificates* (Jerusalem: Bialik Insti-tute, 2002), 259-298 [Hebrew]; Boaz Arpali, "The Jewish Revolution and the Old Testament: Berdichevsky's and Tchernichovsky's Read-ing of the Bible," in Avner Holtzman, Gideon Gatz, and Shalom Rat-zabi, eds., *Around the Dot: Studies on M. Y. Berdichevsky, Y. H. Brenner and A. D. Gordon* (Beersheba: Ben-Gurion University Press, 2008), 31-67 [Hebrew].

13. Berdyczewski, "Feelings of the Heart," 22. See more on this in Nicham Ross, "The Religious Assault Against Neo-Hasidic Trends in Zionist Yeshiva," in Yaacov Yadgar, Gideon Katz, and Shalom Ratzabi, eds., *Beyond Halacha: Remapping Tradition, Secularity, and New-Age Culture in Israel* (Beersheba: Ben-Gurion University Press, 2014), 98 [Hebrew]. See the references to further literature in note 90 there.

For the more faith-related aspects of Berdyczewski's writings, see "'My Soul Thirsts for God: On the Place of the Book 'Horev' in M. J. Berdyczewski's Works," in Holtzman, *Berdyczewski: Studies and Certifi-cates*, 349-371 [Hebrew].

Berdyczewski described the hero of his story "Machanayim" thus: "His mind was emptied of his ancestral inheritance, and his heart still lay in the grave of his ancestors" ("Machanayim," in *Collected Works*, 7:59 [Hebrew]).

According to Avner Holtzman, Berdyczewski was torn between two competing impulses: a drive to replace the rabbinic, ancestral Jew-ish tradition with something of equal value from European culture, and no less powerful a drive to preserve, eternalize, and document that tradition. "The history of Berdyczewski's work is the history of the tear in his heart." See Avner Holtzman, *Toward the Tear in the Heart: M. J. Berdyczewski—The Formative Years (1887–1902)* (Jerusalem: Bialik Institute, 1995), 12 [Hebrew]; Michal Barbell, "Writing Secularism: The Renewed Hebrew Literature and Secularization," in Avriel Bar-Levav, Ran Margolin, and Shmuel Feiner, eds., *Secularization in Jewish Culture* (Raanana: Open University of Israel Press, 2012), 1:216–217, 408–414 especially [Hebrew].

14. Y. H. Brenner, "In Journalism and Literature (On a Vision of Destruction)," in *Writings* (Tel Aviv: HaKibbutz HaMeuchad, 1977-1984), 3:487 [Hebrew]. This essay provoked an angry reaction from Ahad Ha'am, prompting him to write a mighty polemic that led to what was known as "The Brenner Affair," in which almost every writer in Hebrew literature and the Zionist movement expressed an opinion. For a comprehensive analysis of this affair, see Nurith Govrin, *The Brenner Affair: The Fight for Free Speech* (Jerusalem: Yad Yitzhak Ben-Zvi, 1985) [Hebrew].

Brenner and Berdyczewski had a complicated, dialectical relationship, which was the subject of an illuminating analysis by Menachem Brinker. See Menachem Brinker, "Brenner's Judaism," *Proceedings of the Israel Academy of Sciences and Humanities* 7, no. 7 (1986): 211–228 [Hebrew]; Eliezer Schweid, *Toward a Modern Jewish Culture* (Tel Aviv: Am Oved, 1986), 157-181 [Hebrew].

According to Yehezkel Kaufmann, Brenner went much farther in dismissing the Jewish people's Diaspora past than did Berdyczewski. Brenner saw only gloom. He blamed the Jews of the Diaspora for allegedly clinging to the ghettos and their miserable, dependent lives. In a litany of aspersions against Diaspora Jewry, Brenner justified the negative judgments against Jews by anti-Semites. Brenner's criticism was apparently based on a desire to arouse the Jews to fix their situation, but it contains deep tones of self-directed anti-Semitism. See Yehezkel Kaufmann, *Exile and Estrangement: A Socio-Historical Study on the Issue of the Fate of the Nation of Israel from Ancient Times to the Present*, vol. 2, book 2 (Tel Aviv: Dvir, 1930), 405-417 [Hebrew].

In another study, Kaufmann sees Brenner as "the beginning of Zionist anti-Semitism," a notion that in his opinion constituted a surprising development of Theodor Herzl's own ideas. See Yehezkel Kaufmann, *Between Paths: Chapters in the Study of National Thought* (Haifa: Hebrew Reali School, 1952), 153–155 [Hebrew].

15. Y. H. Brenner, "Feelings and Reflections (On the God-Seekers)," in *Writings*, 3:371 [Hebrew]. I learned from a conversation with my friend Assaf Inbari that hidden in Brenner is a profound religiosity, as is evident in his great works *Breakdown and Bereavement* and *From Here and There*. Inbari argues that like Berdyczewski's, Brenner's soul was torn between his aversion to the Jewish tradition within which he was raised and the religious longings that filled him.

16. Y. H. Brenner, "Our Self-Evaluation in Three Volumes," in *Writings*, 4:1225 [Hebrew]. That said, I must add the reservation that Brenner is included in the corpus of Zionist thought because he did not give up on the two "traditional" anchors referred to above: he fought fiercely for the principles of the Land of Israel and the Hebrew language (and his language was steeped in terms he had absorbed in his traditional education); and he was profoundly troubled by the plight of the Jewish people, not as an abstract cultural entity or a historical idea, but as a concrete social group that was seeking an existential solution for its tragic predicament. This latter characteristic is emphasized in particular by Avi Sagi, who analyzes Brenner's Judaism as an existentialist outlook centered on a sense of identification and solidarity with the Jewish collective, a sense of a shared fate with Jewish suffering and sorrow. Avi Sagi, *To Be a Jew: Joseph Chayim Brenner as Jewish Existentialist* (London: Continuum, 2011).

17. Moti Zeira describes the radical secular mindset thus: "Even the revolutionaries, who wanted to reinvent everything, brought their homes and biographies with them. Most of these pioneers came from homes in which Jewish culture was a significant part of their spiritual world. They brought, against their will, almost all their memories and melodies." Zeira, *Torn Apart We Are: The Affinity of the Labor Settlement in the 1920s to Jewish Culture* (Jerusalem: Yad Yitzhak Ben-Zvi, 2002), 346 [Hebrew]. See also David Canaani, *The Second Aliyah and Its Attitude to Religion and Tradition* (Tel Aviv: Sifriat Poalim, 1976) [Hebrew]; Muki Tzur, *Doing It the Hard Way [Le-lo Kutonet Passim]* (Tel Aviv: Am Oved, 1976),

95–122 [Hebrew]; Shmuel Almog, "Religious Values in the Second Aliya," in Anita Shapira, Shmuel Almog, and Jehuda Reinharz, eds., *Zionism and Religion* (Jerusalem: Zalman Center, 1994) [Hebrew].

18. The poet and art critic Shva Salhoov penned a clear expression of her pain at the lack of pain expressed by the new secularists: "This great drama, the emptying of faith from the world, is no longer the context that defines the life of the new secular Jew. It is the obvious state of being, given that its dynamic functioning as the generator of a new phenomenon has ebbed and faded.... This process, the smashing of the tablets, must not be wiped from our cultural consciousness." Shva Salhoov, "Strangers and at Home," in Dedi Zucker, ed., *We the Secular Jews: What Is Secular Jewish Identity?* (Tel Aviv: Yediot Books, 1999), 149 [Hebrew].

19. Ahad Ha'am, "Torah from Zion," in Ahad Ha'am, *At the Crossroads,* part 4, 127 (Dvir: Tel Aviv) [Hebrew].

20. See Plato's discussions on the place and role of music in society in *The Republic,* book 3.

21. Yair Sheleg, "The Jewish Bookcase—Jewish Studies Are Back in Fashion," *The New Religious Jews: A Contemporary Look at Religious Society in Israel* (Jerusalem: Keter, 2000), 300–309 [Hebrew]; Rachel Werczberger and Naama Azulay, "The Jewish Renewal Movement in Israeli Secular Society," *Contemporary Jewry* 31, no. 2 (2011): 107–128; Naama Azulay and Ephraim Tabory, "From Houses of Study to Houses of Prayer: Cultural-Religious Developments in Secular Society in Israel," *Issues in Israeli Society* 6 (2008): 121–156 [Hebrew]; Naama Azulay, "'We Are Hebrews and We Will Serve Our Own Hearts': The Jewish Renewal Movement in Israeli Secular Society" (Ph.D. diss., University of Bar Ilan, 2010) [Hebrew]; Talia Sagiv and Edna Lomsky-Feder, "An Actualization of a Symbolic Conflict: The Arena of Secular 'Batei Midrash,'" *Israeli Sociology* 8, no. 2 (2007): 269–299 [Hebrew]; Yair Sheleg, *The Jewish Renaissance in Israeli Society: The Emergence of the New Jew* (Jerusalem: Israel Democracy Institute, 2010), 27–105 [Hebrew]; Guy Ravid and Moran Barman, *Analysis of the Field of Jewish Renewal in Israel* (Tel Aviv: Midot, 2013 [Hebrew], available at: http://www.midot.org.il/Sites/midot/content/File/hithadshut_yehudit/hithadshut_file_03.pdf. In "An Actu-

alization of a Symbolic Conflict," Sagiv and Lomsky-Feder speak of "learning secularists." Donniel Hartman draws a distinction between "secular Jews" and "secular Israelis" in "The Six Tribes of Israel," *Darsheni* 2 (2010): 2-9 [Hebrew]; Gideon Katz and Nir Keidar distinguish between the approach of "Judaism as culture" and that of "secularism as Jewish alienation," in Katz and Keidar, "Judaism from the Perspective of Secular Israeli Intellectuals," *Democratic Culture* 14 (2013): 93-152.

22. Berl Katznelson, "Revolution and Tradition," in Arthur Hertzberg, ed., *The Zionist Idea: A Historical Analysis and Reader* (Philadelphia: The Jewish Publication Society, 1997), 392.

4 MYSTICAL SECULARISM

1. Yitzhak Elazari-Volcani, "The National Theology," *Revivim* 3-4 (1912): 100 [Hebrew].

2. Gershom Scholem, "Declaration of Loyalty to Our Language: Gershom Scholem's Letter to Franz Rosenzweig on 26 December 1926," in *Another Thing: Chapters on Heritage and Revival (B)*, ed. Avraham Shapira (Tel Aviv: Am Oved, 1989), 59-60 [Hebrew]. The poet Yehuda Amichai similarly feared that the return to the Land of Israel might be dangerous to secularism, for it might revive the religious and messianic senses in the settlers' subconscious. "This is a country whose dead are in the earth / In place of coal and gold and iron / They are the fuel for the coming of messiahs." Quoted in Glenda Abramson, *The Writing of Yehuda Amichai: A Thematic Approach* (Albany: State University of New York Press, 1989), 137. David Biale links the "void" Scholem finds in the Hebrew language to the one Bialik identifies in his essay "Revealment and Concealment in Language," and argues that both authors borrowed this term from the Kabbalistic tradition, giving it a secular dimension. Biale, *Not in the Heavens: The Tradition of Jewish Secular Thought* (Princeton: Princeton University Press, 2010); see Hayim Nahman Bialik, "Revealment and Concealment in Language," in *Complete Works of Hayim Nahman Bialik* (Tel Aviv: Dvir, 1947), 202-204 [Hebrew].

3. Scholem, "Declaration of Loyalty to Our Language," 60 [Hebrew].

4. Ibid.

5. A. D. Gordon, "Man and Nature," in *Writings of A. D. Gordon*, 3 vols.

(Jerusalem: HaSifria HaZionit, 1951–1954), 2:128 [Hebrew] (hereafter "Man and Nature" [Hebrew]).

6. Gordon, *"Levirur ra'ayonenu misodo,"* in *Writings of A. D. Gordon*, vol. 2:195 [Hebrew].

7. Gordon, *"Levirur ra'ayonenu misodo,"* 2:180 [Hebrew]. For a broad and deep study of Gordon's important essay see Eliezer Schweid, *The Foundation and Sources of A. D. Gordon's Philosophy* (Jerusalem: Bialik Institute, 2014) [Hebrew].

8. For the association of nature with God, see Avraham Shapira, *The Kabbalistic and Hasidic Sources of A. D. Gordon's Thought* (Tel Aviv: Am Oved, 1996), 263–270 [Hebrew]. Nonetheless, we should not necessarily conclude that Gordon may be seen as a pantheist, and there are some who reject this view of his thought. See for example Einat Ramon, *A New Life: Religion, Motherhood, and Supreme Love in the Works of Aharon David Gordon* (Jerusalem: Carmel, 2007), 145 [Hebrew]. See also Eliezer Schweid, *The Individual: The World of A. D. Gordon* (Tel Aviv: Am Oved, 1970), 123 [Hebrew].

9. A. D. Gordon, "Man and Nature," in *A. D. Gordon: Selected Essays*, trans. Frances Burnce (New York: League for Labor Palestine, 1938), 251 (further references to "Man and Nature" are to this translation unless "[Hebrew]" is specified). See also Gideon Katz, "Irrationalism and National Revival in A. D. Gordon's Thought," in Avner Holtzman, Gideon Katz, and Shalom Ratzabi, eds., *Around the Dot: Studies on M. Y. Berdichevsky, Y. H. Brenner and A. D. Gordon* (Beersheba: Ben-Gurion University Press, 2008), 321–344 [Hebrew]. For the Hasidic and Kabbalistic roots of Gordon's thought, see in particular Shapira, *The Kabbalistic and Hasidic Sources of A. D. Gordon's Thought* [Hebrew].

10. In light of his profound spirituality, and the fact that he never completely disavowed religious observance, many question whether Gordon fully embraced secularism. According to Gideon Katz, Gordon did indeed meet the definition of "a secular Jew" because he resolutely rejected the supposition that the Jewish religion was given from the heavens, through divine revelation. Gordon rejected the thesis of the Torah's transcendental and supra-historical origins, arguing that

the religion was a matter of history and the work of human beings. Gideon Katz, "The Secular Basis in the Thought of A. D. Gordon," *Iyunim Bitkumat Israel (Studies in Zionism, the Yishuv, and the State of Israel)* 11 (2001): 465–485 [Hebrew]. However, a riposte to this argument might be found in Gordon's own remarks that religiosity does not require a god, citing the Buddhist religion as proof (Gordon, "Man and Nature"; see also "The Account We Must Settle with Ourselves," in *Writings of A. D. Gordon*, vol. 1).

The scholar Einat Ramon, in contrast, resolutely defines Gordon as a religious philosopher. Traditional scholarship about him, she argues, tended to ignore his religiosity because he wrote about it primarily in the context of secular-nationalist discourse, and in that context he was regarded as one of the intellectual shapers of socialist Zionism. Ramon, *A New Life*, 12 [Hebrew]. Ramon notes that this view is now changing, a turn that is first seen in Schweid, *The Individual* [Hebrew]. Schweid points to the fact that writers on Gordon tended to view him in comparison to nineteenth-century Western thought and therefore missed important elements in his teachings, which must be understood mainly in the context of the traditional Jewish sources from which they came (7–12). Two of Schweid's students have broadened and deepened this line of inquiry further: Shapira, in *The Kabbalistic and Hasidic Sources of A. D. Gordon's Thought* [Hebrew] and Sara Strassberg-Dayan in *Individual, Nation, Humanity: The Conception of Man in A. D. Gordon and Rabbi Kook* (Tel Aviv: HaKibbutz HaMeuchad, 1995) [Hebrew]. Ramon distinguishes in Gordon's thought between religious sentiment, which he saw as the foundation of human authenticity, creativity, morality, and culture. and organized, formal religion, with its dogmas, rituals, and laws, which he considered stifling idolatry. Einat Ramon, "Religion and Life: The Renewal of Halakhah and the Jewish Religion in the Works of Aharon David Gordon," *Zmanim* 72 (2000): 76–88 [Hebrew]. (See a similar distinction in Strassberg-Dayan, *Individual, Nation, Humanity*, 96 [Hebrew].)

Ron Margolin takes a similar position: like Ramon, he sees Gordon's thought as an opening to non-halakhic, innovative Jewish religiosity. Ron Margolin, "Yearning for the Spirit: Israeli Religiosity Without Halakhic Commitment," *Deot* 40 (2009): 8-11 [Hebrew].

Speaking of the relationship between religious sentiment and religion, Gordon says that every individual experience of the sublime could be transformed into static official dogma: "Religion took on a frozen form for eternity, a form that is the complete opposite of religion's original purpose." Gordon, "The Account We Must Settle with Ourselves," 352 [Hebrew].

11. Martin Buber, "Jewish Religiosity," in Martin Buber, *On Judaism*, ed. Nahum Glatzer (New York: Schocken, 1972), 80.

12. Ibid.

13. William James, *The Varieties of Religious Experience: A Study in Human Nature* (Oxford: Oxford University Press, 2012).

14. Note that Gordon himself rarely used the term "mystical" and perhaps even saw it as derogatory. See, for example, Gordon, "Man and Nature," 174; see also Gideon Katz, "Below the Threshold of Consciousness," in Holtzman, Katz, and Ratzabi, *Around the Dot*, 336 [Hebrew]; and Shapira, *A. D. Gordon's Thought* [Hebrew].

Gordon writes with a hint of confession and personal crisis: "Yet the religious form was made holy, and in the end, superseded content in value. Such a point did this reach that the earnest soul possessed of deep religious feeling and of profound thought was forced either to adjust itself by seeking a compromise with the old and petrified religious form, or to retire within itself.... It is little wonder that vital, searching thought, which scans and probes all things, left the fold. With it farther and farther away from religion in general went the living soul that strives for regeneration." "Man and Nature," 214. "It's common to think a national religion must be the product of divine revelation, which is static and frozen for all eternity." Gordon, "The Account We Must Settle with Ourselves," 350 [Hebrew].

15. Gordon, "The Account We Must Settle with Ourselves," 350 [Hebrew].

16. See Katz, "The Secular Basis in the Thought of A. D. Gordon," 468 [Hebrew].

17. Gordon, "Man and Nature," 187. For a broad discussion of Gordon's use of these terms, see Schweid, *The Individual*, 101-116 [Hebrew]; and Sha-

pira, *The Kabbalistic and Hasidic Sources of A. D. Gordon's Thought,* 93-108 [Hebrew].

18. Gordon, "Man and Nature," 174-175.

19. Gordon, *"Levirur ra'ayonenu misodo,"* 191 [Hebrew]. See also Gordon, "Man and Nature," 94-101 [Hebrew].

20. Gordon, *"Levirur ra'ayonenu misodo,"* 201 [Hebrew]. "Only when the first ray of light of human thought shone forth was the division made between the soul of man and the soul of universal creation." Gordon, "Man and Nature," 210. Gordon goes on to argue that awareness means first discerning that one is *separate* from the world.

21. Gordon, "Man and Nature," 148 [Hebrew].

22. Gordon, "Third Letter," in *Writings of A. D. Gordon,* 1:364 [Hebrew].

23. Schweid, *The Individual,* 7 [Hebrew], 90.

24. This approach finds expression particularly in Ahad Ha'am's essay "On the Jewish Treasure in the Hebrew Language," in which he stresses the importance of studying and understanding Judaism as the basis for its preservation, operating from the assumption that "study is great as it leads to love"—that is, an understanding of Judaism would produce and strengthen a feeling of nationhood. This sentiment had been preserved naturally in the past through the observance of the practical religious commandments, for which the study of Judaism was an enlightened, modern substitute. Ahad Ha'am, *Complete Works* (Dvir: Tel Aviv, 1974), 104-105 [Hebrew].

This idea recurs in several of Ahad Ha'am's letters, in which he emphasizes the advantages and superiority of the beit midrash over synagogues as a means of preserving the Jewish way of life, even during the Jewish Enlightenment, and he demonstrates a clear preference for study over prayer. See his letter to Dr. Judah Leon Magnes (18 September 1910) in Ahad Ha'am, *The Letters of Ahad Ha'am,* 6 vols. (Tel Aviv: Dvir, 1961), 6:43-44 [Hebrew]. On the other hand, note that Ahad Ha'am has not only an intellectual interest in scholarship but also an emotional connection to it. In "Torah from Zion," he describes his attitude toward the secular nationalists in almost mystical terms, in a manner that is closer to Gordon's way of expressing himself. See also the discussion in Rina Hevlin, *Double Commitment: Jewish Identity Be-*

tween Tradition and Secularization in the Thought of Ahad Ha'am (Tel Aviv: HaKibbutz HaMeuchad, 2001), 75-95 [Hebrew]. See also Gideon Katz's essay on Ahad Ha'am in Gideon Katz, *The Pale God: Israeli Secularism and Spinoza's Philosophy of Culture* (Boston: Academic Series Press, 2011).

5 HALAKHIC SECULARISM

1. David Biale cites Bialik, writing that Ahad Ha'am had such a profound influence over him that it was as if every word Ahad Ha'am wrote were addressed to him and his most hidden thoughts. David Biale, *Not in the Heavens: The Tradition of Jewish Secular Thought* (Princeton: Princeton University Press, 2010). See also Bialik, "On Ahad Ha'am," in *Spoken Words (Devarim Shebe'al-Peh)* (Tel Aviv: Dvir, 1935), 2:191-210 [Hebrew].

2. Haim Nahman Bialik, "Halacha and Aggadah," in Haim Nahman Bialik, *Revealment and Concealment: Five Essays*, trans. Leon Simon (Jerusalem: Ibis, 2000), 86-87.

3. Ibid., 80-81.

4. Hayim Nahman Bialik, "On Ohel Shem and Oneg Shabbat," in *Spoken Words*, 2:160-161 [Hebrew].

5. Bialik did not only speak about the need for Shabbat, he also acted on it. He initiated an event that took place every Saturday afternoon in Tel Aviv called "Oneg Shabbat." It was a gathering of intellectuals and artists, which attracted a wide audience. The meetings combined music with lectures on intellectual and cultural topics. For more on Bialik's enterprise, see Shmuel Avneri, "How Did Bialik's 'Oneg Shabbat' Electrify the Yishuv? 1926-2006: 80 Years to the 'Third Enterprise' of the National Poet,' *Mayim Midlav* 18 (2006) [Hebrew]; Zvi Zameret, "We Must Make Our Shabbats Cultural Bonfires: Unorthodox Zionist Positions on Shabbat," in Gerald Blidstein, ed., *Sabbath: Idea, History, Reality* (Beersheba: Ben Gurion University Press, 2004), 99-122 [Hebrew].

6. Bialik's comments were made in a conversation with the author Hillel Bavli, cited in Avneri, "How Did Bialik's 'Oneg Shabbat' Electrify the Yishuv?" 360 [Hebrew].

7. See the movement's website: www.rebooters.net/engage. The "Shabbat Manifesto," with ten principles for keeping Shabbat in a modern way, is at www.sabbathmanifesto.org.

8. See Randi Zuckerberg, *Dot Complicated: Untangling Our Wired Lives* (New York: HarperCollins, 2013).

9. Bialik himself admitted toward the end of his life that he had once confessed to Ahad Ha'am: "Sometimes I have a desire to wear a *tallit* and *tefillin* and go to synagogue, and mix with all the Jews who still bear the burden of these commandments." Bialik, "On Ahad Ha'am," 210 [Hebrew].

6 IS SECULAR JUDAISM STILL JUDAISM?

1. Ronald Dworkin, *Law's Empire* (Cambridge: Harvard University Press, 1986), 228–229.

2. The former British chief rabbi Lord Jonathan Sacks presents a similar illustration in Jonathan Sacks, *Radical Then, Radical Now: On Being Jewish* (London: Bloomsbury, 2000).

3. Ahad Ha'am felt it important to emphasize that his path was not merely one more stream of Zionism but a new conception of Judaism. Ahad Ha'am, "The Torah in the Heart," in *Complete Works* (Dvir: Tel Aviv, 1974), 53 [Hebrew].

4. Ahad Ha'am was not the only person who made this argument. Even figures at the heart of socialist Zionism argued that the pioneering, secular Zionism was the true successor of traditional Judaism. Ya'akov Hazan, the spiritual leader of the Hashomer Hatzair youth movement and one of the heads of the Mapam Party (which eventually became part of the modern Meretz Party), said something similar: "I see us, the free Jews, as the true heirs of our culture, of all the good, beauty, and humanity that this culture instilled in us, for which the religion was its clothing and soul for generations. We, the free Jews, have been charged not only to fight for our liberty, but also to rescue the Jewish religion— its dignity—from itself." Ya'akov Hazan, *New Beginnings* (Tel Aviv: Sifriat Poalim, 1988), 144 [Hebrew].

5. When Ahad Ha'am made his proposals, it was not the first time that Jews were being asked to save Judaism by developing a new understanding of it. Ahad Ha'am wrote that Rabbi Yohanan ben Zakkai similarly changed Judaism when he left Jerusalem as it fell to the Romans and founded a new beit midrash at Yavne. In the same way, Ahad

Ha'am wrote, Jews who wished their people to survive had to apply themselves to developing a knowledge of Judaism. Ahad Ha'am, "The Treasures of Judaism," in *Complete Works*, 104–105 [Hebrew].

Nathan Rotenstreich has observed that Ahad Ha'am was creating his own pedigree or "chain of transmission" within the Jewish tradition—from Moses to the Prophets, through Rabbi Yohanan ben Zakkai and the Pharisees (and we have seen that Maimonides was also included in the continuation of this dynasty) to cultural Zionism. See Nathan Rotenstreich, "Discussions in Ahad Ha'am's Teachings," in Rotenstreich, *Philosophical Issues* (Tel Aviv: Dvir, 1962), 373–397 [Hebrew].

6. Secularism should not be identified with atheism, just as religion should not be identified with theism. See the incisive discussion in David Benatar, "What's God Got to Do with It? Atheism and Religious Practice," *Ratio* 19, no. 4 (December 2006): 383–400.

7. Baruch Kurzweil, *Our New Literature: Continuation or Revolution?* (Jerusalem: Schocken, 1964), 201–213 [Hebrew]. For a discussion of this critique as one in a series of Ahad Ha'am's criticisms of Berdyczewski, Nordau, Brenner, and Klatzkin, see Gideon Katz, "Debates About the Thought of Ahad Ha'am," in Avriel Bar-Levav, Ran Margolin, and Shmuel Feiner, eds., *Secularization in Jewish Culture* (Raanana: Open University of Israel Press, 2012), 2:827–869 [Hebrew].

8. My argument might be read in conjunction with David Biale's *Not in the Heavens: The Tradition of Jewish Secular Thought* (Princeton: Princeton University Press, 2010). Biale's book is an impressive and far-reaching attempt to offer a radically different interpretation of secularism. The arguments presented in this book are different from his, but the project is the same: to show that secularism is not necessarily the opposite of the Jewish religious tradition but is also rooted *in* it and represents its continuation.

9. In the words of Yehezkel Kaufmann, the great scholar of the biblical Jewish faith: "The basic idea of Israelite faith is that God is supreme over all." Yehezkel Kaufmann, *The Religion of Israel: From Its Beginnings to the Babylonian Exile*, trans. Moshe Greenberg (Chicago: University of

Chicago Press, 1960), 60. See also Micah Goodman, *Moses' Final Oration* (Or Yehuda: Kinneret, Zemora, Dvir, 2016), 86–89 [Hebrew].

10. Babylonian Talmud, Sanhedrin 11a, translated by Rabbi Adin Even-Israel Steinsaltz, available from the Sefaria Library at Sefaria.org.

11. Babylonian Talmud, Bava Metzia 59b, translated by Rabbi Adin Even-Israel Steinsaltz, available from the Sefaria Library at Sefaria.org.

12. Babylonian Talmud, Berakhot 32b, translated by Rabbi Adin Even-Israel Steinsaltz, available from the Sefaria Library at Sefaria.org.

13. Maimonides, *The Guide of the Perplexed*, trans. M. Friedländer (New York: Dutton, 1885), pt. 1, chap. 59. See also Micah Goodman, *Maimonides and the Book That Changed Judaism: Secrets of "The Guide for the Perplexed"* (Philadelphia: Jewish Publication Society, 2015).

14. Exodus 19:23 (JPS Bible).

15. Peter Berger, *The Sacred Canopy: Elements of a Sociological Theory of Religion* (Garden City, N.Y.: Doubleday, 1969), 105–125.

16. See Moshe Halbertal, *Interpretative Revolutions in the Making* (Jerusalem: Magnes, Hebrew University Press, 1999), esp. chap. 8 [Hebrew].

17. Maimonides' position was rejected by Nachmanides, who argued that midrash halakha was in fact a way of elucidating layers that existed in the depths of the text. For a presentation of the debate between the two thinkers and the interpretive positions they represented, see Ariel Picard, *Seeing the Voices: Tradition, Creativity and the Freedom of Interpretation in Judaism* (Tel Aviv: Yediot Books, 2016), 53–57 [Hebrew].

18. Maimonides, *Mishneh Torah*, Book of HaMadda (Knowledge), chap. 1, translated by Simon Glazer, available from the Sefaria Library at Sefaria.org.

19. Rabbi Abraham ibn Daud, Hasagot HaRaavad on Mishneh Torah, Repentance 3:7, translated by Simon Glazer, available from the Sefaria Library at Sefaria.org.

20. Rabbi Moses Taku, *Ketav Tamim* (Jerusalem: Dinur Center, 1984) [Hebrew]. See there the introduction by Joseph Dan on Rabbi Taku's struggle against the Jewish philosophers who denied the corporeality of God and ignored the literal meaning of the prophetic texts.

21. I heard this incisive sentence from Leibowitz in person in 1992.

22. Amos Oz and Fania Oz-Salzberger, *Jews and Words* (New Haven: Yale University Press, 2014).

23. Babylonian Talmud, Menachot 29b, translated by Rabbi Adin Even-Israel Steinsaltz, available from the Sefaria Library at Sefaria.org.

24. Midrash Tanchuma, Parashat *Chukat*, section 8, available from the Sefaria Library at Sefaria.org.

25. Midrash Rabbah, Parashat *Acharei Mot*, 22, section 1, available from the Sefaria Library at Sefaria.org.

26. Note that Oz and Oz-Salzberger qualify their use of the term "Judaism." See *Jews and Words*, 165–168 and 190–199.

27. Amos Oz was more explicit in his article "A Full Cart or an Empty One," republished in "Between Zionism and Hellenism: Amos Oz on the Meaning of Secular Judaism," *Haaretz*, 28 January 2019, available at https://www.haaretz.com/israel-news/culture/.premium.MAGAZINE-amos-oz-there-is-no-judaism-without-debate-over-the-meaning-of-judasim-1.6875342.

28. Assaf Inbari, an Israeli novelist and journalist, argues that the evidence of so-called "secular" Israelis' profound participation in religious rituals and acts compels Israelis to recognize that a secular majority is a myth and to stop leaving Judaism in the hands of religious and ultra-Orthodox Jews. "The secular stream," he writes, "should have come forward as a Jewish group fearful for the image of Judaism and its enlightened, egalitarian and democratic realization." See Assaf Inbari, "The End of the Secular Majority," *Haaretz*, 3 February 2012, available at https://www.haaretz.com/1.5181093.

PART III INTRODUCTION

1. In this book I do not try to cover all the ideas in the Religious Zionist world but concentrate on three major schools of thought. Among the areas I do not touch on are the neo-Hasidic Religious Zionism expressed in the philosophies of Rabbi Shimon Gershon Rosenberg, Rabbi Menachem Froman, and others, and the neo-Lithuanian Religious Zionism shaped by the thought of Rabbi Joseph B. Soloveitchik, based at the Har Etzion Yeshiva.

1. Rabbi Abraham Isaac Kook made varied and even mutually contradic-
    tory comments about secular Jews. On one hand, he said that they were
    superior to ultra-Orthodox Jews, because of their concern for the Jew-
    ish collective and nation-building. Rabbi Abraham Isaac Kook, *Eight
    Folios* (Jerusalem: Mishpachat Hamechaber, 2003), folio 2, verse 21,
    p. 270 [Hebrew]. On the other, he wrote in one of his earlier articles that
    there was a greater difference between observant and nonobservant
    Jews than between Jews and gentiles, and that observant Jews should
    denounce the "evil" secularists and keep them at a distance. Rabbi Abra-
    ham Isaac Kook, "Advice from Afar," in *The Treasures of Rabbi Abraham
    Isaac Kook*, ed. M. Y. Tzuriel (Rishon LeZion: Rishon LeZion Yeshivat
    Hesder, 2002), 73–74. See also Aviezer Ravitzky, *Messianism, Zionism,
    and Jewish Religious Radicalism* (Tel Aviv: Am Oved, 1993), 119–140 [He-
    brew], which notes the great change in Rabbi Kook's attitude toward
    secular Zionism and the pioneers after he immigrated to Israel in 1904.
    During the First World War, Rabbi Kook lost his optimism about the
    human spirit, and his attitude toward secular Zionism changed as well.
    It is clear from several pieces he wrote at the time that he believed that
    hope for the redemption actually lay with the Haredi (ultra-Orthodox
    Jews). See Kook, *Eight Folios*, folio 7, verse 296, p. 468 [Hebrew]; Rabbi
    Abraham Isaac Kook, *Letters of Rabbi Abraham Isaac Kook* (Jerusalem:
    Rav Kook Institute, 1984), vol. 3, letter 871 (9 Shevat 5678), 155–159
    [Hebrew]. See also A. Abramovitz, "The Statesmanlike Theology of
    Rabbi Zvi Tau and His Circle" (Ph.D. diss., Ben Gurion University, 2014),
    191–198 [Hebrew].

2. The concept of a "national spirit" (Volksgeist) was devised by the Ger-
    man philosopher Johann Gottfried Herder, who greatly influenced
    nineteenth-century European philosophers, including Hegel. For the
    evolution of the concept of modern nationalism, see Henry Wasser-
    mann, *People, Nation, Fatherland: Observations on the Emergence, Growth,
    and Demise of Nationalism-Generating Concepts* (Raanana: Open University
    of Israel Press, 2007), 412 [Hebrew].

3. Benjamin Ish-Shalom and Eliezer Goldman argue that Rabbi Kook took

all his ideas from modern thought, and his use of Kabbalistic terms was mainly philosophical and not indebted to genuine Kabbalistic sources. Conversely, Rabbi Joseph Avivi argues that Rabbi Kook presents a precise and consistent interpretation of the theory of spiritual worlds propounded by the original Kabbalists and Rabbi Isaac Luria. See Joseph Avivi, "History: A Higher Need," in Moshe Bar-Asher, ed., *Jubilee Volume for Rabbi Mordechai Breuer* (Jerusalem: Akdamon, 1991), esp. 762–771 [Hebrew]. Most scholars, including Shalom Rosenberg, Tamar Ross, Jonathan Garb, and others, fall between the two camps, taking into account both sources of inspiration. Recently Rabbi Yoel Bin-Nun argued that there was no meaningful difference between the views of Ish-Shalom and Avivi. See the introduction in Yoel Bin-Nun, *The Double Origin: Inspiration and Authority in the Teachings of Rabbi Kook* (Jerusalem, Bnei Brak: HaKibbutz HaMeuchad, 2014) [Hebrew], which presents the various approaches and their arguments at length.

4. This association, which would later be developed by Rabbi Kook's disciples, has been fiercely criticized. Some critics argue that the deification of the Jewish people turns a moderate sense of nationhood into a dangerous form of nationalism. See Yosef Ahituv, "On the Use of Divine Images of Israeli Nationhood in Certain Circles of Religious Zionism," in Avi Sagi, ed., *The Book of Michael* (Jerusalem: Keter, 2007), 383–398 [Hebrew].

5. Kook, *Eight Folios*, fol. 1, v. 71, pp. 19–20; Abraham Isaac Kook, "Lights of the Revival," in his *Lights* (Jerusalem: Rav Kook Institute, 1963), 63. Rabbi Kook explains the difference between heretics, who must be ostracized, and secularists, who must be brought into the fold, thus: heretics have abandoned the Jewish people, while secularists have only abandoned the Torah while remaining committed to the Jewish people. See Kook, *Letters of Rabbi Abraham Isaac Kook*, vol. 2, letter 555 (Sivan 5673), 186–189 [Hebrew].

6. Rabbi Kook's argument concerning the unconscious religiosity lurking behind secularism was met with massive criticism from Rabbi Yosef Chaim Sonnenfeld, one of the great ultra-Orthodox leaders of the age and the rabbi of the Eda Haredit, a radical anti-Zionist sect, in Jerusalem. "What do we care about their insides?" he asked. "God will show

the heart, but we humans have only things that are revealed." Cited in Ravitzky, *Messianism, Zionism, and Jewish Religious Radicalism*, 159 [Hebrew].

7. The Redemption, according to Rabbi Zvi Yehuda Kook, was a prolonged process of revelation, by which he meant the revelation of the Israeli national soul. "And things will become clear from within us, from our faith, not from beyond us. And they will be revealed with each and every step of the revelation of the holy soul of *Klal Israel*—All of Israel." Rabbi Zvi Yehuda Kook, *From the Redemptive Torah: On the Order of the Weekly Parshas* (Jerusalem: Nahalat Zvi, 1988), 167 [Hebrew].

   Gideon Aran has proposed a somewhat different formulation. He describes the combination of Zionism and religion by the students of Rabbi Zvi Yehuda from Gush Emunim thus: "The faithful of the Gush [Emunim] do not adhere to the Torah and the commandments, nor do they adhere to Zionism in its conventional form, but they believe that their religiosity and their Zionism are one and the same. The Gush's revolution of faith can be summarized as the process from Religious Zionism to a Zionist religion." Gideon Aran, *Kookism: The Roots of Gush Emunim, the Subculture of Jewish Settlers, Zionist Theology, Contemporary Messianism* (Jerusalem: Carmel, 2013), 21 [Hebrew].

8. Rabbi Abraham Isaac Kook, *Lights of the Torah: 13 Chapters on the Value of the Torah, Its Study, and Its Teachings* (Merkaz Shapira: Yeshivat Or Tzion, 2003), 33 [Hebrew].

9. Rabbi Zvi Tau, *Those Who Hope in the Lord Will Renew Their Strength* (Jerusalem: Ki Ein Be'Ein Yira'u, 2004), 16 [Hebrew]. This is the background, at least in part, for the splintering of the Mercaz HaRav Yeshiva into two constituent streams and the establishment of a yeshiva that perceived itself as even more devoted to the Jewish national soul because it went farther in blocking foreign influences. See Ishay Rosen Zvi, "The Creation of Metaphysics: The Debate in the Mercaz HaRav Yeshiva—A Critical Study," in Avi Sagi and Dov Schwartz, eds., *A Hundred Years of Religious Zionism*, 3 vols. (Ramat Gan: Bar Ilan University Press, 2003), 3:421-445 [Hebrew]. For the character and teachings of Rabbi Tau, see Oz David Bluman, "The Return to Metaphysics: Sanctity and Consciousness in the Teachings of Rabbi Zvi Israel Tau" (Master's

thesis, Bar Ilan University, 2012) [Hebrew]; Abramovitz, "The States-manlike Theology of Rabbi Zvi Tau and His Circle" [Hebrew].

10. Yair Sheleg, *The New Religious Jews: A Contemporary Look at Religious Society in Israel* (Jerusalem: Keter, 2000), 94–102 [Hebrew].

11. Rabbi Zvi Tau, *To the Faith of Our Times* (Jerusalem: Hosen Yeshuot, 1999–2012), pt. 3, p. 152 [Hebrew].

12. This crisis of confidence in the secular State of Israel generated many different trends in the Religious Zionist movement. Some reacted through self-seclusion, others by hoping to take over the country. See Yedidia Stern, "Not Meeting the Challenge," in the Shabbat supplement of *Makor Rishon*, 16 May 2016 [Hebrew]. For a deeper analysis of the crisis of Religious Zionism following the Gaza Disengagement, see Micah Goodman, *Catch-67*, trans. Eylon Levy (New Haven: Yale University Press, 2018).

13. Quoted in Avinoam Rosenak, *Cracks: Unity of Opposites, the Political and Rabbi Kook's Disciples* (Tel Aviv: Riesling, 2013) [Hebrew]. It must be said that the vast majority of Religious Zionists do not feel that the Disengagement created this crisis. The belief in the mystical interpretation of secularism and the messianic significance of Zionism was not a core component in the lives of most middle-class Religious Zionists. It was central only for elite minority groups—the rabbinic and more religiously hardline groups in the Religious Zionist movement. But these groups represent a dominant force in the spiritual leadership of the Religious Zionist movement, and for them the crisis of faith in secular Israel shook the foundations of their religious consciousness.

14. Note that Rabbi Kook pointed out this possibility and perhaps even foresaw it. See Rabbi Abraham Isaac Kook, "On the Course of Ideas in Israel," in his *Lights*, 103 [Hebrew].

15. I first learned about the possibility of this alternative from my teacher, the late David Hartman. See David Hartman, *A Living Covenant: The Innovative Spirit in Traditional Judaism* (Woodstock, Vt.: Jewish Lights, 1997).

8 NON-DIASPORIC JUDAISM

1. Ben-Gurion wrote in his famous letter to the "Sages of Israel" in 1958: "No Jewish collective in Israel is like the Jewish collectives in the Diaspora. Here we are not a minority subjected to pressure from foreign cultures, and here there is no fear that Jews will assimilate into non-Jewish society." For the original Hebrew letter, see the website of the Israel State Archives: http://www.archives.gov.il/en/chapter/state-of -israel/. Yoav Sorek has proposed that precisely because Zionism represents the realization of the messianic vision, it should prompt a change in the interpretation of Judaism. That is, contrary to what I have argued—that Jewish renewal is an alternative to the messianic interpretation of Judaism—Sorek argues that the Jewish renewal be rooted in that interpretation. See Yoav Sorek, *The Israeli Covenant* (Tel Aviv: Yediot Books, 2015) [Hebrew].

2. Jeremiah 7:4-7 (JPS Bible).

3. The Hebrew original says *"hegemon,"* but it is questionable whether the *Zohar* meant a "Christian bishop," as the term meant in medieval Hebrew, or "Roman magistrate," as it meant in Mishnaic Hebrew. In any case, it seems that the conversation was geared toward the argument over the true word of God, which reflected, of course, the Jewish-Christian polemic. See also Wilhelm Bacher, "Judaeo-Christian Polemics in the Zohar," *Jewish Quarterly Review* 3:4 (July 1891): 781-784 [Hebrew].

4. *The Zohar: Volume Six*, ed. and trans. Daniel C. Matt, Zohar Ki Tissa 188a (Stanford: Stanford University Press, 2011), 60.

5. Ibid., Zohar Ki Tissa 188b, 61.

6. Much has been written about the *Zohar*'s approach to gentiles. For a scholarly overview, see Elliot R. Wolfson, "Re/membering the Covenant: Memory, Forgetfulness, and the Construction of History in the *Zohar*," in Elisheva Carlebach, John M. Efron, and David N. Meyers, eds., *Jewish History and Jewish Memory: Essays in Honor of Yosef Hayim Yerushalmi* (Hanover, N.H.: University Press of New England, 1998), 233n17. For the prevailing trend in Kabbalah, see Moshe Halamish, "The Attitude to the Nations of the World in the Kabbalists' World," in Aviezer Ravitzky, ed., *From Rome to Jerusalem: Joseph Baruch Sermoneta*

Memorial Volume (Jerusalem: Hebrew University, 1998), 223–238 [Hebrew]. Halamish's rich and wide-reaching essay presents different approaches to foreign nations taken in the Kabbalistic world.

7. See Micah Goodman, *The King's Dream* (Or Yehuda: Kinneret, Zmora-Bitan, Dvir, 2012), 135–212 [Hebrew].

8. I present and develop this argument in my book *Moses' Last Oration* (Or Yehuda: Dvir, 2014), 172–177 [Hebrew].

9. See Micah Goodman, *Maimonides and the Book That Changed Judaism: Secrets of "The Guide for the Perplexed"* (Philadelphia: Jewish Publication Society, 2015).

10. Yosef Kaplan and Avraham Grossman, *Kehal Yisrael: Jewish Self-Rule Through the Ages*, 3 vols. (Jerusalem: Zalman Center, 2004), vol. 3: *The Modern Era* [Hebrew].

11. See the discussion in Chapter 2, "The New Orthodoxy," above.

12. Hosea 6:6 (JPS Bible).

13. See data in Pew Research Center, *A Portrait of Jewish Americans: Findings from a Pew Research Center Survey of U.S. Jews* (Washington, D.C.: Pew Research Center, 2013), pp. 7–19, available at https://www.pewforum .org/2013/10/01/jewish-american-beliefs-attitudes-culture-survey/.

14. Tamar Hermann, Gilad Be'ery, Ella Heller, Chanan Cohen, Yuval Lebel, Hanan Mozes, and Kalman Neuman, *The National-Religious Sector in Israel, 2014* (Jerusalem: Israel Democracy Institute, 2014), 191 [Hebrew]. Abridged English version available at https://en.idi.org.il/media/4663 /madad-z-english_web.pdf.

15. Moshe Halbertal, *Interpretative Revolutions in the Making* (Jerusalem: Magnes, Hebrew University Press, 1999) [Hebrew].

16. See Yoav Sorek, *The Israeli Covenant* (Tel Aviv: Yediot Books, 2015), 176 [Hebrew]; Responsa Chatam Sofer, Part A, 148 [Hebrew], available through the Sefaria Library at Sefaria.org.

17. Pew Research Center, *A Portrait of Jewish Americans*, 9.

18. Ibid., 37. Among Orthodox Jews, the rate of marriage to non-Jews is 2 percent, among Conservative Jews 27 percent, among Reform Jews 50 percent. Among Jews who define themselves as being of "no religion," 69 percent are married to non-Jews.

19. I first presented and published this idea in late 2015 in the weekend

supplement of the newspaper *Makor Rishon*. The article provoked many reactions. One of the most important responses was that with all due respect to Zionism, the Exile was not over yet. Most Jews still live beyond the borders of the Land of Israel, and my idea applied only to those who live in Israel. This observation is correct and should be emphasized. Jews who do not live in Israel, including the hundreds of thousands of Israeli expatriates who make no use of the diasporic defense mechanisms of self-seclusion and Orthodox religious observance, are at risk of losing their Jewish identity. Judaism in its conservative, reclusive form is redundant in Israel but remains necessary outside it.

20. For Rabbi Abraham Isaac Kook, this was a two-way street: Judaism interpreted Zionism as messianic, and the Zionist renewal enabled a Jewish renewal. Yoav Sorek provides a good illustration of this. He argues that the renewal of Judaism will not come about through the renewal of the Jewish religion but through recognition that Judaism is not a religion at all. Sorek, *The Israeli Covenant* [Hebrew].

9 SEPHARDIC RABBIS AND TRADITIONALIST JUDAISM

1. Chazon Ish, *Faith and Trust*, trans. Yaakov Goldstein (New York: Judaica Press, 2009).

2. Cited in Paul Mendes-Flohr and Jehuda Reinharz, *The Jew in the Modern World: A Documentary History* (New York: Oxford University Press, 1995), 197.

3. Rabbi Ben-Zion Meir Hai Uziel, *Mishpatei Uziel, Questions and Responsa Part 1: Lifestyle and Yoreh De'ah* (Jerusalem: HaRav Uziel, 2010), 9 [Hebrew]. See also Shalom Ratzabi, "Halakha and Orthodoxy," in Yosef Salmon, Aviezer Ravitzky, and Adam Ferziger, eds., *Orthodox Judaism: New Perspectives* (Jerusalem: Magnes, 2006), 482 [Hebrew].

4. Hayim David HaLevi, "These and These Are Words of the Living God (Ways to Interpret Halakha)," in HaLevi, *Appoint for Thyself a Teacher* (Tel Aviv: Rav Kook Institute, 1982), part 5, pp. 300–301 [Hebrew].

5. Ibid.

6. Ibid.

7. For a more detailed study of the attitude of the founders of the Reform Movement to the concept of "revelation" and the question of God's involvement in prophecy, see Michael Meyer, *Judaism Within Modernity: Essays on Jewish History and Religion* (Detroit: Wayne State University Press, 2011).

8. Jacob Katz, "Orthodoxy as a Response to the Departure from the Ghetto and the Reform Movement," in *Halakha in Straits: Obstacles to Orthodoxy at Its Inception* (Jerusalem: Magnes, Hebrew University, 1992), 9-20 [Hebrew]. This idea was discussed in depth in Chapter 2 above.

9. Zvi Zohar, who has been conducting a comprehensive, years-long study of the halakhic outlook of the Jewish sages of the Sephardic-Mizrahi world, has tried to analyze the reasons for their moderate and open-minded approach to modernity compared to the Ashkenazi tradition, which has inclined toward self-seclusion and halakhic conservatism. Among his explanations, he highlights in particular one factor inherent in the unique nature of the Sephardic tradition: "While the former [the Ashkenazi] advocate a dynamic halakha, the latter [the Sephardi] associate loyalty to the Torah with the preservation of the premodern status quo." Zvi Zohar, "Torah Sages and Modernity: On Orthodoxy, Mizrahi Sages, and the Shas Movement," in Meir Roth, ed., *Religious Zionism: A New Perspective* (Ein Tzurim: Ne'emanei Torah ve-Avoda, 1998), 167 [Hebrew]. See also Zvi Zohar, *The Luminous Face of the East: Studies in the Legal and Religious Thought of Sephardic Rabbis of the Middle East* (Tel Aviv: HaKibbutz HaMeuchad, 2001), esp. 353-364 [Hebrew]; Zvi Zohar, "Carved on the Tablets: On the Characteristics of Sephardic-Mizrahi Halakha in the Modern Age," *Dimui* 10 (1995): 14-23 [Hebrew]; Zvi Zohar, "The Independence of the Contemporary Posek with Regard to Halakhic Precedent," in Ze'ev Safrai and Avi Sagi, eds., *Between Authority and Autonomy in Jewish Tradition* (Tel Aviv: HaKibbutz HaMeuchad, 1997), 304-320 [Hebrew]; Zvi Zohar, "An Alternative: A Typology of the Sephardic-Oriental Rabbi in the Recent Past," in Yedidia Z. Stern and Shuki Friedman, eds., *Rabbis and the Rabbinate: The Challenge* (Jerusalem: Israel Democracy Institute, 2011), vol. 1, 505-523 [Hebrew]. My own remarks above were deeply influenced by Zvi Zohar's work.

An interesting and fruitful debate has emerged on this subject between Zohar and Benjamin Brown. See Benjamin Brown, "Sephardi Rabbis and Religious Radicalism: Toward a Revision," *Akdamot* 10

(2000): 289-324 [Hebrew]; Zvi Zohar, "Orthodoxy Is Not the Only Authentic Halakhic Response to Modernity: Sephardic and Ashkenazic Religious-Halakhic Cultures Are Different," *Akdamot* 10 (2001): 139-151 [Hebrew]; Benjamin Brown, "'European' Modernization: Orthodox Response and the Causal Linkage," *Akdamot* 11 (2002): 153-160 [Hebrew].

For the development of this debate, see also the position of Nissim Leon, "The Haredization of Oriental Jewry in Israel," *Iyunim Bitkumat Israel (Studies in Zionism, the Yishuv, and the State of Israel)* 16 (2006): 85-107 [Hebrew]; Nissim Leon, *Soft Ultra-Orthodoxy: Religious Renewal in Oriental Jewry in Israel* (Jerusalem: Yad Yitzhak Ben-Zvi, 2010), 21-54 [Hebrew].

10. Moshe Shokeid tells a similar story about the historian Yehuda Nini. Nini, who was born in an old Yemenite village in Israel and moved to the adjacent town, was frequently asked by the village elders why he did not come to synagogue on Shabbat. When he answered that he could not walk so far by foot, they suggested that he drive and park his car at the entrance to the village. Moshe Shokeid, "Recent Trends in the Religiosity of Middle Eastern Jews," in Shlomo Deshen and Moshe Shaked, eds., *Jews of the Middle East* (Jerusalem: Schocken, 1984), 88 [Hebrew].

11. Many examples for this can be found in Yaacov Yadgar, *Masortim in Israel: Modernity Without Secularization* (Jerusalem: Keter, 2010) [Hebrew]. Yadgar emphasizes the dominant element of choice in the identity of traditionalist Jews in contrast to that of religious and secular Jews: a conscious choice to belong to this identity, and also a constant choice of a lifestyle stemming from the freedom permitted by this identity (47-82 [Hebrew]).

12. See Meir Buzaglo, "The New Traditional Jew and the Halakha: A Phenomenology," in Moshe Orfali and Ephraim Hazan, eds., *Progress and Tradition: Creativity, Leadership and Acculturation Processes Among the Jews of North Africa* (Jerusalem: Bialik Institute, 2005), 187-204 [Hebrew]. Shlomo Deshen notes the two traits that characterize Mizrahi Judaism: the dilution of traditional customs and sustained adherence to core beliefs. Deshen, "The Religion of Jewish Immigrants from North Africa and the Middle East," in Moshe Shokeid and Shlomo Deshen, eds., *The*

Generation of Transition: Continuity and Change Among North African Immigrants in Israel (Jerusalem: Yad Ben-Zvi, 1999), 243–244 [Hebrew].

Moshe Shokeid emphasizes the importance of the institution of the synagogue in the traditionalist conception of Judaism, and the anchoring of Judaism in circles of family and society over the individual's observance of mitzvot. He observes that even "identification with the synagogue community, which is also a form of participation that does not include a full religious life," is considered by traditionalist communities a rung on a religious ladder that is different for every participant according to each individual's character and circumstance. "The uniqueness of this form of religion is in its participants' emotional state and sense of attachment, not necessarily their consistency in observing the commandments. ... This religious tolerance, and the limited number of religious demands made of the public in their day-to-day lives, may seem unusual for observers whose perspective is anchored in the Ashkenazi tradition." Shokeid, "Recent Trends in the Religiosity of Middle Eastern Jews," 88 [Hebrew]. Shokeid quotes one political activist from the Mizrahi-led Tami Party who claimed that whereas the Ashkenazi-led National Religious Party insisted on observance of the 613 commandments, for the Tami Party "even 100 commandments are enough!" (83).

13. Buzaglo, "The New Traditional Jew and the Halakha," 189–191 [Hebrew].

14. See Yossi Yonah and Yehuda Goodman, eds., *Maelstrom of Identities: A Critical Look at Religion and Secularity in Israel* (Tel Aviv: Van Leer Institute, HaKibbutz HaMeuchad, 2004) [Hebrew]. See in particular Yonah and Goodman's introduction (9–45), and Yehuda Goodman and Shlomo Fischer, "Understanding Religion and Secularity in Israel: The Secularization Thesis and Its Conceptual Alternatives" (349–390). Yaacov Yadgar argues that the "traditionalist" category was originally invented by the Ashkenazi-Israeli establishment in order to cope with population groups who did not define themselves according to the Ashkenazi secular-religious dichotomy. Yadgar, *Masortim in Israel*, 11–14 [Hebrew].

15. Meir Buzaglo, *A Language for the Faithful* (Jerusalem: Keter, 2008).

16. Buzaglo presents an example of the different trends in religious rulings

of ultra-Orthodox and traditionalist rabbis in Buzaglo, "The New Traditional Jew and the Halakha," 196 [Hebrew].

17. Buzaglo, "The New Traditionalist and the Halakha," 202 [Hebrew]. Secularism existed in Muslim countries because of the European colonial presence. There were regions and countries where the Enlightenment and secularism had more influence and others where they had less, but in none of them did the European presence create such a severe reaction among Jews as among European Jewry. See Avriel Bar-Levav, "Secularization and the Jews in Islamic Countries," in Avriel Bar-Levav, Ron Margolin, and Shmuel Feiner, eds., *Secularization in Jewish Culture* (Raanana: Open University of Israel Press, 2012), 1:293-342 [Hebrew]; Lital Levy, "The Haskala and Secularism in the Literature of Jews of Muslim Lands," in Bar-Levav, Margolin, and Feiner, *Secularization in Jewish Culture*, 1:521-549. See also Avriel Bar-Levav, "Secularization and the Jews in Islamic Countries," in Yochi Fischer, ed., *Secularism and Secularization: Interdisciplinary Perspectives* (Jerusalem: Van Leer Institute, 2015), 170-196.

Many traditionalist Jews experienced the collision with modernity and secularism, in their radical and all-encompassing forms, in Israel, of all places. They reacted differently from the Jews of western Europe. Whereas western European Jews responded to modern values by changing halakha, disconnecting from it, or retreating inside it, Mizrahi Jews reacted by diluting their commitment to halakha, while emphasizing the familial and communal dimensions of their Jewish identity. See Shokeid, "Recent Trends in the Religiosity of Middle Eastern Jews," 78-91 [Hebrew]; Deshen, "The Religion of Jewish Immigrants from North Africa and the Middle East," 237-249 [Hebrew].

18. Buzaglo, "The New Traditionalist and the Halakha," 197-198 [Hebrew].

19. See, for example, the description in Daniel Ben-Simon, "Religious or Secular," in Dedi Zucker, ed., *We the Secular Jews: What Is Secular Jewish Identity?* (Tel Aviv: Yediot Books, 1999), esp. 102-105 [Hebrew].

20. Charles Liebman and Bernard Susser argue that contrary to conventional wisdom, the Jewish Israeli public does not comprise two camps but three: two extreme groups (one religious, one secular) who together make up 30 percent of the population and generally define the terms

of the political debate, and a silent, moderate majority of 70 percent, whose relationship to Judaism can be defined as traditional. Liebman and Susser, "Judaism and Jewishness in the Jewish State," *Annals of the American Academy of Political and Social Science* 555, no. 1 (January 1998): 15–25. Elazar Weinrib argues on the basis of these figures: "The struggle over the character of the State of Israel is essentially happening between these two 'vocal' minorities.... The two extreme minorities, the religious on the one hand and the secular on the other, are in fact competing over the soul of this silent majority." Weinrib, *Religion and State: Philosophical Aspects* (Tel Aviv: HaKibbutz HaMeuchad, 2000), 9 [Hebrew].

21. The search for an Israeli middle way has elicited a lot of interest in recent years. In the past decade, three books have been written that undo the religious-secular dichotomy: Moshe Meir, *Two Together: A New Religious-Secular Philosophy* (Jerusalem: Magnes, 2012) [Hebrew]; Yoav Sorek, *The Israeli Covenant* (Tel Aviv: Yediot Books, 2015) [Hebrew]; and Elhanan Shilo, *Existential Judaism* (Jerusalem: Schocken, 2017) [Hebrew]. Since I have already discussed Sorek's book, I shall briefly address the other two.

Meir and Shilo have similar motivations. Both fear the growing gulf between religious and secular societies in Israel, and both have devised philosophies that attempt to bridge it. But Shilo looks for the middle ground between religion and secularism. He proposes a soft form of religion based less on authority and more on individual free will. In Shilo's argument, this middle ground could allow religious liberals, the formerly religious, and secular Israelis who want a connection with Judaism to integrate. Moshe Meir, in contrast, is not looking for the space between the different options but a path that spans them both in a dialectical fashion. Meir imagines a religious-secular Jew as someone who does not live *between* religion and secularism but inhabits *both* of them at the same time.

10 PARALLEL WORLDS, PARALLEL DIVISIONS

1. Maimonides, *Eight Chapters of Maimonides on Ethics*, trans. Joseph Isaac Gorfinkle (New York: Columbia University Press, 1912), 35.

2. Rabbi Shem-Tov ibn Falaquera, *Sefer ha-Ma'alot* (Jerusalem: Makor, 1969), 11-12 [Hebrew], originally published in the thirteenth century.

3. Rabbi Abraham Ibn Ezra, *Commentary on the Creation* available through Sefaria Library at Sefaria.org.

4. Rabbi Meir ben Ezekiel ibn Gabbai, *Avodat HaKodesh* (Jerusalem: Ha-Aḥim Leyin-Epshtayn, 1953), 169 [Hebrew]. The discrepancies and differences between these two philosophical options are outlined in my book *The King's Dream* (Or Yehuda: Kinneret, Zmora-Bitan, Dvir, 2012) [Hebrew], 270-279.

5. Responsa 69 of Rabbi Asher ben Jehiel, cited in Baruch Efrati, "The Torah's Attitude to Philosophy," *Daat* (2005) [Hebrew].

6. The tension between the streams spanned different times, characters, and places. But the main sphere of contention between the two populations was probably the series of debates around the writings of Maimonides. Between the late twelfth and early fourteenth centuries, four different arguments raged over Maimonides' philosophy. In this series of debates, the rationalists and anti-rationalists collided, ostracized one another, and demarcated two very different ways of thinking. Raphael Jospe has outlined and summarized the philosophical aspects of the various polemics in *Jewish Philosophy in the Middle Ages* (Boston: Academic Studies Press, 2009), 551-570.

7. Babylonian Talmud, Ketubot 16b-17a, translated by Rabbi Adin Even-Israel Steinsaltz, available from the Sefaria Library at Sefaria.org. Researchers of the Talmud generally assume that there is a discrepancy in how the Babylonian Talmud presents this debate. The historical debate took place around a hundred years before the destruction of the Second Temple, and it was recounted and presented by the Talmud hundreds of years later. Of course, the following discussion makes no pretense of replicating the historical debate between the two schools. My aim is only to provide a philosophical and literary analysis of the debate in light of the later sources that related it.

8. Babylonian Talmud, Ketubot 17a, translated by Rabbi Adin Even-Israel Steinsaltz, available from the Sefaria Library at Sefaria.org.

9. Ibid.

10. My attempt to decipher the debate between Beit Shammai and Beit

Hillel in light of the kinds of proofs each side used was influenced by the method I found in Haim Shapira and Menachem Fisch, "The Debates Between the Houses of Shammai and Hillel: The Meta-Halakhic Issue," *Iyyunei Mishpat (The Tel Aviv University Law Review)* 22, no. 3 (1988): 461–497 [Hebrew].

11. Babylonian Talmud, Eruvin 13b, translated by Rabbi Adin Even-Israel Steinsaltz, available from the Sefaria Library at Sefaria.org.

12. *Vayikra Rabbah*, 34:3. Translation from Samuel Rapaport, *Tales and Maxims from the Midrash* (London: Routledge, 1907), 128. This story has further parallels and theological implications. For more see Yair Lorberbaum, *Image of God: Halakhah and Aggadah* (Jerusalem: Schocken, 2004), 306–314 [Hebrew].

13. One can base the statement that Beit Shammai and Beit Hillel have different perceptions and attach different values to human experience on the following two examples, among others:

> 1. As the Sages taught: Beit Shammai say: The heavens were created first and afterward the earth was created, as it is stated: "In the beginning God created the heaven and the earth" (Genesis 1:1), which indicates that heaven came first. And Beit Hillel say: The earth was created first, and heaven after it, as it is stated: "On the day that the Lord God made earth and heaven" (Genesis 2:4).
>
> Beit Hillel said to Beit Shammai: According to your words, does a person build a second floor and build the first floor of the house afterward? As it is stated: "It is He Who builds His upper chambers in the heaven, and has founded His vault upon the earth" (Amos 9:6), indicating that the upper floor, heaven, was built above the earth. Beit Shammai said to Beit Hillel: According to your words, does a person make a stool for his feet, and make a seat afterward? As it is stated: "So said the Lord: The heavens are My seat, and the earth My footstool" (Isaiah 66:1). But the Rabbis say: Both this and that were created as one, for it is stated: "Indeed, My hand has laid the foundation of the earth, and My right hand has spread out the heavens; when I call to them, they stand up together" (Isaiah 48:13), implying that they were created as one (Babylonian Talmud,

Chagigah 12a, translated by Rabbi Adin Even-Israel Steinsaltz, available from the Sefaria Library at Sefaria.org).

2. The Sages taught in a baraita that Beit Shammai say: The burnt-offering of appearance must be worth two silver coins, and the Festival peace-offering need be worth only one silver ma'a. The reason the burnt-offering must be worth more is that the burnt-offering of appearance goes up entirely to God, which is not so with regard to the Festival peace-offering, as parts of a peace-offering are eaten by its owner while other portions are consumed by the priests. . . .

And Beit Hillel say: The burnt-offering of appearance must be worth one silver ma'a and the Festival peace-offering must be worth two silver coins. . . . The Gemara asks: And Beit Hillel, what is the reason that they do not say in accordance with the opinion of Beit Shammai? Beit Hillel would respond to both claims of Beit Shammai. With regard to that which you said, that the burnt-offering of appearance is superior because it goes up entirely to God, on the contrary, the Festival peace-offering is superior, as it has two consumptions, by God on the altar and by people (Babylonian Talmud, Chagigah 6a, translated by Rabbi Adin Even-Israel Steinsaltz, available from the Sefaria Library at Sefaria.org).

When Jews make a pilgrimage to Jerusalem, they are commanded to make two sacrifices: a "burnt-offering of appearance" and a "festival peace-offering." The offering "of appearance" is a burnt offering: it is completely consumed at the altar. It is dedicated in its entirety to the Almighty. The festival offering, however, is a "peace-offering": part of it is sacrificed at the altar, but most is eaten by human beings. There is a debate between Beit Shammai and Beit Hillel over which sacrifice we should invest more money in: the sacrifice that is dedicated entirely to God, or the one in which human beings partake as well. Predictably, Beit Shammai glorifies more the sacrifice that is focused on God, while Beit Hillel believes that we should invest more in the sacrifice that people will enjoy as well.

14. My distinctions are influenced by and based on Menachem Fisch and Haim Shapira's work on the debate between Beit Shammai and Beit

Hillel. They demonstrate and bolster the position that Beit Hillel was rationalist and anti-traditionalist, while Beit Shammai was traditionalist and anti-rationalist. See Shapira and Fisch, "The Debates Between the Houses of Shammai and Hillel" [Hebrew].

15. The rabbis of the Talmud rejected the notion that Hillel the Elder had canceled an explicit commandment from the Torah, arguing that in effect the validity of debt cancelation was only *derabanan*—rabbinically ordained. See Mishnah Gittin 36:71, available through the Sefaria Library at Sefaria.org.

16. The famous debate between Rabbi Joshua ben Hananiah and Rabbi Eliezer ben Hurcanus in the Talmudic story "The Oven of Akhnai" represents a disagreement between two approaches: Rabbi Eliezer's traditionalist approach, which holds that humanity has no authority to independently interpret the scriptures and tradition, and an anti-traditionalist and rationalist approach, which holds that it is *God* who has no authority to intervene in the process of interpretation. The debate between these rabbis is but a rehearsal of the debate between Beit Shammai and Beit Hillel. Rabbi Eliezer is the representative of Beit Shammai's school of thought, and Rabbi Joshua belongs to the school of Beit Hillel. For more see David Brezis, *Between Zealotry and Grace* (Ramat Gan: Bar Ilan University Press, 2015), 184–192 [Hebrew]. This debate would go on to appear in multiple guises throughout Jewish history. One fascinating example can be found in Avi Sagi's comparison between the conservative, traditionalist position of Rabbi Meir ibn Gabbai and Rabbi Solomon Luria's stance against subservience to the written word. For more see Avi Sagi, *The Open Canon: On the Meaning of Halakhic Discourse* (London: Continuum, 2007).

17. The traditionalist nature of Beit Shammai's approach is elucidated by Vered Noam's research. Noam shows that there is a profound similarity between many of Beit Shammai's positions on halakha and those of the sect that lived in Qumran. In light of this, Noam concludes that Beit Shammai held "an ancient, severe, and demanding conception of halakha, rooted in authority and tradition rather than logical arguments and elaborate distinctions." Noam, "Beit Shammai and the Sectarian Halakha," *Jewish Studies* 41 (2001–2): 67 [Hebrew].

18. Babylonian Talmud, Eruvin 14b, translated by Rabbi Adin Even-Israel Steinsaltz, available from the Sefaria Library at Sefaria.org.

19. Ibid.

20. Menahem Kahana has demonstrated that Beit Hillel's tolerance for the positions of Beit Shammai was not purely theoretical: Beit Hillel actually believed that whoever followed Beit Shammai's interpretations of halakha was still obeying the commandments. See Menahem Kahana, "On Halakhic Tolerance as It Evolved: An Early and Forgotten Disagreement Between Beit Shammai and Beit Hillel," *Tarbiz* 83, no. 3 (2015) [Hebrew].

21. Mishnah Yadayim 3:5, available from the Sefaria Library at Sefaria.org.

22. For a clear expression of the differences between Beit Shammai and Beit Hillel on the question of cultural boundaries, consider the eighteen rulings in which Beit Shammai defeats Beit Hillel. They contain expansive legal interpretations that aim to erect higher barriers between Jews and gentiles, including the prohibitions on bread, oil, and wine prepared by gentiles. Mishnah Shabbat 17:72, available from the Sefaria Library at Sefaria.org.

23. Babylonian Talmud, Yoma 72, translated by Rabbi Adin Even-Israel Steinsaltz, available from the Sefaria Library at Sefaria.org.

24. Babylonian Talmud, Shabbat, translated by Rabbi Adin Even-Israel Steinsaltz, available from the Sefaria Library at Sefaria.org.

11 SELF-CONFIDENCE AND FEARS ABOUT IDENTITY

1. Rabbi Avraham Yeshaya Karelitz, *Collection of Letters* (Jerusalem: Grenimann, 1954), pt. B, letter 24, p. 38 [Hebrew].

2. Menachem Marc Keller has discussed the development and spread of the idea of "the diminution of the generations" from the Talmud to the Middle Ages in *Maimonides on the "Decline of the Generations" and the Nature of Rabbinic Authority* (Albany: State University of New York Press, 1996). Rabbi Abraham ibn Ezra did not believe that the generations were growing gradually inferior; nor did Maimonides believe that the passage of time necessarily heralded a deterioration. The concept of the "diminution of generations" was not the accepted, official position of Judaism in the Middle Ages. For the position of ibn Ezra, see Uriel

Simon, *The Ear Discerns Words: Studies in Ibn Ezra's Exegetical Methodology* (Ramat Gan: Bar Ilan University Press, 2013), 9–10 [Hebrew]. For Maimonides' conception of history, see my doctoral research: Micah Goodman, "Historiography and Historiosophy in the Thought of Maimonides and Nachmanides" (Ph.D. diss., Hebrew University of Jerusalem, 2005).

3. See Avi Sagi, *The Open Canon: On the Meaning of Halakhic Discourse* (London: Continuum, 2007).

4. Literary representations of this fear can be found in such works as *The Fourth Dream* by David Melamed (Tel Aviv: Sifriat HaPoalim, 1986) [Hebrew], which describes the doomsday on which Judaism completes its takeover of Israel. Yishai Sarid has written another apocalyptic novel in this genre: *The Third* (Tel Aviv: Am Oved, 2015) [Hebrew]. A further contemporary example is an artwork that was recently exhibited by the student Yosi Even Kama as a final-year project in Visual Communications at Shenkar College, depicting a dystopian reality in the year 2023, when Israel becomes the "State of Judea" ruled by the nationalist religious movement.

5. Menachem Brinker, "The Uniqueness of Secular Jews," in his *Israeli Thoughts* (Jerusalem: Carmel, 2007), 45 [Hebrew]. According to Brinker's analysis, secular Judaism suffers from having come onto the world stage at a very late stage, for it lacks symbols with which modern-day secular Israelis could express themselves. In the absence of secular symbols, secular Israelis are compelled to express themselves with religious symbols. Brinker describes the semi-automatic attraction of secular Jews to the ancient religious tradition as the never-ending mission of secular Jews.

6. Theodor Herzl, *Old New Land*, trans. Lotta Levensohn (Princeton, N.J.: M. Wiener, 1997). See the discussion on this subject in Gideon Katz, *The Pale God: Israeli Secularism and Spinoza's Philosophy of Culture* (Boston: Academic Series Press, 2011); and Yaacov Yadgar, Gideon Katz, and Shalom Ratzabi, eds., *Beyond Halakha: Remapping Tradition, Secularity, and New-Age Culture in Israel* (Beersheba: Ben-Gurion University Press, 2014), 50–64 [Hebrew].

7. One representative example of secular Jews who close themselves off from tradition for fear of its power can be found in Ram Vromen, "Secu-

lar Israelis, Save Your Children!" *Haaretz*, 2 May 2015 [Hebrew]. Our position in this country, as was revealed so clearly in the elections," he writes, "compels us to act before our way of life is brought to an end."

12 THE ISRAELI MIDDLE GROUND

1. Gideon Katz, "The Culture War in Israel," in Avriel Bar-Levav, Ran Margolin, and Shmuel Feiner, eds., *Secularization in Jewish Culture* (Raanana: Open University of Israel Press, 2012), 898 [Hebrew]. Katz bases this observation on a study by Charles Liebman. See Charles Liebman, "The Culture Wars in Israel: A New Mapping," in Anita Shapira, ed., *State in the Making: Israeli Society in the First Decades* (Jerusalem: Zalman Shazar Center, 2001), 249–264 [Hebrew]. See also Charles Liebman, "Secular Judaism and Its Prospects," *Israel Affairs* 4, nos. 3–4 (1998): 29–48.

2. See a series of reports by Yair Ettinger on this subject in *Haaretz* in late 2015: Yair Ettinger, "Is Orthodox Judaism on the Verge of a Historic Schism?" *Haaretz*, 27 July 2015, available at https://www.haaretz.com /jewish/.premium-is-orthodox-judaism-on-the-verge-of-a-historic -schism-1.5379629; Ettinger, "Has Modern Orthodoxy in America Reached Its Breaking Point?" *Haaretz*, 30 August 2015, available at https://www.haaretz.com/jewish/.premium-has-modern-orthodoxy -reached-its-breaking-point-1.5392522; Ettinger, "A Quiet Coup: Young Religious Women Are Flocking to the Israeli Army," *Haaretz*, 25 November 2015, available at https://www.haaretz.com/a-quiet-coup-young -religious-women-are-flocking-to-the-israeli-army-1.5402164.

   The divisions within Religious Zionism have not been explored in comprehensive research on religious society in Israel, as the researcher Kimmy Caplan has observed. Caplan demonstrates why the common treatment of Religious Zionism as a single, uniform social sector is flawed and represents one of the great missed opportunities of academic research. See Kimmy Caplan, "The Scholarly Study of Jewish Religious Society in Israel: Achievements, Missed Opportunities, and Challenges," *Megamot* 51, no. 2 (2017): 207–250 [Hebrew].

3. Yuval Noah Harari, *Homo Deus: A Brief History of Tomorrow* (New York: Harper Perennial, 2017).

4. See especially T. M. Luhrmann, "Religion Without God," *New York*

Times, 24 December 2014, available at http://www.nytimes.com/2014
/12/25/opinion/religion-without-god.html. To find Luhrmann's fascinating and important studies on the role of religion in modern society,
I recommend visiting her website: luhrmann.net.

5. For Mitchell's central place in the history of psychology, see Gadi Taub,
    "The Revolution in Psychoanalysis, from Freud to Relational Psycho-
    analysis," in his *Against Solitude*, vol. 1: *Impressions* (Tel Aviv: Yediot
    Books, 2011) [Hebrew], 49–78.

6. There is probably a profound connection between the open-minded
    thought of Sephardic rabbis in the modern era and the rationalism of
    the Middle Ages. Maimonides devised his philosophy in the same Arab
    cultural environment that produced the Sephardic rabbis of the mod-
    ern day. The scholar Zvi Zohar argues that Rabbi Uziel and Rabbi Hayim
    David HaLevi are modern representatives and heirs of the Golden
    Age in Spain. See Zvi Zohar and David Hartman, "Maimonides and
    Sephardic-Oriental Rabbis in Modern Times: A Comparative Analy-
    sis," in Avi Sagi and Zvi Zohar, eds., *Renewing Jewish Commitment—The
    Work and Thought of David Hartman*, 2 vols. (Jerusalem: Shalom Hartman
    Institute and HaKibbutz HaMeuchad, 2001), 2:607–608 [Hebrew].

7. Mekhilta of Rabbi Ishmael, Massekta de-Bahodesh, Jethro, 4, translated
    by Rabbi Shraga Silverstein, available from the Sefaria Library at Se-
    faria.org.

8. Jerusalem Talmud, Chagigah, 9a:1, available from the Sefaria Library at
    Sefaria.org. See also Rabbi Bahya ibn Paquda, *Duties of the Heart (Chovot
    HaLevavot)*, originally published 1040 C.E., translated by Rabbi Yosef
    Sebag, available from the Sefaria Library at Sefaria.org: "'It is good that
    you should take hold of this, and also from this you shall not withdraw
    your hand' (Koheles [Ecclesiastes] 7:18), which means 'Be not overly
    righteous'—Do not be extreme in the ways of the righteous who sepa-
    rate from this world. . . . Likewise, do not be extreme in the ways of the
    wicked who strengthen after this world." See also Shlomo Weissblit,
    "The 'Middle Way' in Jewish Thought," *Mahanayim* 5 (1992): 162–169
    [Hebrew].

AFTERWORD

1. Adam Alter, *Irresistible: The Rise of Addictive Technology and the Business of Keeping Us Hooked* (New York: Penguin, 2015).

2. Sherry Turkle, *Reclaiming Conversation: The Power of Talk in a Digital Age* (New York: Penguin, 2015). For a summary of Turkle's conclusions, see her *New York Times* editorial: Sherry Turkle, "Stop Googling. Let's Talk," *New York Times*, 26 September 2015, available at https://www.nytimes.com/2015/09/27/opinion/sunday/stop-googling-lets-talk.html. See also Lee Rainie and Kathryn Zickuhr, "Americans' Views on Mobile Etiquette," 26 August 2015, Pew Research Center: Internet and Technology, available at http://www.pewinternet.org/2015/08/26/americans-views-on-mobile-etiquette/. For a concise overview of the research on this subject, see J. M. Twenge, "Does Online Social Media Lead to Social Connection or Social Disconnection?" *Journal of College and Character* 14, no. 1 (2013): 11–20. For an anthropological analysis with less critical conclusions about the influence of social media on young people's social lives, see for example danah boyd, *It's Complicated: The Social Lives of Networked Teens* (New Haven: Yale University Press, 2014).

3. Turkle, *Reclaiming Conversation*, 22–23.

4. Ibid., 21; Twenge, "Does Online Social Media Lead to Social Connection or Social Disconnection?"

5. Eldar Habusha, "They Take a Selfie and Lose Themselves," *Haaretz*, 14 December 2015 [Hebrew]. See also Oz Almog and Tamar Almog, *Generation Y: Generation Snowflake* (Chicago: Vallentine Mitchell, 2019). The Almogs' study paints a comprehensive sociological portrait of the young generation in Israel.

6. The transition from screens to virtual- or augmented-reality glasses will further enhance the temptation to escape our physical surroundings for the virtual reality, because wearable technology will threaten one of the only advantages that the nondigital world still has over its digital rival—its tangibility.

7. On this growing phenomenon, see Rachel Malek Buda, "Shomer Shabbos: Why Have Keren Peres and Avri Gilad Disconnected from Their Cell Phones?" in *Makor Rishon*, 7 November 2016 [Hebrew], available at https://www.makorrishon.co.il/nrg/online/11/ART2/845/817.html.

ACKNOWLEDGMENTS

This book was written over the space of four and a half years, and I finished writing it four times. Each time I finished writing one draft, I reread it and recognized with great frustration that I had not written the book I had set out to write. A few weeks later, I would find myself rolling up my sleeves and trying to rewrite it from scratch. In the first version I tried to devise a theory that was post-religious and post-secular, seeking to contribute to the development of an Israeli Judaism that would transcend sectoral divisions. The second version dealt with the relationship between Judaism and Zionism. It sharpened my perception that secular Zionism, like Kabbalah and Hasidism, is a movement that revitalizes Jewish life. The third draft dealt primarily with the tension between Judaism and Western culture, and with the notion that Western values can help Jews reinterpret Judaism, while Judaism can help them defend themselves from the more serious problems in the Western lifestyle.

After I had finished writing the book three times, I understood that my dilemmas were the same as my existential questions about life. I inhabit the lively space where the religious and secular worlds overlap, I sense the clash and the opportunity at the core of the relationship between Judaism and Zionism, and I feel torn between my Jewish soul and my Western spirit. Only upon grasping that the different versions of the book reflected versions of my own personal sentiments could I write the book you see before you. This is the full edition, bringing together everything that was contained in previous drafts.

It took me many years to understand that my journey was the one my parents had sent me on. I was raised and educated by two people who are proof of the possibility of living a happy and productive life in the zone between two worlds. This book is dedicated to both of you, Mom and Dad, my greatest teachers, with gratitude and love.

I am not alone on this path. I am joined by many dear and good friends. I thank all the partners, teachers, students, supporters, and friends of the Beit Prat Yisraeli—The Israeli Midrasha community, which under the leadership of director Anat Silverstone and Keren Apfelbaum has become a lively institution with an intellectual and collegial climate that has allowed my thoughts to flourish.

I could not have written this book alone, without the help and support of dear friends who read drafts at different stages, spotted mistakes, offered fresh perspectives, and helped me find the voice I was searching for: Robert Hirt, Asael Abelman, Ariel Levinson, Roni Magidov, Shay Zarchi, Shai Gilis, Rani Alon, Roni Rosenberg, Ofer Glanz, Micha Jesselson, Jonny Klahr, Avi Garfinkel, Shraga Braun, Assaf Inbari, Vered Noam, Azri Levi, Oved Yehezkel, and Regev Ben-David. A special thanks to Ariel Steinberg for his support in the writing process from its initial stages.

Amy Klein and Brian Lefsky have backed dreams and pushed me day by day to overcome obstacles and fulfill those dreams. Boaz and Kylie Lifschitz have walked with me hand in hand in an effort to turn vision into reality. I thank them all, from the bottom of my heart, for their friendship and cooperation.

This manuscript was enriched thanks to the perceptive and illuminating perspectives of Tom Segev, Jay Pomerenze, Yossi Beilin, Yair Lapid, and Rabbi Danny Segel. Thank you for your enormous contributions to the composition of this book. A special thanks to Yivniyah Kaploun for his tremendous work and contributions to this book at every stage of its growth.

Thanks also to those who read parts of the book and contributed from their individual areas of expertise to the strengthening of its ideas and arguments, including Rabbi Yitzhak Ben David, Dr. Udi Abramovitz, Milcha Elimelech, Rabbi Michael Marmor, Aner Dascallu, Dr. Ariel Picard, and Dr. Meir Buzaglo. A special thanks to Leah Beinhaker for her many contributions to my work, going back years. I thank Eliran Zered for his deep and thorough contribution as my research assistant for this project. Eliran's work was exemplary and professional, and he enriched the book with a firm academic underpinning in research, without which the ideas presented here would have been less grounded.

The idea of writing two books that attempt to conceptualize the philosophy of a new Israeli middle way was born in a conversation with Efrat Shapira Rosenberg. I thank Efrat for her contribution to the development of this book and *Catch-67*.

I thank Dr. Donniel Hartman and the entire wonderful team at the Hartman Institute for the lively intellectual space they are nurturing and their encouragement and support for my research and writings. And I thank my Hebrew publishers, Yoram Roz, Eran Zemora, Yael Naamani, Sarit Rosenberg, Imri Zertal, Daniel Dollinger, Irit Yosilevitch, Shir Aviv, and the rest of the dedicated team at Kinneret, Zmora-Bitan, Dvir for their thorough and professional handling of the manuscript. Thank you to Heather Gold and Susan Laity at Yale University Press for the devoted, perceptive, and punctilious handling of this manuscript.

During the writing of this book, my wife's uncle Michael Fried, whom I came to see as my own uncle, passed away. Michael was one of the most challenging and fascinating people I have ever had the privilege of speaking to, and he very much wanted to read this book in English. He will never do so, but Uncle Michael's children and his nearest and dearest are my fellow dreamers, and his, in the quest for an Israeli Jewish awakening.

Eylon Levy was more than the translator of this book: he is a true traveling companion, an intellectual interlocutor, and a good friend. Thanks to his dedication, wisdom, and professionalism, Eylon not only translated the book from Hebrew into English but also turned an Israeli book into something more universal. Thank you, Eylon, for the whole journey we are taking together. Thank you also to Yael Andrea Levy for the inspired and creative idea for the title of this English edition, solving the puzzle of how to translate the untranslatable Hebrew title.

This book concludes the second series of books I have written. The first series deals with classical Jewish thought and includes three books; the second series deals with modern Israeli thought and includes two books. This literary enterprise was from the beginning the vision of Shmuel Rosner, and it could not have come about without his wisdom, creativity, and rigor. I thank him for our years of partnership and friendship.

And thank you to Tzipi—for everything.

INDEX

Beit Hillel (continued)
  as rival of Beit Shammai,
    153-160, 163, 164-165, 166,
    235-236n10, 236-237n13, 237-
    238n14, 239n20, 239n22
Beit Prat, 146, 165
Beit Shammai, 50, 90, 238n17; as
  rival of Beit Hillel, 153-160, 163,
    164-165, 166, 235-236n10, 236-
    237n13, 237-238n14, 239n20,
    239n22
Ben-Gurion, David, 16-17, 34,
    197n12, 201n5, 227n1
Berdyczewski, Micha Josef, 22, 25,
    28, 37, 197n12, 199n19, 206n6,
    207n11, 208-209n12, 209-
    210n13, 210n14; and secular
    Judaism, 37, 48-49, 51-52, 59,
    80, 93, 149, 161, 166
Berger, Peter, 85
Bergmann, Samuel Hugo, 44-45
Biale, David, 203n1, 213n2
Bialik, Hayim Nahman, 45, 161, 175,
    176; "In the City of Slaughter,"
    25-27, 198n13; on Jewish reli-
    gious law, 27-28, 39, 71-73, 75,
    78, 79, 100, 177, 190; on our re-
    lationship to the past, 71-73;
    on the Sabbath, 73, 75, 190;
    "On the Slaughter," 198-199n15
Bin-Nun, Rabbi Yoel, 224n3
Birnbaum, Nathan, 21
Brenner, Yosef Haim, 210-211n14,
    211n15; on secularism, 52, 53,

92, 161, 203n1, 205-206n3; on
    Zionism, 21, 22, 211n16
Brinker, Menachem, 167, 240n5
Buber, Martin, 45; on religion and
    religiosity, 65-67
Buzaglo, Meir, 137, 139, 140

Campbell, David E., 193n9
Caplan, Kimmy, 241n2
Caro, Joseph, 72
chavaya (immediate experience),
    67
Chazon Ish, 129-130, 134, 163-164
Chowers, Eyal, 197n11
consumerism, 8, 178
cultural isolationism: in Israel, 164-
    165, 168; and secular Judaism,
    160-162
cultural secularism, 79; as applied
    to Judaism, 47-60. *See also*
    Ahad Ha'am

derabanan, 90-91
Deshen, Shlomo, 231n12
Deuteronomy, book of, 115
Diaspora Jews, 210n14; as contrast-
    ed with Israeli Jews, 16, 98-99,
    113-114; and Jewish identity,
    113-114, 119-120, 123, 126-127;
    strength of, 117-121; Zionist
    views of, 22-23, 25, 27
digital technology. *See* technology
d'oraita, 90
Dworkin, Ronald, 78-79

binic leadership of, 15-16, 164;
and the Redemption, 111; religious divisions in, 17-19, 36-38,
40; secularism in, 36-38, 43-54,
163-169, 171-173, 202n9; Sephardic Judaism in, 129, 131-134;
settlements in, 38; status-quo
agreement in, 34-35; "trap of
moderation" in, 146-147. *See
also* Judaism; Zionism
Israeli Judaism, 43-45. *See also* secular Judaism
Israeli music, 54, 55

Jabotinsky, Ze'ev (Vladimir), 23,
196n9, 198n13
James, William, 66
Jehiel, Asher ben, 152
Jehiel, Rabbi Nathan ben, 200n2
Jeremiah, on religious ritual, 114-115
Jewish identity: assimilation as
threat to, 125-126; for Diaspora Jews, 113-114, 119-120,
123, 126-127; instability of,
166, 168-169, 171; in Israel,
97-101, 113-114, 123, 127; and
the Torah, 112; and the *Zohar*,
118-119
Jewish nationalism, 48; and secular
Zionism, 105-110
Jewish people: assimilation of, 32,
98, 113, 121-122, 123, 125; as the
Chosen People, 119-120; and
memories of past weakness,

115-116; strength and weakness
of, 25-28, 115-120; survival
of, over time, 111-112, 121-122;
Zionists' critiques of, 21-27. *See
also* Diaspora Jews; Judaism;
religious Jews
Jewish religious law, oral versus
written, 90-91. *See also* halakha
Jewish renewal, 54-60, 93, 229n20;
and Sephardic Judaism, 129
Jewish secularism. *See* secular
Judaism
Jewish society, women in, 3-4, 124
Jewish texts, 55, 57; interpretation
and study of, 85-92, 118-120.
See also Hebrew Bible; Maimonides; Talmud; Torah
Jospe, Raphael, 235n6
Judaism: in America, 75, 99; authoritarian form of, 17-19;
books relating to, 55, 57; conflicting ideologies within, 15-
19, 31-33, 34-35; critiques of,
23-25; discrimination within,
176; guilt and judgmentalism
associated with, 2; as an intergenerational conversation,
89-93; many forms of, 43-45,
129; messianic, 103-110; and
openness to new ideas, 151-
153, 160-161, 164-165, 177, 178;
Orthodox, 3-4, 32-33, 34-35,
70, 78, 91, 114, 125, 126, 135;
prejudices relating to, 99-100;
purpose of, 112-114; and the

Judaism (continuerd)
rabbinical establishment,
15–16; Reform movement in,
32–33, 133–134, 135; and religious tradition, 8–9, 47–48, 171;
Spinoza's critique of, 23–24;
strength and weakness as
shifting themes in, 114–121;
and tensions between modern values and ancient traditions, 2–5, 24–25, 31–33. *See also*
Ashkenazi Orthodoxy; Jewish
renewal; mystical secularism;
Reform movement; religious
Jews; Religious Zionism; secular Judaism; secular Zionism;
Sephardic Judaism; traditionalist Judaism; Zionism
judgmentalism, and Judaism, 2

Kabbalah/Kabbalists, 55, 84; on the
Divine, 88, 104; on truth, 160
Kama, Yosi Even, 240n4
Katz, Gideon, 172, 214–215n10,
241n1
Katz, Jacob, 32, 124, 134, 200n4
Katznelson, Berl, 45, 56, 61, 204n5
Kaufmann, Yehezkel, 210–211n14
Keller, Menachem Marc, 239n2
Kishinev, massacre at, 25–26,
198n13
Knesset Israel (Assembly of Israel),
104, 106
Kook, Rabbi Abraham Isaac (Rav

Kook), 101, 223n1, 223–224n3,
224n4, 224n5, 224–225n6,
229n20; on the Redemption,
225n7; and Religious Zionism,
103–106, 109, 110, 127; on the
Torah, 105–106
Kurzweil, Baruch, 81

lamentations, following suffering
and tragedy, 25–26
Leibowitz, Yeshayahu, 3, 77, 89
Liebman, Charles, 233–234n20
Luhrmann, Tanya Marie, 174
Luria, Rabbi Isaac, 224n3
Luria, Rabbi Solomon, 238n16
Luz, Ehud, 194n9

Mahmoody, Betty, *Not Without My
Daughter*, 39–40
Maimonides, 50, 80, 113, 121, 152,
160, 177, 235n6, 239–240n2,
242n6; Aristotle as influence
on, 150–151; *Eight Chapters*,
149–150; on God, 83, 86, 88–89,
99, 120; *Guide for the Perplexed*,
10–11, 86, 99; on midrash halakha, 86
malkuth, 104
Margolin, Ron, 215–216n10
Matrix (film), 175
Melamed, David, *The Fourth Dream*,
240n4
Melamed, Rabbi Zalman, 110
Mercaz HaRav Yeshiva, 225n9

midrash halakha, 85–86

minyan, 3, 137

Mishnah, 55, 90–91, 92

Mitchell, Stephen, 174

Mizrahi Judaism, 101, 135–137, 140–141, 233n17

modernity, 191n2, 197n11; appeal of, 32; as challenge for Diaspora Jews, 123, 125; conservative concerns regarding, 192–193n6; and European Jewry, 135–137, 233n17; and Middle Eastern (Mizrahi) Jewry, 135–137; and the relevance of religion, 9, 16, 174

monotheism, and the secularization of nature, 85

Moses, 84, 90; on God's love, 119–120; on power, 115–116

music. *See* Israeli music

mystical secularism, 61–70, 79, 100

Nachmanides, 197–198n12

Nachshon, Commander, 58–59

Near East, ancient, Hebrews in, 112

Nietzsche, Friedrich, 112

Nini, Yehuda, 231n10

Noam, Vered, 238n17

Old Yishuv, 34

Orthodox Judaism (Religious Zionism), 32–33, 34–35, 70, 78, 135; and assimilation, 125; in conflict with modern society, 3–4; criticism of, 91; prejudices relating to, 100–101; and Zionism, 126. *See also* Ashkenazi Orthodoxy

Oz, Amos, 49, 89, 91, 206n6

Oz, Kokbi, 54

Oz-Salzberger, Fania, 89, 91, 206n6

Palestine: Jewish settlements in, 38–39; as part of Israel, 34

Peretz, I. L, 198n13

Plato, 54

Popper, Karl, 5

Postman, Neil, 186

postmodernism, 10–11

prophets, 114–115; as God's messengers, 82; on morality versus ritual, 122–123. *See also* Isaiah, book of; Jeremiah, on religious ritual

Proverbs, 117

Psalms, 83

Putnam, Robert D., 8, 193n9

Raavad (Abraham ibn Daud), 88

Rabbah, Rabbi, 90

Ramon, Einat, 215n10

reason: and faith, 10–11; and interpretation of the Torah, 151–153; and judgment, 163–164

Reboot, 74, 190

Redemption, 225n7; and Religious Zionism, 103–105, 109–110, 111, 127

Reform movement (in Judaism), 32–33, 133–134, 135

religion/religiosity, 65–66; and charitable giving, 193n9; failure of, 2–5; and mental health, 191–192n4. *See also* Judaism

religious Jews: inner conflict experienced by, 4–5, 10–11; and intellectual integrity, 2–3; and secular Jews, 172–173, 176–177; Zionists' critiques of, 21–29

religious tradition: and secularism, 9–11, 18–19, 179; and sense of belonging, 8–9, 47–48, 178. *See also* faith

Religious Zionism, 100–101, 127, 136, 142, 149, 171, 172, 180, 226n13, 241n2; and Mizrahi approach to religion, 136, 141; paradox inherent in, 103–108; purpose of, 121; and the Redemption, 103–105, 109–110. *See also* Orthodox Judaism

Rhineland massacres, 25–26

Rosenberg, Shalom, 224n3

Rosner, Shmuel, 197–198n12

Ross, Tamar, 224n3

Rotenstreich, Nathan, 194n3

Sabbath, sanctity of: Bialik's views on, 73, 75, 190, 204n5; as a break from technology, 189–190; revitalization of, 73, 75, 189–190

Sacks, Lord Jonathan, 98

Sagi, Avi, 211n16, 238n16

Sakharof, Berry, 54

Salhoov, Shva, 212n18

Sarid, Yishai, *The Third*, 240n4

Scholem, Gershom, 44, 45; on the revival of the Hebrew language, 62–64

Schweid, Eliezer, 215n10

science: in conflict with religious belief, 2–3, 10, 175; and monotheism, 85. *See also* technology

secular humanism, 6

secularism: failure of, 5–9; forms of, 44–45; and happiness, 6–7; in Israel, 36–38, 43–54, 163–169, 171–173, 202n9; and religious tradition, 9–11, 18–19, 171, 175; and spirituality, 69. *See also* halakhic secularism; mystical secularism; secular Judaism; secular Zionism

secular Judaism, 5; continuity in, 78–81, 142; fears associated with, 166–169; foundational debates within, 50–54, 79–81, 149, 161–162; intergenerational conversation relating to, 89–93; interpretation of texts as applied to, 85–89; in Israel, 36–38, 43–54, 163–169; and the Jewish renewal, 54–60, 93, 229n20; and Jewish tradition, 50–60, 64, 85–89, 100, 240n5; and sovereignty, 56–57; as a stream of Judaism, 92–93; and traditional texts, 55, 57, 85–89; and Zionism, 18–19, 35–38. *See also* Ahad Ha'am; Bialik, Hayim Nahman; Gordon, A. D.; secularism; secular Zionism

secular Zionism, 180; and Jewish nationalism, 105–110; Rav Kook's perspective on, 103–106, 109, 110; and Mizrahi approach to halakha, 141

Sephardic Judaism, 129, 131–134, 230n9

Sephardic rabbis, 101, 177, 242n6

sephirot. See emanations

settlements in Israel, justifications for, 38–39

Shapira, Anita, 198n13

Shapira, Haim, 236n10, 237–238n14

Sheleg, Yair, 108

Shilo, Elhanan, 234n21

Shokeid, Moshe, 231n10, 231–232n12

Shulchan Aruch, 72

Six-Day War, 168; and antipathy toward religion, 38

Sofer, Rabbi Moses (Chatam Sofer), 125, 130, 134

Sonnenfeld, Chaim, 224–225n6

Sorek, Yoav, 227n1, 229n20

sovereignty, and secularism, 56–57

Spengler, Oswald, 112

Spinoza, Baruch, 23–24, 196–197n10

spirituality, and secularism, 69

Susser, Bernard, 233–234n20

Syrkin, Nachman, 21

Taku, Rabbi Moses, 88

Talmon, Jacob, 191n2

Talmud, 55, 57, 82–83, 86, 92, 180; and religious law, 129, 138, 200n2

Talmudic sages, 82–86, 124

Tau, Rabbi Zvi, 107, 108, 225–226n9

Taylor, Charles, 197n11

Tchernichovsky, Shaul, 22, 24

technology: addiction to, 182; disconnecting from, 74, 188; emotional cost of, 183–185; impact of, 181–182, 185–186; and isolation, 8, 178; our relationship with, 185–190; and the Sabbath, 189–190; and virtual reality, 243n6

teshuva, and becoming newly religious, 179

Tocqueville, Alexis de, 7, 8, 36–37

Torah, 84, 112; in a changing world, 131–134; homosexuality as judged in, 4; immutability of, 129–130; interpretation of, 31, 32, 124, 151–153, 156–157, 179–180; and Jewish nationalism, 107–108; Rav Kook's teaching on, 105–106; study of, 89–91, 107, 108; on strength and weakness in the Jewish people, 115–120

traditionalist Judaism, 232n12; conceptualization of, 141–142; and faithfulness, 139; flexibility of, 137–140; and the halakhic

traditionalist Judaism (continued)
system, 137–139; and Mizrahi
Judaism, 137, 140–141, 142
truth: as applied to the Torah, 151–
153; faith as, 1; Kabbalists' view
of, 160; quest for, 174
Turkle, Sherry, 183–184, 187, 188

Uganda Scheme, 17
United Nations, and partitioning of
Israel, 33–34
United Nations Special Committee
on Palestine (UNSCOP), 34
United States of America: consum-
erism in, 8; Judaism in, 75, 99;
separation of church and state
in, 36, 37
Unplug Yourself, 74
Uziel, Rabbi Ben-Zion Meir Hai, 131,
134, 242n6

values, tension between, 173–174
virtual reality, 243n6
Volcani, Yitzhak, on religious tradition, 61–62
Vromen, Ram, 240–241n7

Weinrib, Elazar, 234n20
women: dilemmas faced by, 39–40;
in Jewish society, 3–4, 124, 176

Yadgar, Yaacov, 202n9, 202n11,
231n11, 232n14
Yannai, Rabbi, 31
Yehuda, Rabbi Zvi, 225n7
Yirmeya, Rabbi, 83
Yizhar, S., 51
Yose, Rabbi, 118

Zeira, Moti, 53, 211n17
Zionism, 194n4, 195–196n8; and
anti-Semitism, 22–23; debate
surrounding, 97; dual identity
of, 17–19; and halakha, 130; in
Israel, 16–19, 113–114; and Mizrahi Judaism, 136; as modern
ideology, 16–17; religious, 44;
as response to modernity, 126–
127; as revolt against Judaism,
17, 29; and the Sabbath, 75;
secular, 44; and secular Judaism, 35–38; skepticism regarding, 111; socialist, 65. *See also*
Judaism; Religious Zionism
Zionists: as critics of religious Jews,
21–29; and halakha, 24–25
Zohar, 117–119, 120, 227n3
Zohar, Zvi, 230–231n9, 242n6
Zuckerberg, Mark, 74
Zuckerberg, Randi, 74

EINSTEIN
NOT RELIGIOS